CHRISTIAN FINDINGS AFTER FIFTY YEARS

A Retrospective Summary

BY

FRANK BALLARD

D.D., M.A., B.Sc., &c. (Lond.)

ARTHOR OF

The Miracles of Unbelief; Clarion Fallacies; Haeckel's Monism False; Theomonism True; The True God; Does it matter what a Man Believes?; Christian Essentials; The People's Religious Difficulties; Christian Reality in Modern Light—Fernley Lecture, 1916; *Does Faith need Reasons?; Modern Determinism, False and True; Eddyism—A Delusion and a Snare; Christian Theism Justified; Christian Truth concerning the Lord's Supper; Why does not God Intervene?; Why not Modern Unbelief?; Reality in Bible Reading; The Mystery of Painlessness; Twentieth Century Christianity, &c.*

Published for the Author

London
THE EPWORTH PRESS
J. ALFRED SHARP

First Edition, February, 1927.
Second Edition, September, 1927.
Third Edition, October, 1927.
Fourth Edition, August, 1929.

MADE AND PRINTED IN GREAT BRITAIN BY
RUSH & WARWICK, LTD., HARPUR PRINTING WORKS, BEDFORD.

CONTENTS

With grateful remembrance
to ALL who
during past years have spoken or written
so many words of
kindly sympathy

I

APOLOGIA

When through a period of years one has tried in many ways, and not a few publications, to express one's thoughts concerning certain great religious themes, it may seem somewhat superfluous to refer to them again. The reasons for so doing, as in the following pages, are such as these : the growth and modification of one's convictions, with the passing years; the manifestly increasing need for plain teaching as to what Christianity really is, and means; the desire to contribute something, at least, towards the truer understanding and development of Christ's Kingdom on earth, before the call comes to other service. Some foundation truths, moreover, call for and will bear constant repetition. But I confess frankly that during the course of fifty years, the gradual enlargement of mind and heart has compelled me to think and feel very differently now, from what I did at the beginning of my ministry. Then, I should have endorsed probably all that has recently been set forth so strenuously in Dr. J. G. Machen's much discussed book entitled *What is Faith?* But the following pages will show in how many ways—with all respect, but with also all deliberation and emphasis—I am compelled to differ from him and from the school of thought which he represents. For such blending of the new with the old there is good warrant, not only in Christ's own definite direction (Matt. xiii. 52), but in the immeasurable gains which come from so doing in every department of modern human life. In every realm of life except religion, the necessity and advantage of growth are acknowledged, whatever the cost of ensuing changes. The repudiation of such necessity, is, however, most pronounced where it ought to be most freely acknowledged, namely, in theology. It is easy enough to call theology the ' Queen of the sciences,' but so vast and complex are the subjects for consideration, and so helplessly limited are human perceptions, that there, if anywhere, frank confession of ignorance should be combined with more than willingness to unlearn as well as to learn. The sense of one's ignorances and limitations becomes continually more intense and humiliating. The ever-deepening certainty is that, apart from the Christian assurance and hope, one's whole being and doing, even in a lengthy life, amount to little more than the insignificant movements of an infinitesimal speck, that exists upon a speck, which itself goes round and round a mere speck, in a boundless universe. And yet—the Apostolic exhortation—' Finally, brothers, whatsoever things are true '—appeals to every moral being, and by it Christianity stands or falls.

At the close of the most remarkable chapter in his remarkable book,[1] Prof. Seeley remarked that—' We are to remember that nothing has been subjected to such multiform and grotesque perversion as Christianity.' Such an estimate, staggering though it may be, is not only endorsed in history, but confirmed around us now, on every hand, by the multiplied and irreconcilable differences of creed and practice which keep apart all the main sections of modern Christendom. There is no prospect whatever of any real unanimity, let alone union, between Romanism and Anglicanism; or between Anglicanism and the Free Churches in this country. Indeed, as to these latter, not only are Presbyterianism, Congregationalism, and the Baptist fraternity, entirely distinct from each other and from Methodism, but even the attempt to form one organic whole out of the three sections so much alike as Wesleyan Methodism, Primitive Methodism, and the United Methodist Church, has

[1] *Ecce Homo*—Everyman's Library Edn. p. 136.

been met with dogged and sometimes bitter opposition. There are also not a few other bodies of avowed Christians which cannot be ignored, even if they only represent eccentric minorities. One has but to cultivate the acquaintance of Plymouth Brethren, Christadelphians, Russellites, Mormons, Eddyists (misnamed 'Christian Scientists'), British Israelites, Seventh Day Adventists, Theosophists, &c., to appreciate the utter impossibility of anything like unanimity in doctrine or practice, throughout the nominally Christian world of to-day. How much, or how little, this is matter for lamentation, must be left for discussion elsewhere. The main consideration here, is that all these professing Christians must be credited with intelligence and sincerity. It is equally certain that no one of them holds a complete, faultless, and final monopoly of Christian truth. Whence then arises all these irreconcilable differences? Plainly from the varying interpretations and representations of such fundamental matters as are considered in the following pages.

But where any real irenicon is apparently impossible, is it not sheer madness, or intolerable presumption, to dare to speak in one small volume upon twenty great themes any one of which needs and deserves, from far abler hands than mine, a whole volume, or even volumes, for its fair consideration? Indeed it would be so, if these brief findings were dogmatic pronouncements, claiming to settle keenly disputed questions. But they are not. They simply express the thoughts which have crystallized into convictions, in the mind and heart of an ordinary individual who has tried, at least, to think honestly and earnestly about them during half a century. They may mean little or nothing to others. To him they cannot but mean much. And there is neither madness nor immodesty in a final attempt to set forth plainly what one has found after long, long search, as a real,

even if small, contribution to that truth and love which
alone can make human life worth living. The convictions here embodied are at least as sincere as their
finding has been costly, and have been as carefully considered as they may sometimes seem to be dogmatic.
They express those realities of internal vision which must
go with me as I follow the many whom here I have
known, and revered, and loved, into that great hereafter which, when realized, makes all the present, with
all its cares and fears, its joys and griefs, its conflicts
and ambitions, to be but a drop in an infinite ocean.

I cannot but add that so far as one little life-course
has permitted, all these findings have been ratified in
experience. However many and great have been the
failures from my own Christian ideals, the absolute
certainty which nothing in the universe can shake, has
been and is, that in the exact proportion as I have been
true to the spiritual and ethical principles which are
inseparable from the convictions here recorded, my
whole being, alike in itself and in all its relations to
others, has been the very best—giving that term its
highest and fullest connotation—of which it is capable.
That certainty constitutes the finally compelling motive,
and sufficing Apologia, for the pages which follow. They
are not intended for experts in any realm, but for
ordinary men and women—the ' common people ' who
heard Jesus ' gladly '—who are necessarily engrossed
with life's daily cares and duties, and yet desire as much
as any recluse, and need as much as any student, to
know the truth which will make them free. May He
who said, as no other has ever said or could say—' I am
the way, the truth, and the life '—accept and use what
is here recorded, for the purposes of His Kingdom, both
here and hereafter.

                                                    F. B.

Sheffield, 1926.

' Whatsoever things are true.'

II

THEOLOGICAL CONCEPTIONS

(1) GOD

It may now be taken for ganted, as beyond reasonable question, that man is a religious animal. The few apparent exceptions which have been so industriously hunted up by unbelief, only serve to emphasize the rule. There is abundant warrant for assuming that religion is not a mere sense of awe or fear, but a recognition of definite relationship between the human individual and the measureless power by which he is so manifestly surrounded. Yet Mr. Herbert Spencer's 'unseen and eternal energy from which all things proceed,' can never be the basis of a real religion. For the individual human being, as a person, can only cultivate real relations with another personality. Moreover, even when the personality of God, as the Creator and Upholder of all, is conceded, it becomes true beyond all question, that the nature of religion depends upon the estimate of the character of that personality. It is not proposed in these pages even to summarize, let alone set forth in worthy detail, the rational grounds for believing in the existence of God, or the reality of His personality. That has been done plentifully in numberless volumes. Nor is it contemplated to answer once more[1] the many objections urged in these days against such belief. What is intended is simply a brief statement of the thoughts

[1] In two of my other works I have endeavoured to contribute some small share to such defence of Christian principles, viz. *Theomonism True—God in Modern Light,* and *Christian Theism Justified* (Epworth Press). What is there stated remains, I think, true.

concerning God, which, after the careful consideration of half a century, seem to me most true, and most needed in the religious atmosphere of to-day, as related to the great human environment. In a word, the thought of God determines the nature of religion. If the old maxim 'like priest, like people,' has in it any truth, it is even more true that like God, like priest. Other religions than Christianity must here be left out of account. What does Christianity mean by 'GOD'? All Christians are supposed to believe in the same God. But do they? We have seen in how many respects Christians differ. Upon what do their differences ultimately turn? Undoubtedly upon their thought of God. That really decides everything, theological or practical. Dr. Denney, after exhaustive scrutiny in search of a formula of faith which all living Christians could accept, finally suggests —'I believe in God, through Jesus Christ our Lord.' But the very breadth of his terms defeats their purpose. Before any man can use such a formula as intelligently as honestly, he must know what is meant by 'God' and 'Lord.' Dr. Garvie says that—'It is Christ's revelation of God as Father, with its prophetic preparation, and its apostolic interpretation, which is the object of Christian faith.' But there are thousands of Christians, and myriads of non-Christians, for whom such a statement is neither sufficient nor true. Sufficient it certainly is not, without further thought. Jesus everywhere indeed assumed a heavenly Father's omnipresence, omniscience, immanence, transcendence. But these terms all mean more to us than to His contemporaries. At best and utmost, the Apostolic interpretation was geocentric. What they thought of stars, we do not know. Nor could they know what we cannot but think. Dr. Watts wrote :

> The God that rules on high,
> That all the earth surveys,

That rides upon the stormy sky,
And calms the roaring seas,—
This awful God is ours,
Our Father and our love.

But he suggested far more than he knew. For that awfulness, in all its overwhelming force, has now come to be appreciated as never before. We are compelled to bear in mind what the early Christians did not know, that whilst light travels at the rate of 186,000 miles per second, there are suns—with probably attendant worlds—in the universe, whose light has to travel for millions of years before it reaches us. James wrote—' the devils also believe and shudder.' Well they may. But it is just this unspeakable awfulness which easy-going Christianity ignores. For want of it, the ordinary thought of God is in many senses far too anthropomorphic. Even in churches which profess to believe in His Fatherhood, He is, as often represented, neither good enough nor great enough to be the valid basis of modern Christian faith. The God of ecclesiasticism, whether Roman, or Greek, or Anglo-Catholic, is too small for modern intelligent worship. To realize for one moment the awfulness of astronomy's revelation concerning the magnitude of the universe, makes it for ever unthinkable that the only God of all should care whether men worship him in black, or white, or green, or red. In His sight, whether man-made rubrics are obeyed, or forms observed, or shibboleths pronounced, matters nothing. These all but infinitesimal trifles are of no value whatever compared with the final declaration of Jesus, that ' God is Spirit, and they that worship Him must worship in spirit and in truth.' All worship forms beyond that, are but human fads and fancies. To make them compulsory, is to reduce God to a petty Eastern despot.

Nor is the God of evangelical theology, as hitherto generally represented, good enough for Christian faith

2

to-day. Many current references to sin which are said to be 'orthodox,' make Him to be a selfish, impatient, unsympathetic, and meticulous tyrant. In regard to the older conceptions of Him, as a judge who would not hesitate to condemn many of His creatures to fearful torment for ever and ever, with all the ghastly additions of mediaeval theology, these have mercifully been dismissed to the limbo of exploded superstitions. But even yet, in many pulpits and sermons which are accounted evangelical, the attitude of God towards human beings is such as no true father or mother on earth would feel towards their child, even if he were sometimes wayward or disobedient. Furthermore, when, in accordance with the whole of Christ's representation of God, it is pointed out that the 'wrath of God' never is or can be, towards even the worst offenders, what is meant in our ordinary speech by 'anger,' it is said to be loose or dangerous doctrine. To teach that the 'anger' of God is, only and always, the grief and yearning love of a Father's heart, elicits a warning against too soft and easy views of the divine majesty.

But every such caveat is uncalled for. The majesty and sovereignty of God, according to the teaching of Jesus, are the very basis of His unchanging tenderness. If God is the universal Father, then John's sublime summary is true—'God is love.' That love can never be 'angry' in the common, malignant, human sense. There never was, is, or will be, any 'wrath of God' which is not the expression of love. That is absolute, unlimited, eternal truth. By it all else in Christian faith must be estimated. The choice alike for mind and heart, is either— 'the God and Father of our Lord Jesus Christ, the Father of mercies, and the God of all comfort'—or none at all—Christian Theism, or blank Agnosticism. Thus in his *Conquest of Fear,* Mr. Basil King has truly summarized what should be present-day Christian conviction.

God, who ever since His sun first rose, and His rain first fell, has been making Himself known to us, is by our generation a little better understood. God, whom we have tried to lock up in churches, or banished to Sundays and special holy days, is breaking through all our prohibitions, becoming more and more a force in our homes and schools, in our shops and factories, in our offices and banks, our whole human environment. Into His light we advance slowly, unwillingly, driven by our pain. But we advance.

To affirm so much as this, is certainly to make great assumptions. Even Theism as against Atheism and Agnosticism; Christian Theism as against Deism and Pantheism; a doctrine of Divine Triunity as against Unitarianism. Having dealt with these, rationally, else-where[1] I must here be content to ratify those expressions of conviction. But the whole case must be re-considered in modern light. Even Christ's revelation was, by His own avowal, incomplete. The Biblical representation of God is manifestly and necessarily imperfect. The revelations of modern science are quite as valid and imperative for Christian faith, as anything in the Canon of Scripture. Even Fundamentalists, who declaim so vehemently against evolution, cannot and dare not maintain the Ptolemaic astronomy which underlies the New Testament, or deny the revolution in religious thought which came through Copernicus. But if the further teaching of the Holy Spirit, of which Jesus spoke, may include Copernicus, Galileo, and Newton, so may it also welcome all that is now shown to be true through the labours of Darwin, or Lyell, or Einstein, and all the consequences of the discovery of the main principles of evolution. The faith that cannot face ' whatsoever things are true,' is neither Christian nor valid. Whatever becomes of the ceaseless logomachies between

[1] See *The True God; Theomonism True; Why not Atheism, Agnosticism, Pantheism? Christian Theism Justified; Christian Essentials; Christian Reality in Modern Light;* all published by the Epworth Press.

Fundamentalist and Modernist, some things should be clear and final. Even the following, as a reverent minimum.

(1) The definite belief in the real Fatherhood of God, which is the very essence of the Christian faith, is not derived from science, nor from philosophy. Nor does it rest upon the representations of the Old Testament. It rests, only and wholly, upon the Christ of the Gospels, in all that He was, as well as in all that He said and did, together with His tragic death and marvellous resurrection. In this respect the witness of one far from orthodoxy, is worth recounting. Says Mr. R. L. Hartt[1]—

The first mortal ever to believe in the Fatherhood of God was the Nazarene. He was the first ever to speak of God constantly as His Father. He was the first ever to speak of God constantly as the Father of all mankind, and to bid us address Him as such in our prayers. He was the first to proclaim boldly and unequivocally that God was love, and only love, and could never be anything else. That has been the secret of His influence ever since.

Our modern terms almighty, omnipotent, omniscient, omnipresent, immanent, transcendent, were never on His lips. But His use of the word ' Father,' in reference to God, implies and includes them all, in a happier and more hopeful setting than the cold light of science, or the verbal meanderings of philosophy. He assumed and asserted the highest ideal that our minds and hearts can put into the term ' Father.' It includes not only all the tenderness of Motherhood, but all that is wisest, noblest, deepest, best, in the love of parents for their children. This is the absolute *sine quâ non* of Christian faith. If only it had been kept in the full view which Jesus most certainly intended, Christianity would have been saved from the theological monstrosities which have blackened its history and prevented its hold upon humanity. It is simply impossible to think of the

[1] In *The Man Himself*, p. 115.

Heavenly Father whom Jesus affirmed, and credit Him
with such immoralities as ' election ' and ' predestination,'
in the Augustinian Calvinistic sense.   Or with what
has been taught under the names of ' original sin,' ' total
depravity,' ' eternal punishment,' by ' evangelical '
theology. One of the strangest and most tragic problems
in religion is how so many men, otherwise good and
intelligent, could ever have been able to believe such
things, when the unmistakable words and whole attitude
of Jesus were before their eyes.

(2) It is still stranger how theologians yet shrink
from the implications of Christ's doctrine concerning
this divine Fatherhood. Thus even Dr. Garvie, one of
the best representatives of modern Christian thought,
protests that Jesus ' taught a retributive revelation of
God, not only as forgiving but punishing, because
retribution is included in redemption.'   But the half-
truth in such a statement is very likely to mislead. For
if ' punishing,' or ' retribution,' connotes the direct
infliction of suffering, *ab extra*, on the part of God as
Father, then it is not true. Nor does any reference to
Heb. xii. justify it. παιδεία there mentioned, has all
too long been sadly mistranslated as ' chastening,' that
is, punishing with stripes. That term conveys far too
much of the notion of a parent's caprice, instead of the
whole conception of parental discipline which, proceeding only and always from love, makes the offender
his own judge, and the inflictor of his own punishment.
There is no need to protest that ' righteousness as well
as love ' must enter into the conception of the divine
Fatherhood. For that Fatherhood could never be other
than righteous. If it be true that ' all's love, and yet all's
law,' it is no less true that ' all's law, and yet all's love '
—' Whatsoever a man sows, that will he also reap '—
requires no external executioner. And the very pain
which the offender thus inevitably inflicts upon himself,

is in itself deterrent proof of the Father's love.
Even as the blister raised by playing with fire, is but
proof of the presence of the beneficent heat through
which we live.

(3) Again; it is only too true that even yet, thanks
to the tenacity of Augustinian Calvinism, very many
in ' evangelical ' churches shrink from the full truth of
the universality of the divine Fatherhood as Jesus
declared it. Mr. Spurgeon did not hesitate to say, and to
print, that ' The doctrine of the universal Fatherhood of
God is a lie.' Some other Christian teachers with great
influence have echoed that avowal, even calling it a
' damnable ' doctrine. A popular Missioner in an evangelical church recently declared that he ' did not know of
anything working such irreparable ruin, as the doctrine
of the universal Fatherhood of God, and its corollary,
the brotherhood of man.' Thus, after nearly two
millenniums, Christ's own manifest teaching is being
openly flouted by his avowed disciples.[1] And then it
is thought strange that Christianity does not everywhere
prevail! The real wonder is that it still exists at all.

But thanks to a false estimate of the Old Testment,
and the picking out of a few isolated passages in the New
Testament, the character of God has been all too often
misrepresented, even in Christian churches, as that of an
Eastern despot, rather than a Father. Sovereignty, not
fatherhood, was the pious shibboleth of generations
past which called themselves Christian. It is only within
the last fifty years that the true doctrine of God, as
Jesus and Paul declared it—' One God and Father of all,
who is over all, and through all, and in all '[2]—has been
generally accepted throughout Christendom. And even
yet, there are those in the churches who oppose.

[1] For full statement of the whole case, I must refer to my
published booklet—*Father of All*—(Epworth Press).
[2] Not ' in you all '—as in the A.V.—where ' you ' is undoubtedly
a gloss. See my *Reality in Bible Reading*, p. 181.

(4) But the time has come to say quite plainly, without any hesitation or limitation, that this truth concerning the nature of God and His relation to all mankind, as a Father—without any consideration of faith, or creed, or sex, or clime, or time—is the distinctive and unequivocal revelation of Jesus Christ. It is the only thought of God which the whole New Testament, when fairly interpreted by itself in modern light, permits. It is the Alpha and Omega of Christian theology, and by its truth Christianity stands or falls.

The oft quoted phrase concerning the ' central doctrine of the Cross ' is simply not true, whatever be the reverent appreciation which is intended. The apostle's plain words in 1 Cor. xv. 14, 17, indeed, ought to have prevented the coining of such a phrase. If we are willing to take an illustration from our bodies, as he did, there is no ' central ' organ of the body—neither heart nor brain—though there are several vital organs. Behind and within all alike, there is that mystery which we call ' vitality.' It is indefinable, but all else depends upon it. Even so, in the whole body of truth which constitutes the Christian Gospel, whilst there are certain great vital fundamental truths, without which Christian faith could not be Christian, these all are ultimately dependent upon, derived from, and expressive of, that divine Fatherhood which is implicit in the constantly quoted but little realized words—' God so loved the world, that He gave His only Son, that whoever believes in Him should not perish but have eternal life.' For in this case, as throughout the New Testament, the primary meaning of ' eternal ' is not quantitative—as if it were the mere expression of personal continuity after death—but qualitative, as is made so plain in the 17th chapter of the same Gospel (John xvii. 2). Its essence is the true knowledge of God, as the loving Father of all, with the comfort, inspiration, benediction, of daily communion with Him.

Thus in regard to the two Great Commands which, as Jesus interpreted them, constitute the Christian law of life, it is the reality of the divine Fatherhood which alone can make possible and binding the first; so that it may in turn become the dynamic of the second. It is the ' world,' not the church; humanity, not saints or converts, that God ' SO ' loved, as to assure them, in Jesus, of the reality of His universal and eternal Fatherhood. That, and nothing else, or less, is the Christian Gospel.

(5) To such a conception of God as the preceding summary assumes, there can be but one real objection— that it is too good to be true. Mr. Robert Blatchford, in his anti-Christian crusade, expressed this with unmistakable lucidity. ' There is no Heavenly Father watching over us. He is but the baseless shadow of a wistful human dream.' As to the wistfulness, there is no question. The gravamen of disbelief turns upon the old and hackneyed pseudo-dilemma concerning the mystery of pain and evil. If God is so good a Father, He must wish to end it all—and if He be ' Almighty,' He must be able. Therefore, since that double mystery continues its gruesome record, the belief in a universal divine Fatherhood is but a ' baseless shadow.' That is soon said, and confessedly it is not easily answered. Both head and heart demand to be heard. With the intellectual part I have already dealt so often and so fully elsewhere,[1] that mere repetition would be here unprofitable. But it may be helpful to face quite frankly that vision of the heart which is so often tragically obscured. No one can reach middle life, let alone old age, without meeting with many cases of individual suffering and premature death,

[1] See *Christian Theism Justified*, Part III. *The Mystery of Pain —a Fair Estimate* (Epworth Press).

in which the assurance of divine Fatherhood seems mockingly unthinkable. All our deepest, tenderest feelings are apparently ruthlessly disregarded. It is useless to attempt to conceal the fact, that, in very many such cases, nothing is left but trust in the dark. No theology, no sermons, no hymns, no texts, will ever explain to me why my mother should have been taken away in her youth, leaving a year-old babe with a broken-hearted father, who took only a short time to die of grief. Nor, on the wider scale, ignoring one's own sorrows, to take one fact typical of so many, can any honest preaching mitigate the dreadfulness of the fact that 30,000 human beings perished in the eruption of Krakatoa in 1883; whilst every year in India, 20,000 human beings die from snake bite; to say nothing of epidemics of disease, or of famine, in which not long since in only one part of India 300,000 men, women, and children perished. Sir F. Younghusband has, in his pathetic book entitled *Within*, pitifully related how his own motor-accident, added to all his observations in India and elsewhere, compelled him at last to give up all his belief in Divine Providence, or a Heavenly Father. No sensitive soul can fail to feel the tragic force of such considerations.

A real solution of the whole vast problem is, in this life, not forthcoming. Yet there are at least two elements in the case which must on no account be omitted, or underrated. For a fair statement of the immeasurable greatness and significance of what may be called ' the other side,' I must be content to refer to another publication.[1] But part of it may here be profitably reiterated.

This mystery of pain is confessedly the crux of Christian Theism. The question of questions is whether we can retain our faith in face of such happenings. And this in plain terms is the answer. If on rational principles faith is shaken by the mystery of pain, upon the very same principles it is restored, established,

[1] *The Mystery of Painlessness* (Epworth Press).

and made unshakably triumphant by the greater mystery of painlessness. If God is rightly credited with all that dark side of human existence which is not definitely due to moral evil, then certainly, in all honesty, He must also be regarded as the ultimate source of all that bright and happy side of human being, which is manifestly not man's own creation. When, thereafter, these two estimates are compared, it becomes plain beyond denial, that the bright side exceeds the dark, as truly and as much as the light and heat of the mid-day sun, exceed the cold illumination of the nightly moon.

But in addition to that, we are alike free, and bound, to meet without evasion another question which is as decisive as it is simple. That is, the plain but tremendous query whether we can deliberately credit the Christ of the Gospels with being either deceiver or deceived? One or the other He must have been, if the divine Fatherhood upon which He laid such stress in His teaching, and gave His whole incomparable life and cruel death to prove, be but a 'wistful human dream.' For my own part, I cannot, cannot, believe Him to have been either. For assuredly, in either case, the difficulties for rational thought which then arise, are immeasurably greater even than those which so trouble us in life's perplexities and pains. Until the Gospels are destroyed and forgotten, and the whole New Testament shown to rest upon sheer delusion, it will be simply impossible for human minds and hearts to think of the Jesus there depicted as a self-deluded fanatic, or a self-seeking charlatan. His deliberate assurance—'He who has seen Me, has seen the Father'—has shone through all the dark ages of the past, and will irradiate the better centuries to come. Meanwhile, the essence of Christian faith must consist in realizing this sublimest of all truths which He reveals, and applying it, so far as in us lies, to our whole human environment.

(6) It will probably appear strange to the thoughtful reader that no specific reference has been made above

to the theological doctrine of the Trinity. But the following reasons may suffice by way of explanation.

(i) The Christian doctrine of the Trinity is far too difficult and abstruse to be wisely considered in a few words. Its justification must be sought in more elaborate treatises. In his last book, Dr. Garvie has well illustrated this in saying that the orthodox terminology must be dismissed, as not only not helpful, but even a hindrance to intelligent conception. But to ordinary men and women it will not be very helpful to say that as to the term, 'person,' in the formula 'three persons in one God'—'there is a convergence of the two conceptions of personality as social, and of society as personal. If we apply these conceptions to the doctrine of the Trinity, the first may help us to conceive the unity in differences and the second the differences in unity.' [1]

(ii) This doctrine can only properly be appreciated after the truth concerning Christ and the Holy Spirit has been fairly considered.

(iii) It is purely a matter for intellectual apprehension, and must be left to the capacity, temperament, and training of each individual believer.

(iv) It is certainly not an absolute necessity for all that the New Testament means by 'salvation.' The 'damnatory clauses' of the 'Athanasian Creed' are as unwarranted as they are intolerable, and utterly contrary to all Christ's spirit and teaching. The dogged persistence of some Anglican clergy—against earnest protest—that they shall be read in public, only illustrates all that must in truth be said concerning the 'perversions' of ecclesiasticism.

(v) A Unitarian may be quite as real a Christian as the Trinitarian. The old-time contempt if not hatred, with which Unitarians were regarded, has no warrant in the New Testament. None of the texts usually quoted

[1] *The Christian Doctrine of the Godhead*, p. 375 (Hodder).

by Fundamentalists justify it.   Rather was it the outcome
of theological conceit and ecclesiastical pride.   Christ's
own warning in Mark ix. 38 to 40, was wholly ignored.

(vi) That which cannot be comprehended may well be
left in abeyance for that which can.   Beyond doubt this is
what is actually done by ninety-nine out of every hundred
'orthodox' Christians.   The Trinity is inconceivable;
the Fatherhood is plain.   The realities of Christian faith
and hope and love and service, do not depend upon
clearness of apprehension of the relations between Father,
Son, and Spirit, in the Godhead; any more than the
appreciation of wireless messages and music depends upon
exact understanding of the ultimate nature of electrons,
or the construction of thermionic valves.   According
to the New Testament, we may think of and pray to
God as our Heavenly Father; we may think of and
pray to Christ Jesus as our Saviour; we may think of
and cry to the Holy Spirit as our Advocate, Comforter,
everlasting Friend in need,—the Guide of the Christian
Church, and Revealer of ever-growing truth.   There we
must, and may, leave all the rest.

(2)   JESUS   CHRIST

Any attempt to summarize the whole truth concerning
Jesus Christ in few words, is as certainly foredoomed
to failure as would be the idea of putting the ocean into
a teacup.   More volumes have been written concerning
Him, than in regard to any other human being.   Whole
libraries have been compiled relating to the mystery of
His person, and the nature of His work, the significance
of His death, and the extent of His influence.   And yet,
week by week, the flood of such literature rolls on, with
promise of increase rather than diminution.   In view of

such multitudinous expressions of conviction, on the part of the clearest minds and purest hearts humanity has known, it would be unpardonable presumption for an ordinary individual to assume judicial capacity for estimating such efforts, or undertaking to decide for others where so many have been in conflict. All he can venture to do is to state his own convictions, as the result of ceaseless reading, thinking, working, praying, during many years. I am only concerned here with what seems to me, finally, to be true. ' Who is Christ? ' remains the greatest enigma of the ages intellectually, and whether my convictions do really embody ultimate truth, or whether they have any value for others, may be set aside. They are mine, and I believe them to be true, and so far worthy of regard. That is the sole significance of the following brief but sincere and careful synopsis.

It has been said, times without number, that ' Christianity is Christ.' Condensed aphorisms are often misleading; but in this case there is much to be said for it. Christianity is undoubtedly summed up for all time in Christ's own words—' Believe in God; believe also in Me.' Its essence is in the love and service of God as a Heavenly Father, revealed, exhibited, and proved in Jesus Christ,—' He who has seen Me has seen the Father.' But however unmistakable that revelation may be, the question of questions remains. Is it really true? The answer to that overwhelming query must be found in Christ Himself. Is He mythical or historical? Could He be either deceiver or deceived? Whence did He come? What really was He? What did He actually do? Why did He die? What then became of Him? These are the persistent, irrepressible, crucial questions, which each succeeding age has to answer for itself. Their significance, for all humanity, is simply immeasurable. If numbers merit any regard, there are more human beings included to-day under the Christian name than under any other kind of religion. But what all these 580,000,000 of Christendom really believe, and feel, and say, concerning Jesus, is indescribable for sheer variety. All the more so, since the diffusion of knowledge and development of science have compelled greater numbers than ever before in the world's history to think for themselves—apart from any findings of church, or priest, or theologian.

The intensity of these ever-increasing differences of estimate and conviction concerning the Christ of the New Testament, recently reached such a pitch as to occasion the publication of a special number of the must influential religious Journal in the world, in which all shades of opinion were expressed with the utmost freedom. The issue of the *Hibbert Journal Supplement* for 1909 was indeed a remarkable collection of deliberate avowals from acknowledged experts in theology, science, and philosophy. It arose in response to the sweeping and bitter attack upon Christ and Christianity by a virulent Agnostic who yet persisted, with brazen misrepresentation, in styling himself the ' Rev.' R. Roberts. To summarize the discussions of this remarkable volume is, of course, here impossible. For once, at all events, the very worst has been incisively said, which the keenest criticism and the most ruthless disbelief can say against the ' orthodox ' or ' evangelical ' conception of Jesus, as the Saviour of the world. Out of the eighteen well-known contributors, it is indeed very significant that only three showed real sympathy with the generally accepted views and teachings of the ' free ' or ' evangelical ' Churches. A careful estimate of this whole verbal whirlpool, leaves one with the feeling that unless there were something inexpressibly superhuman in the soul and substance of Christianity, it never could have survived such a flood of contradictions and denials. It is greatly to be regretted that a corresponding volume was not

issued from another standpoint—whether called 'orthodox' or aught else—in illustration of a protest in Dr.
H. Drummond's contribution, against 'the very common
error of supposing that all candour and wisdom are on
the side of those who so scornfully repudiate what has
been generally believed.' The article from which this
sentence comes, though written from the Unitarian standpoint, is in every sense one of the best in the volume,
and its conclusion is as true as reassuring—'Christianity
has still its grandest victories to win. It is still the one
commanding influence that fights against the cruelty and
selfishness in human hearts.'

For the average Christian believer, all questions
concerning Jesus are still answered by assumptions based
upon the New Testament. It cannot, however, be
denied, that besides the fact that there may be numberless varying interpretations of the New Testament, there
remains always, inevitably and impressively, the further
question as to whether the original text which contains
the account of Jesus and His teachings, is reliable and
authoritative. There are, it is true, myriads of devoted
Christians, distinguished alike by lofty character and
unquestionable devotion, to whom all such inquiries are
unnecessary, if not dangerous. Nor, in all ordinary
churches, is any theme more unwelcome and thankless
than reference, in the broadest sense, to 'Christian
evidences.' But the modern world becomes every
year less amenable to ecclesiastical authority, and less
disposed to accept theological assumptions, however
conventional or venerable. The question 'What do you
think of Christ?' not only remains for each section of
the Catholic Church to answer, but comes home indeed
to each individual, with keener point and weightier
emphasis than ever before. It is the supreme and
perennial query of the Christian faith, and upon the
answer to it everything else turns, theological, personal,

social, national, international. In an autobiographical summary some assumptions are inevitable—their justification is to be found elsewhere. Four fundamental avowals only may, therefore, here be made.

(i) The historicity of Jesus is now beyond reasonable question, in spite of all that has been urged by Kalthof and Drews in Germany, with Robertson, Anderson, and Sadler, in this country. Dr. F. C. Conybeare, himself an able and pronounced 'Rationalist,' after keenest scrutiny, estimated the work of these critics as 'blundering extravagances' and declared that their hypothesis 'deserves to be summarily dismissed.'[1] So that Dr. Drummond is well warranted, in the article above mentioned, when he says that 'the exalted personality of Christ is as certainly historical, as the battle of Zama or the assassination of Caesar.' Prof. Loof's verdict thus remains in force, 'No science can prevent us from saying that the historical Jesus is the same as the Christ of faith, that is, the Christ who was a man, but also the beginner of a new mankind, and the Christ in whose face we behold the glory of God, our Saviour and our Lord.'[2]

(ii) The difference between Unitarianism and the Catholic faith, is, after all, really unequivocal and immeasurable. It is true, indeed, that by some Unitarians the most real reverence for Christ and devotion to His ethical teaching have been displayed. The attitude of such men as Channing, Martineau, George Dawson, is unimpeachable for deepest and highest appreciation of the character and influence of Jesus. Also, they have accepted to the full His revelation of the universal

[1] *The Historical Christ,* p. 223 (Watts & Co.).
[2] *What is the Truth about Jesus Christ?* p. 240. (T. & T. Clark). If any further evidence is desired concerning the historicity of Jesus it will be found in *The Mythical Interpretation of the Gospels* by T. J. Thorburn (T. & T. Clark); *The Historicity of Jesus* by S. J. Case (Chicago University Press), & Dr. Warschauer's *Jesus or Christ*—(Jas. Clarke & Co.).

Fatherhood of God; as against the pathetic agnosticism of Sir F. Younghusband, or the truculent atheism of a noisy minority calling themselves 'Freethinkers.' Some Unitarians could join with Bernard of Clairvaux, in singing,

> Nor voice can sing, nor heart can frame,
> Nor can the memory find
> A sweeter sound than Thy blest name,
> O Saviour of mankind!

But they could not pray, with Charles Wesley,

> Jesus, Lover of my soul,
> Let me to Thy bosom fly,

nor with Ellerton,

> Saviour, again to Thy dear name we raise
> With one accord our parting hymn of praise,

nor with Faber,

> Sweet Saviour, bless us ere we go,
> Thy word into our minds instil.

No largeness of heart or breadth of sympathy can bridge the gulf between the merely human Jesus, and the eternal Son of God; or join sincerely in the ordinary Doxology. The decisive test is, truly, as simple as profound. It is to answer unequivocally the question, can we pray to Christ, as One who hears and answers prayer? As a man supremely exalted, he may be loved, revered, adored. But unless he be more than man, the worship which prayer involves is out of the question. The truth is vividly exhibited in Rev. xix. 10. But until the whole significance of the New Testament is whittled away to nothing by hyper-criticism, it would seem impossible to question what was the conviction and practice of the Apostles and their converts, in this respect. The representation of Rev. i. 13-18, as it stands, is quite unmistakable.

(iii) The difficulties of evangelical faith for human

3

thought must be frankly acknowledged. The true Deity of Christ, with the associated doctrine of the Trinity, cannot be accepted as a rational demonstration, but as an inevitable deduction from undeniable facts. No definition of the Incarnation can ever be adequate. Nor can it ever be less than a demand upon faith to describe it as the ' Hypostatic Union.' Again, in regard to the Virgin Birth, it must be acknowledged that Christendom is divided. And not without reason. For, on the one hand, it appears to be both a natural and necessary concomitant to the acceptance of His eternal Sonship. Whilst on the other hand, it would seem to be fatal to the New Testament representation that—' He was in all points tempted as we are.' An abnormal birth apparently could not but prevent His ever being a fair example for such as are only of normal birth. The difficulty is not scientific, but moral. It would seem to be impossible in thought to make the humanity of Jesus real enough to constitute a truly human example, without dismissing the Deity which eternal Sonship involves.

(iv) Upon two considerations, therefore, the faith of each believer must turn. First, his own estimate of the reliability of the New Testament account of all that Jesus was, and said, and did. Then, the acceptance of such an interpretation of those records as seems to him to be the only one compatible with objective truth and subjective honesty. There is no present warrant for or indeed future prospect of, any one final dogmatic authoritative decision, as to the historic or legendary character of the birth narratives in our first and third Gospels. There seems to be an equal number of able and sincere scholars on both sides. Romish assumptions are of no more value than in regard to the 'Immaculate Conception,' or Transubstantiation, or Papal Infallibility. Ultimately, it must come to the fulfilment of the Apostle's principle in his letter to the Romans (ch. xiv.)—'Let every man be fully convinced in his own mind.'

Is there, then, nothing about which one may be sure—sure enough to live upon day by day, with duty for the present, and hope for the future? Yes—so far as one can see, the following principles remain among the 'things that cannot be shaken.'

(i) A definite conviction of some kind, whatever it be, and whatever the cost, is the duty and responsibility, as well as privilege, of every rational being. Moffatt's rendering of Gal. vi. 5—'For every one will have to bear his own load of responsibility,'—is as well warranted as timely. The tendency which prevails so largely in the religious world, to take refuge in matters of doubt or difficulty in the authority of the church, or the priest, or thoughtless custom, is as contrary to the mind of Christ[1] as it is unworthy of a moral being. It is simply a mark of mental indolence or ignorance, and explains the vast numbers of those who have given themselves up to the priestly assumptions of Rome, and Anglo-Catholicism.

(ii) In fulfilling this responsibility, and forming definitely one's own convictions, there is neither need nor room for mutual condemnation. 'Orthodoxy' is, after all, a mere verbal delusion. The only 'orthodoxy' for each individual, is that which appears to him to be true, when his mind is clear and his heart pure. 'To his own Master he stands or falls.' The Apostle's exhortation to the Romans (ch. xiv.) is at once the only moral and only Christian attitude. Between Romanist and Protestant, between Methodist and Unitarian, there may be and must be intense difference of conviction. But there ought to be no mutual recrimination, and certainly no dogmatic denunciation. In mind they cannot but stand apart, but in heart they ought ever to be one;

---

[1] Luke xii. 57—'Why do you not yourselves settle what is right?' (Moffatt).

since each must acknowledge and respect the other's intelligent sincerity. The only unpardonable sins are hypocrisy in one's own heart, and scornful condemnation of another's honest belief. The only impassable gulf between avowed Christians, should be failure in the unmistakable character enjoined by their common Lord. Compared with that—as portrayed by the Apostle in his never-to-be-forgotten description of love—in 1 Cor. xiii. —all else, literally all else, is ' nothing.'

(iii) For us mortals, in the realm of Christology as in all other realms, absolute, objective, final truth is unattainable. Relativity is the law of our being. Whether concerning God, or Christ, or even ourselves, we can but find truth enough for our life guidance. Whether this be termed pragmatism, or aught else, matters nothing. In no subject within compass of our thought, can we obtain complete mental definition and satisfaction. A God defined would be God denied : so a Jesus Christ who could be completely analysed and comprehended, would be other than the Christ Jesus of the New Testament. As indeed He Himself said, and the Apostles ever acknowledged. It is enough if, with all our highest powers and utmost scutiny, we find that the Christ of the New Testament deserves to be the object of our trust, our love, our prayers, our life devotion, as Paul did when he wrote to the Corinthians—not what is so poorly rendered both in the A.V. and R.V. but—' We make it our love and our ambition whether we live or die, to please Him.'[1]

(iv) In general, it may and must be said that whatever conceptions concerning the person of Christ are regarded as theologically truest, they ought at the same time to be morally highest and ethically noblest.

[1] 2 Cor. v. 9, where the compound Greek verb expresses the blending of love and honour—surely the strongest motives to all that is best in human nature's possibilities.

Just in the degree in which any avowed Christian believes
his convictions concerning the nature and work of Christ,
to be truer and worthier than those of other men, in
that degree he is bound to exhibit in himself a corresponding superiority of character.   If an ' orthodox '
Christian, or a Methodist, holds that his interpretation
of such experiences as are enshrined in Gal. ii. 20, or
2 Cor. v. 9, involve a truly and utterly divine Christ,
no less than a Christ truly and utterly human, then, at
least, there ought ever to be in his own life a corresponding experience, and in his character a similar loftiness.
Surely this is what Jesus meant when, for all His pros-
pective disciples He framed the test—'If you are courteous
only to your own relations '—as even pagan unbelievers
are—' what *extra* are you doing '—to justify your faith?[1]

(v) It is self-evident that the whole of one's religious
life turns upon his estimate of Christ.   It is impossible
herein to mistake the attitude of the New Testament.
No modern criticism rules out of consideration the
compelled conviction of Thomas,—' My Lord and my
God ! '   Nor can any estimate less than that be harmon-
ized with the Gospels and Epistles.   There is, indeed,
no stated doctrine of the Trinity, in the New Testament.
The Deity of Jesus is there rather implicit than explicit.
But by how much reverence in worship connotes more
than love in service, by so much is it impossible to ascribe
to a merely human teacher, all that is related concerning
the nature, and character, and works of Jesus in the
Gospels, together with the references to Him in the
Epistles.   The whole New Testament, it must in truth
be said, stands or falls with the divine humanity of Jesus.
If He be merely human, these records are the most misleading of all the world's religious literatures.

(vi) Nor is that all.   He is certainly therein declared
to be a Saviour.   The Christian question of questions is

[1] Matt. v. 47 : τί περισσὸν ποιεῖτε ;

—what does ' Saviour ' mean, and involve? As long as language has any meaning, Saviour must signify more than Teacher, or Master, or Leader, or Martyr. If we view humanity as a whole, from what do men need to be saved? Can there be any controversy in regard to the threefold answer to such a query? Assuredly there is enough sorrow in life, and enough fear of death to call for some deliverance. But if pain and sorrow be regarded as life's Upas Tree, it is surely with the root of such misery that men are most concerned. The common Christian term for that root is ' sin.' Those who would be precise without theology, term it ' moral evil.' Be the name what it may, from it above all else, as the main source of the other two, humanity needs to be saved. That is—' From sorrow, fear, and sin.' All that these short terms convey will not go into few words. Nor is it expressed in the myriads of volumes which have been written thereupon. It is true and sufficient to say, when we heed our words, that ' salvation from sin ' brings in its healing train, the being veritably saved from the other two. What is to be understood by ' sin,' and ' salvation,' will be presently considered. The main Christian truth here is that Jesus is in very deed, above all else, the Saviour, because He is what He is, and because He has done what He has done.

As to what He is. The numberless testimonies of believers, from the Apostles to this day, are not to be scorned. They did not lose their heads in renewing their hearts. But the impartiality of the witness of eminent unbelievers, makes it useful also to bear their words in memory. Strauss, the ablest Continental sceptic of the 19th century, testifies

Amongst the personages to whom mankind is indebted for the perfecting of his moral consciousness, Jesus occupies at any rate the highest place. With reference to all that bears upon the love of God and of our neighbour, upon purity of heart, and upon the individual life, nothing can be added to the moral intuition which Jesus Christ has left us.

John Stuart Mill, this country's famous non-Christian logician, declared that

Jesus must be placed, even in the estimation of those who have no belief in his inspiration, in the very rank of the men of sublime genius of whom our species can boast. Nor even now would it be easy, even for an unbeliever, to find a better translation of the rule of virtue from the abstract into the concrete, than to endeavour so to live that Christ would approve his life.

Whilst Mr. Lecky the ' Rationalist' historian, avers that

The character of Jesus has not only been the highest pattern of virtue, but the strongest incentive to its practice, and has exerted so deep an influence, that it may be truly said that the simple record of three short years of active life, has done more to regenerate and to soften mankind, than all the disquisitions of philosophers and than all the exhortations of moralists.[1]

And Dr. Drummond, writing in the *Hibbert Journal* above mentioned, from the Unitarian standpoint, says,

Would not the carrying out of one single commandment of Christ—' Love one another '—change the whole aspect of the world, and sweep away prisons and workhouses and envy and strife and all the strongholds of the devil? Long may it be before the world has cast away the deep and solemn wisdom of Jesus Christ, and ceased to be influenced by His holy impersonation of grace and truth.

To say nothing of one's own convictions and experience, those who are unmoved by such witnesses, may well be left out of account.

As to what He did, being what He was, until the New Testament is shown to be worthless, that also remains beyond expression. Words can never say more than we have before us in Paul's letter to the Philippians

[1] Strauss, *Life of Jesus,* Peop. Edn., 1864, p. 625.
Mill, *Essays on Nature and Theism,* pp. 253-5.
Lecky, *History of European Morals,* vol. ii., p. 88.

(ii. 5 to 8). The exact sense of ' He emptied Himself '—
how much, or how little, it includes of human fallibility—
can never avail to make less than awful the Incarnation
asserted.   Even Dr. Drummond, the Unitarian, writes
that ' such limitations or errors as may be discovered in
the recorded teaching of Jesus, have no effect whatever
on my reverence and love.' Why such humiliation should
necessarily involve the ' death of the cross,' may remain
a mystery for theology, but it can never mean less than
Paul wrote to the Romans—' God commendeth His own
love toward us, in that while we were yet sinners, Christ
died for us.'   In face of the whole overwhelming reality
of this divine-human tragedy, words will probably never
reach farther than those so well known which came to
Dr. Watts, in as real inspiration as Paul's :

> When I survey the wondrous cross
>   On which the Prince of Glory died,
> My richest gain I count but loss,
>   And pour contempt on all my pride.
>
> Were the whole realm of nature mine,
>   That were an offering far too small;
> Love so amazing, so divine,
>   Demands my soul, my life, my all.

More and more it seems to me, after all the watchings
and conflicts of the years, that Calvary is the uttermost
and final expression of the love of God for humanity. In
that sense and that alone, the Cross of Christ is the
essence of Christianity.

In reflecting on all this, that is on Him, the pitiful
failure of every attempt at a summary becomes overwhelming. Well might Paul exclaim—' Thanks be unto
God, for His unspeakable gift ! ' Much that should be
added, goes into two sobering considerations. (i) Taking
a large view, how fearfully far, through all the centuries
and even yet, has Christendom been from Christ's own
ideal. In regard to the common reproach that ' 2,000

years of Christianity' have proved a wretched failure—
as witness the sins, and shames, and miseries, and fears,
of our 'advanced' civilization—the least honest thought
shows that humanity, thus far, has never known 2,000
minutes of real Christianity.   Nor does there seem any
present prospect whatever of civilization being truly
Christianized.

(ii)   The apparent insignificance of any individual
effort in the struggle for Christian reality, as against
ecclesiasticism, clericalism, sacerdotal superstition, and
mere religious convention, can never absolve one from
the sacred duty of self-examination. Christ's own avowal
that the Kingdom of Heaven is 'like leaven' with which
a woman leavens the whole of her meal, takes on immeasurable emphasis in the light of our modern knowledge.   The whole leavening process, we now know, is
due to the vitality and activity of millions of microscopic
living cells, no one of which is too small to take its part.
So, ultimately, does the work and worth of Christianity in
this modern human world depend, not upon theological
accuracy, or the organic union of churches, or mass
movements of revivals, but upon the answer which each
avowed Christian gives to the simple though probing
query, is it true, or not, that—'For me to live is Christ'?

(3) THE HOLY SPIRIT

If, regarded as a whole, the doctrine of the Trinity
be described as a mystery, the truth concerning the Holy
Spirit is certainly an integral part of it. So much so,
that in spite of all the popular stress upon Whitsuntide,
it is little understood, or appreciated, by ordinary
Christian believers.   Beyond some Hymns which are
expressive and beautiful, too often there is little more

than unctuous reference to the ' Holy Ghost.' Happily,
this last word, which now is so out of date as to be not only
meaningless but repellent, is giving way for the far better
term ' Spirit.' But there is much hesitation and confusion
as to the real Christian significance of, or necessity for,
the doctrine of the Holy Spirit. All helpful consideration
of this must turn, again, upon the authority, and sufficiency of the New Testament. More especially, upon the
reliability of the Fourth Gospel—whoever may have been
its author. Relying on that witness, the Holy Spirit is
best known in Christian converse as the ' Comforter ';
although a nearer representation of the original παράκλητος
is the term ' advocate.' The general sense is that of a
teacher or helper, better still perhaps, in the words of
Dr. W. N. Clarke,—the ' Friend in need.' In spite of the
labours of theologians, the actual personality of the Holy
Spirit, and His relation to the divine Triunity, remain
an unsolved and inexpressible mystery. It cannot, of
course, be considered here at length.[1] But one preliminary
remark may well be made. Mystery is no warrant for
dismissal as untrue, or unimportant. For all realities
—beginning with our own consciousness—are equally
lost in mystery, whilst practically we live upon them from
day to day. Accepting then the testimony of the New
Testament, what are we led to believe concerning the
nature and work of the Holy Spirit?

(1) As to the nature or personality of the Spirit—it
must be owned that great differences of conviction are
found in Christendom. The warrant for speaking of
' Him,' or ' His,' as being distinct from the Father and
the Son in the Trinity, is definitely denied by Unitarians.
Whilst by some who are accounted Trinitarians, the Holy

[1] Out of innumerable writings hereupon, two may perhaps be
specified as the best that can be done in human speech. Namely,
the section dealing with this theme in Dr. W. N. Clarke's *Outline
of Christian Theology,* and Dr. A. E. Garvie's reference to it in his
recent book, *The Christian Doctrine of the Godhead.*

Spirit is identified with the Spirit of Christ—as by Dr. Jackson in two recent articles in the *Hibbert Journal.* A very orthodox paper, the *Methodist Recorder,* recently put it thus :

The Spirit of God—that is to say, the divine energy within ourselves, that vital power which prompts in the direction of all that is beautiful and good—is referred to in Scripture under various metaphors. When the Apostle wrote 'Quench not the Spirit,' he was thinking of it as a fire in our hearts which may on the one hand be fanned into a blaze, and may on the other hand be extinguished leaving us cold and dead.

This doubtless expresses what not only many feel, but what may also be said in regard to other New Testament utterances. But it is certainly nebulous, where clear statement is most needed. It must be confessed that the ancient phrase ' Three persons in one God ' is not satisfactory. The term ' persons ' is quite misleading; but it seems impossible to find any truer substitute. Nor does the ' Athanasian Creed ' make it clearer. But these three elements of the case seem both plain and helpful.

(1) The witness of Jesus Himself is unmistakable— unless the plain witness of the Fourth Gospel is jettisoned. His assurance to the bewildered disciples—' When He the Spirit of truth is come, He will guide you into all truth. He will take of Mine, and show it unto you '—admits of only one interpretation, namely, that the Advocate, or Paraklete, or Comforter, was personally distinct from Himself, and from the Father. The same must be said of many other statements in the speech and writing of the Apostles.

(2) In Christ's own words of promise, there is no element of difficulty. His own work is manifestly regarded as incomplete. Its continuance and development by the Spirit whom He Himself would send, appears to be only a natural procedure. But if all that is said concerning

the Spirit's teaching, guidance, comfort, help, really means nothing more than an ' influence ' from the Father, then language has lost its meaning, and the New Testament becomes fatally ambiguous in its whole attitude.

(3)   When Jesus said—' It is expedient for you that I go away—for if I do not, the Comforter will not come ' —how are we to understand such an assurance?   Surely thus.   (i) In revealing the reality of the divine Fatherhood, Jesus inevitably made Himself a problem.   He had to become, through the mystery of the Incarnation, the enigma of the ages.   How much He is so still, is witnessed in the remarkable volume to which reference has been made above.[1]   How much room there yet is for more teaching concerning Him, is manifest in the prevalent differences of conviction which divide Christendom.   It is true that the understanding of the nature and purpose of Christ's whole mission is, on the whole, to-day better than it has ever been, but the need for further teaching is measureless.   (ii) For careful thought, in the light of to-day, it is even easier to believe in, and appeal to, the Holy Spirit, than in regard to Christ Himself.   For whilst the mystery of the Incarnation remains as utterly insoluble in thought as inexpressible in speech, and intellectually it remains not merely incomprehensible but incredible —there is no such difficulty in the doctrine of the Holy Spirit.   If His personality be for the moment assumed, the familiar words of Tennyson find here fullest conceivable scope.

Speak to Him, thou, for He hears, and spirit with spirit may meet;
Closer is He than breathing, nearer than hands or feet.

There is only the question as to how the Divine Spirit can act upon the human.   And that is no question at all; seeing that in our own daily intercourse, spirit acts upon spirit continually, and in a myriad ways.   Ultimately,

[1] *Jesus or Christ?*   The supplement to the *Hibbert Journal* for 1909.

all modern psychology put together does not know how. But every sane consciousness accepts and uses such spirit communion hour by hour.

(II)   In regard to what is technically termed ' the work of the Spirit,' the assurance of Jesus Himself is endorsed by the rest of the New Testament, and accords most definitely and helpfully with every Christian's sense of need, and observation of human nature.   In at least two distinct respects.

(1)   The need for further enlightenment, as to the Person of Christ and the true significance of His Gospel, is too manifest to call for comment.   There may well be, as Paul said, ' diversities of operations, but the same Spirit.'   But the pronounced and often bitter dissensions of Christendom as to what is Christian truth, constitute an unmeasured tragedy.   It is not for us to apportion blame for sincere differences of conviction—yet it is impossible to regard the deep-cut divisions in and between the churches, as the fulfilment of the promise—' He shall take of Mine, and shall show it unto you.'   Somewhere, somehow, there must have been, and must still be, what the New Testament calls resisting, or quenching, the Spirit.   Whatever be the difficulties of theological thought, most assuredly there is more need to-day than ever before for ' some power not ourselves,' to fulfil Christ's promise—' He shall guide you into all truth.'

(2)   If we turn in thought from church and world, to the individual Christian life and character which must be ultimately the real leaven of civilization, four personal needs are unmistakable, and these are just what the divine immanence of the Holy Spirit is pledged by Christ and the Apostles to supply.   Every one who desires to live the Christian life is in constant need of four things, in greater or less degree.   Restraint from evil in all its forms;   prompting to good in all its opportunities; genuine comfort amid life's many sorrows and mysteries

of pain; and at the end of life's conflict, some reliable prospect of an after-death triumph of righteousness and healing of heart wounds. All these are beyond words to portray, but they are unmistakably included in the New Testament representations of the 'work of the Spirit.'

(III) Thus all that is left for Christian reality, is to appreciate and live upon such a sublime and yet homely assurance. Those to whom 'The Spirit,' as represented in the New Testament, is no more than an influence proceeding from God as the Father, or from Christ as the divine Son, must be allowed perfect liberty, with no 'touch of scorn' or condemnation, to carry out their own convictions. But for those to whom the 'personality' of the Holy Spirit is as real as it is indefinable, there come two practical reflections which might well find larger place in sermons or homilies. For

(1) first, here is the overwhelming assurance of a 'Friend in need' in God Himself, the living, loving, and eternal Spirit, close at hand every hour of every day, and everywhere, to lead us into the truth we each most need to know; to hold us back from doing ill; to urge us on to use every opportunity of doing good; to comfort and sustain when life's burdens or sorrows seem to be intolerable; to make as sure as vivid the truth that death is but the gate to higher life. Is not all this too good to be true?

(2) No; not if Christ be true. But there is a condition. An 'advocate' is not merely a 'friend in need,' but, as etymology reminds us, a friend whose help is called for. 'A friend in need is a friend indeed' is always true. But a friend to be such really, has to be not only called for, but accepted, heeded, taken into counsel, trusted. That, ultimately, is the significance and worth of the Christian doctrine of the Spirit. 'Quench not the Spirit' is more than stifling an impulse for good.

It is the wounding of a personal friend. Nothing less
can be the honest meaning of the Apostolic appeal—
'Grieve not the Holy Spirit.' Without the realization
of this, in heart and life, 'orthodoxy' is but a verbal
mockery. With it, such truth is the surest hope of
mankind.

(4) THE BIBLE

It seems impossible in these days to say, in brief, anything new or specially worthy of regard, concerning
the Bible. Dr. W. N. Clarke did indeed say something
well worthy of appreciation in his little book entitled
Sixty Years with the Bible. But far less than the 250
pages he there occupied, can be taken here.[1] Yet some
attempt at a summary of present-day Biblical matters,
is an inevitable part of any religious retrospect of the
last half century. The findings of acknowledged scholars
hereupon, differ immeasurably and irreconcilably. But
taken as a whole, they are as far from representing the
average views of church-goers, as from the attitude of
the man in the street. The vast literature which exhibits
the evolution of Christian thought concerning the Bible,
cannot be summarized. All that is here presented is the
general conclusion reached by an ordinary mind honestly
seeking the truth through many years. We will, therefore,
consider (I) A fair estimate of related facts which may
be regarded as beyond question. (II) A few inferences
therefrom which appear to be as reasonable as resistless.

[1] Although it may not be immodest to mention that some few
years ago, in my Fernley Lecture for 1916, a whole chapter was
specifically given to the same theme. I see nothing to withdraw
in that statement. It has only been confirmed by the intervening
years. But the circulation of such works is very limited—hence
some repetition here may well be worth while.

(III) A summary of the whole case. (IV) General conclusions.

(I)

The following statements of fact one may truly say are beyond contradiction.

(1) The Bible is certainly the best known and most influential of all sacred writings the world has ever known. At the present time it is being circulated all over the globe, to an extent unparalleled in any other religious literature. The records of the British and Foreign Bible Society constitute a development and a romance, the like of which has never been approached by the sacred books of any other religion. The annual report of that Society is a wonderful narrative. Last year (1925), in brief, it exhibits a distribution of over a million complete Bibles, more than a million New Testaments, and over eight millions of smaller portions, all complete in themselves. In various portions the Bible is now translated into at least 586 languages, with an increasing number each year.

(2) Taken as a whole, the Bible is best known, and most influential, throughout all those English speaking nations which are in every sense foremost in the modern world.

(3) The history of its translation from the original tongues is itself an unparalleled romance. From the time of Tyndale to this day, the most remarkable and most influential translation has undoubtedly been the Version of 1611, generally, though not accurately, known as the ' Authorized Version.' For pure and dignified English, the rhythm of which will never be surpassed, it was indeed a wonderful production. Its influence has been, and yet is, measureless. But for accuracy, the Revised Version, which appeared in 1881 to 1884, is vastly superior. In spite of many hindrances and mighty

prejudice, it is slowly but surely making its way. The remarkable performance of Dr. James Moffatt, in his recent translation of the whole Bible, is of real value; though its endeavour to express a more accurate represen- tation of the original in modern homely and natural speech, is fiercely resented by the many to whom sound is more than sense, and old association more important than truth. Besides these, but for the New Testament only, two other renderings have had considerable circulation, and for those who do not read Greek, are of great value, as being both more accurate and more in harmony with the speech of to-day. Of these two— Dr. Weymouth's *New Testament in Modern Speech,* and *The Twentieth Century New Testament*—the latter is on the whole to be preferred. It is specially valuable in en- deavouring to convey to ordinary readers some idea of the chronological order of the various portions.

(4) Whatever translation be adopted, the Bible is certainly and incomparably unique in its reference to God and man, as well as in its record concerning Jesus Christ. This is the more true now, by reason of the comparison with other sacred writings, which the study of comparative religion has made possible.

(5) It is revered and loved by millions of sincere and intelligent men and women, with an unshakable devotion which has been proof against all attempts to destroy it, and would doubtless, if the need arose, be as firm to-day in the defence and preservation of the Bible, as in the times of Diocletian, or the Romish Inquisition.

(6) But there are great and growing differences in the estimate of its significance and inspiration. Two great divisions of opinion are becoming more and more pronounced. On the one hand, those who cling to the past and are now widely known as ' Fundamentalists ' strongly maintain the verbal inspiration of the whole book. With varying intensity they declare that the whole

4

Bible is literally and equally the ' Word of God '; that it contains no error of any kind; is in harmony with modern knowledge; and is all alike binding upon the Christian conscience. There are also many grades of those who are termed ' Modernists.' But generally speaking, their estimate dismisses verbal inspiration as equally untrue and unnecessary; and acknowledges many minor inaccuracies in the letter of Scripture. Modernists come to the study of the Bible with an open mind, prepared to base their conceptions of inspiration on what they actually find. They thus set greatly differing value upon the various portions of both Old and New Testaments. In the former especially, they neither find nor expect to find, what is known as modern science, or what conforms to the literary standards of to-day.

(7) Between these two sections of believers there is, and is likely to continue for some time, a keen and often bitter conflict. The name ' obscurantist' is not euphemistic but it seems to be warranted by the dogged tenacity with which Fundamentalists maintain their views, in spite of everything which can be shown to the contrary. There are certainly some real grounds for their devotion. The lofty Theism of many parts of the Bible, together with its high ethical ideals, its unquestionably great and worthy moral influence, and, above all, its record of Christ and His Gospel, combine to make it unspeakably precious to millions. But the majority of them are quite content to regard the English version of 1611 as God's infallible, all-sufficient, and final word to mankind.

On the other hand, Modernists are increasingly supported in their attitude by the resistless developments of modern knowledge—scientific, historical, and critical —whilst the demands for thorough scrutiny become ever stronger, the proofs of mistakes in the older view ever plainer, the knowledge of the vastness of the universe

more and more impressive, and the understanding of
what Christianity really involves clearer than ever
before. These two great currents of thought and feeling
flow side by side, and neither of them can be prevented,
or extinguished, or ignored. It must be owned that
there is an ever-increasing number of better educated
folk, especially including the young, who strongly feel
that the older views cannot be honestly maintained
in face of facts which cannot be denied. Hence the
question arises, if the former estimate and understanding
of the Bible are to pass away, what have we in their
place? It is a fair question, and merits an unevasive
answer. The following main feature of the case cannot
be ignored.

(i) Outside the Churches, the Bible is not read at
all to-day. For the average citizen it is quite ousted
by newspapers and magazines, or swamped by the
ever-growing flood of fiction. It is no less ignored by
students of science and philosophy. (ii) Inside the
Churches, it is really read only by the few. The superficial
acquaintance with it which was acquired at school, or
in the Sunday School, is assumed as being quite sufficient.
In multitudes of Christian homes—I speak from knowledge—a Bible is scarcely discoverable. (iii) The
comparatively few who read it, do so almost always on
conventional lines. They are as a rule content with the
' Authorized ' version, without note or comment. Even
what is known as ' devotional ' reading is too often
merely another name for the unthinking repetition of a
pious habit. (iv) The ensuing ignorance is very little,
if at all, helped by the reading of what are called 'lessons'
in public worship. As a rule, with few exceptions, that
term is far from the truth. The reading is taken from
the old Version, without any regard whatever to its many
and important errors. The portions chosen for such
reading, especially from the Old Testament, have no

relation whatever to modern life—though the assumption is that the Old Testament is quite as applicable to Christian thought and conduct as the New. The reading itself is generally bad. No true expression is imparted to the words : ecclesiastical tone is substituted for good elocution. On the part of the congregation, little attention is paid, naturally enough, to the whole proceeding. The very last thing which occurs to the average hearer, is that in what is being read there is a real lesson for to-day's life. This summary is no cartoon. It is a simple, lamentable but truthful summary of what personal observation has shown to be the actual procedure, in numberless churches, every Sunday.[1]

Meanwhile, whether the quantity and quality of Bible reading be great or small, nothing can prevent that application of modern knowledge to Biblical matters which is called 'criticism.' It is thus most essential to ask, quite plainly, what such criticism has done, and is doing, in regard to the present-day appreciation and interpretation of the Bible. The term 'criticism' is certainly unfortunate, seeing that to the majority of ordinary people it conveys a notion of antagonism, or destructive purpose, which has no warrant whatever either in the real meaning of the word, or in its employment by earnest Bible students. Especially does this apply to the term 'higher criticism,' which is often sneered at by those who ought to know better, as if it claimed moral superiority. Whereas, the least instructed student knows well that it does nothing of the kind, but is simply a name for that further examination which

---

[1] Quite recently a high authority on religious teaching—Canon X—deliberately asserted, in a leading London daily, that there are in the United Kingdom less than 2,000 intelligent readers of the Bible. For such a startling assertion the writer gave two long columns of careful statements as proof. Even if we shrink from the figures, there can be no honest doubt that the assertion as to the comparative paucity of careful and open-minded Bible readers, is only too true.

follows, when the 'lower,' or textual, scrutiny has done
its part in making sure the original texts. Criticism
really represents nothing more than the natural and
necessary scrutiny which must be associated with the
desire for truth, in any and every realm of thought.
Every man who objects to criticism is himself a critic;
and is doing the very thing to which he objects. The
notion that Christian faith consists simply in blind
acceptance of what we are told, or have been accustomed
to, is sheer superstition. It is disowned not only by
Christ Himself, but by all who have learned of Him.

When it is asked what has criticism done for the
Bible as a whole?—the following five-fold gain may be
definitely specified.

(i) It has made plain and emphatic what is almost
universally ignored, that the Bible is not really a book
at all, but a library. As Dr. Thistleton Mark has said,
it is a 'progressive literature.'[1] It is a collection of the
writings of at least forty different authors; under entirely
different circumstances; with wholly different tempera-
ments and intentions; extending over hundreds of years;
without any anticipation whatever of their writings being
ever gathered into one exclusive volume. The late
Dr. Monro Gibson—a mellow scholar and genial conservative—did not hesitate to declare that to 'treat the
Scriptures as if the whole collection were only one book'
was 'extraordinary perversity and unfairness.' Said he,

Of all the unfair devices for weakening the evidences of
Christianity, this is perhaps the very worst. And it is surprising
that so many good Christians allow it, and even encourage it—
sometimes demand it. So great is the mischief arising from this,

[1] In his excellent volume on *The Appeal of the Bible To-day*.
For the ordinary reader who has an open mind, no better statement,
in brief, of the modern position can be found. Published by Nelson
& Sons, it deserves the widest circulation, as a truthful and wise
eirenicon in the conflict between Fundamentalist and Modernist.
See especially the chaper (p. 9) on 'A progressive literature.'

that even for convenience it would seem a pity that the sixty-six or more books which form our Bible, are so constantly bound together in one volume.

This witness is true; but nothing short of modern criticism would induce the religious public to acknowledge it.

(ii) Only so, moreover, would the vast importance of chronological order in the books of the Bible be apprehended. Probably ninety-nine out of every hundred Christians still think of Genesis as having been first written, then Exodus, and so on, right through to Revelation. For very many, also, the antique and misleading chronology of Abp. Ussher, which appeared in the margin of the Version of 1611, continues to be regarded as inspired truth.

(iii) Modern criticism has also made manifest and shown the importance of a progressive revelation, in the true order of the various portions. It thus clearly distinguishes the revealing of God and His purposes in the Bible, from the alleged revelation to one man, in one age, which is so fanatically claimed for the Koran.

(iv) It brings into necessary and rightful prominence the superiority of the New Testament to the Old, spiritually, theologically, and ethically. The careful scrutiny involved shows the New Testament to be not the contradiction, but the culmination of all the contributions of historians, psalmists, and prophets, to the Jewish conception of God and His attitude towards mankind.

(v) It has thus set the minds of Christians free for ever, from the former difficulties which were inseparable from regarding the Bible as being all of equal value and authority. This conception had, indeed, become as intolerable, morally and spiritually, as the attempt to ' harmonize ' the opening chapters of Genesis with modern science was manifestly impossible.

These all are undoubtedly so great gains for all

who value the truth, that it may be well to state simply
the unquestionable facts which remain for Christian
faith.

(1)   As to the Old Testament.   It is certain that
chapters 1 to 3 in Genesis are neither exact science nor
literal history. We know that this world was not made
in six days 6,000 years ago; that Adam and Eve are
not the names of one real man and woman from whom
the whole human race has sprung; that there was no
' Fall of man ' consisting of the eating of the fruit of a
certain tree, and then hiding from a God who could not
find them, in a garden. The whole creation epic is but a
purified version of previously existing Babylonian lore;
wonderful indeed in its freedom from gross polytheistic
traditions, but a purely spiritual representation suited
to the needs and capacities of the times, and having
no relation whatever to modern scientific conceptions.
The story of the Fall is but vivid allegory; certainly
with vast significance and imperishable lessons; but
needing to be interpreted in the light of our present-day
knowledge of anthropology and psychology; whilst
chapters 3 to 11 of Genesis are largely folk-lore, which
need not be dismissed as wholly untrue, but must not be
regarded as literal history in regard to each individual.
The historic portions are of greatest interest and value,
but not necessarily free from all errors. The Psalms are
certainly not all to be attributed to David; though there
is no sufficient reason for denying that any of them are
his. The Prophets must all be understood and interpreted
in the light of their varying national environment.

As regards the relations between the Old and New
Testaments, the New Testament undoubtedly begins
with the Old, and would be incomprehensible without
it. It is also plain that Jesus Himself knew and revered
the Old Testament, using it with intelligent care for His
own teaching purposes. But it is no less manifest that

He did not endorse it *en bloc*. His attitude of criticism and even rejection of some of its ideals, was much more bold and significant than is generally acknowledged. As for those of His references which seem to be contrary to modern critical findings, it is sufficient to mark that, for His purpose of spiritual teaching, it was as natural as necessary to accept the generally received beliefs of his fellow-countrymen. Any attempt at critical examination or correction, would have been as utterly fatal to His purpose, as entirely beyond their comprehension. It would have been as if, to-day, a lecturer on English history to an ordinary audience, should pause at every mention of a date, to discuss authorities for it; and at every notable event, to give all the contradictory estimates of opposing writers concerning it.

(2) As to the New Testament. The following items are so fully demonstrated that only blind fanaticism can deny or ignore them. (i) Whilst much may be said from the spiritual and practical standpoint, for the position of the four Gospels at the beginning of the New Testament, it is quite as necessary in this case as for the Old Testament, that much more notice should be taken of the true chronological order of the 27 portions of which it is composed. A very helpful attempt at this is found in the *Twentieth Century New Testament*. But little attention is paid to it by ordinary Bible readers. The popular notion undoubtedly is that the Gospels were first written, and then all the succeeding portions, in the order with which we are familiar. Hence arises not only the utter ignorance concerning early Christian history which obtains in all the churches, but also the common and michievous notion that the reference to ' this book,' in the closing verses of Revelation, applies to the whole New Testament—or as some declare, to the whole Bible —instead of to that portion only. (ii) It has to be acknowledged that there is a ' Synoptic ' problem which

cannot be wisely or honestly ignored. The relations between the three Gospels are both historically complex and spiritually important.

(iii) There is also a ' Johannine problem ' which is neither solved nor likely to be. For whilst some critics of eminence, such as Dr. Drummond and Mr. Nolloth, still insist that the author was the son of Zebedee, the beloved disciple, others, apparently the majority, equally learned and Christian, attribute it to John the Elder. There is, moreover, a general consensus of opinion that it is not so much a plain historical record, as a dramatized or spiritualized summary of personal recollections, in which the events related are more or less allegorical; whilst the discourses cannot always be taken as literal reproductions of Christ's words, but vivid recollections dramatically represented.

(iv) On the other hand the ' Acts of the Apostles ' which were for some time regarded as historically doubtful, and due to the activities of opposing Petrine and Pauline sections in the early church, have been so definitely confirmed by recent researches—especially those of Sir William Ramsay—that the reliableness of this record is now beyond all reasonable question.

(v) In regard to the other portions of the New Testament, whilst the Pauline authorship of the letters to the Romans, Corinthians, and Galatians, is now beyond dispute, it is equally sure that he was not the writer of Hebrews, which must apparently remain anonymous. There is also some doubt as to the authorship of what are called the ' Pastoral Epistles,' that is, those to Timothy and Titus.

(vi) Numberless volumes have been written and discussions expended upon the last portion in the New Testament, sometimes called the ' Apocalypse.' The authorship still remains undetermined. There is no warrant for the title affixed in the R.V. as well as the A.V.—' The

Revelation of St. John the Divine '—though it is often
regarded as being by the same author as the Fourth Gospel.
But it has become increasingly clear, in spite of the
ceaseless publications and activities of all kinds of
'Millenarians,' that this highly figurative and dazzlingly
symbolic book was never intended to be a kind of cryptic
summary of far-reaching future events, but is only
truly interpreted in the light of the environment of the
Churches at the beginning of the Second Century. It
was really written for the support and encouragement of
believers, during the fiery trials of pressing and threatening persecutions. Its cryptic style was absolutely
necessary because of the prevailing terror, but was entirely
intelligible to those for whom it was intended. Its Millen-
arian interpretations are intimately bound up with the
former estimate of the book of David, which the most
careful modern scrutiny has now shown to be untenable.[1]

(II)

The preceding summary represents at least the
minimum which must be acknowledged as resulting
from the unprecedented investigation into Biblical
matters during recent years, more particularly the last
half century. Much more has confessedly been alleged
by extremists on both sides. But the truth or untruth
of their allegations must be left for students to estimate.
For the vast majority of those who are known as Christian
believers, members or adherents of Christian churches,
it is equally certain that they will not be led by extremists,
and that they will come to feel increasingly, even if slowly,
such results as are outlined above. It remains, therefore,
to ask what is the personal or practical effect of these

[1] An excellent statement of the modern position in regard to
this book will be found in the late Dr. F. W. Farrar's volume in the
Expositor's Bible series published by Hodder & Stoughton. The
brief summary in Dr. Mark's book mentioned above, is also clear
and reliable.

resistless influences, upon ordinary Christian faith?
What is the loss or gain for Christian reality?

(1)   Let us first contemplate what may seem to be
losses.

(i)   It is simply impossible for us to read our Bibles
as our fathers did. The England of the 17th century so
vividly pictured by J. R. Green in his *Short History*
as the 'people of one book,' has passed away never to
return. The whole mental atmosphere of Great Britain
has changed immeasurably, even since the days of John
Wesley. We live now in another world, and all our
thoughts, estimates, and convictions, are inevitably
affected. Dr. Peake has only expressed the truth in his
valuable volume hereupon—when he says that

> The Bible has irretrievably lost the place once accorded to it
> by the consent of Christendom, and this is coming to be realized by
> an ever-increasing number.

(ii)   It is no less true, in spite of all the lamentations
and fulminations of Fundamentalists, that the former
estimate of the Bible as being so verbally inspired that
every word in it is 'the word of God,' and that it is
absolutely free from all errors, can no longer be maintained. The 'Authorized' version, in spite of its literary
excellence, contains many real mistakes, and is responsible
for much misrepresentation of Christian truth. The
suggestion of perfect original autographs, is too false as
well as flimsy to merit notice.

(iii)   It is now made clear that the Bible cannot be
truthfully regarded as an equally inspired whole, but
is composed of parts which differ greatly in spiritual
value and authority. There is no warrant for putting
the Old Testament upon the same level as the New,
for all purposes of Christian thought and life. The time-
honoured practice of quoting indiscriminately picked
passages and isolated verses, without regard to their

context, as applicable to Christian doctrines, needs, and duties, must be set aside for something truer and better.

(iv) The spiritual value and application of the Old Testament must always be estimated in accordance with Christ's revelation of God, and general New Testament principles. Thus the actions and characters of Old Testament heroes are by no means always examples for Christian emulation, but must be judged in the light of their times. So too in regard to the ideals of Prophets and Psalmists. They are not, and cannot be, Christian, seeing that to them there was no Gospel of Christ. The deep fundamental principles of their belief in God, with corresponding moral and spiritual conceptions, may be fully appreciated so far as they go. But the real lesson to be learned from them is always *a fortiori,* as expressed in the opening words of the letter to the Hebrews. If the saints and psalmists of old had such ideals, comforts and inspirations, under the influence of a restricted and only partially developed theism, how much more should we respond to the higher ideals and mightier stimulus which come from ' the light of the knowledge of the glory of God, in the face of Jesus Christ.'

(v) It is of the very greatest importance that the true understanding and appreciation of the Bible, and especially the relations between the Old and New Testaments, should be made clear to young people. The vast developments in both the matter and manner of our modern school teaching, especially in secondary and technical schools, are beyond measure. After such training through the week, to bring our young people to Sunday school or public worship, simply to hear in Bible reading and interpretation what satisfied their grandmothers, is as utterly unworthy of Christian intelligence, as manifestly contrary to Christian principles and ideals.

(2) If these considerations, which cannot be denied or dismissed, seem to be discouraging for ordinary Christian life, it is only necessary to bear in mind the other side with equal care and sincerity. The loss of what is untrue is always definite gain, and the gains in the present case are immeasurable. The cost of truthful understanding is overwhelmingly repaid.

(i) We have first the dismissal of all fear as to ' Bible difficulties.' When the Bible is treated as it ought to be, there are no ' difficulties.' An ' honest Bible ' has nothing to fear. The old difficulties which used to be so strongly alleged as to science, or history, or morality, were only difficulties in that they clashed with pre-conceived theories concerning Biblical inspiration and authority. Which theories the Bible itself neither suggested nor endorsed. They were but the imagination of theologians.

There are no scientific difficulties, because it is now acknowledged that it is no part of the function of the Bible to teach science; as certainly it was no part of its commission or intention to anticipate modern science. There was no more need in olden times for modern science in order to convey spiritual truth, than there was that the water they drank should have been always contained in vessels of modern Wedgwood pottery. Moral and spiritual truth can be as forcefully conveyed in allegory as in history, in poetry as in prose, and in fiction as in fact. At the time when the Old Testament scriptures were written, there was, of course, no science at all in the modern sense. Men spoke as simply and naturally of surrounding phenomena as we still do, when we say that the ' sun rises ' later in winter than it does in summer. As it would be sheer pedantry to declare that such sayings are unscientific, so is it but the pedantry of scepticism, or of Fundamentalism, to demand that the sublime vision of the first chapter of

Genesis should conform with all that we now know from modern physics or geology.[1]

In the same way the modern appreciation of the Bible sets us free from all the alleged 'moral difficulties' which formed so large a part of the blatant attacks upon the Bible in the 19th century. Some of the Old Testament representations concerning God's nature and character were shocking enough, on the old theory of inspiration. But they trouble us no longer. We now see that the ancient writers could not be expected to think of God as Christ reveals Him, nor can the men of that age be justly judged according to Christian ideals. The revelation concerning God was as necessarily progressive, as education still has to be for every ordinary child. Whilst as to some of the prominent human characters in the Old Testament, they must be judged according to their own knowledge and environment. Whether it be Jacob, or Joseph, or Samuel, or David, they cannot be expected to rise to a standard of ethics which they never knew. For us they are not examples, but reminders of Christ's word that—'unto whomsoever much is given, of him shall much be required.'

(ii) We have also learned to estimate at their proper value, the manifold inaccuracies which occur in the Bible, alike in the original texts, and the various translations. No human work is perfect, so that the manifest inperfections in the Scriptures do not now trouble us. They are simply indications of the humanness of the writers. When some Fundamentalists reply—one re-

[1] It is really as pitiful as surprising, to find a good and able man like Mr. E. W. Maunder using all his astronomical knowledge through some thirty odd pages of his book—*The Astronomy of the Bible*—to demonstrate that in the case of Joshua, in chapter x., 12 to 14, the sun and moon did actually 'stand still in the sky' through 'the slackening rotation of the earth'—on the ground that 'all things are possible to God.' Surely the implications of such a suggestion are to-day unthinkable. The whole account is neither more nor less than an extract from a poem written to glorify Joshua's victory.

cently did, with loudest profession of devotion to truth—
that all the Scriptures are wholly divine, because the
writers were just ' God's pens,' he only casts shadows
upon the divine character, and contumely upon human
nature. The mistakes of both originals and translations
are plain before our very eyes.[1] But we have learned
not only to recognize honestly the 150,000 various
readings in the Greek New Testament, and the very
many untranslatable passages in the Old—which
are absolutely fatal to ' verbal inspiration '—but also
to estimate them aright. They are of no concern at all
to those who desire substantial truth rather than verbal
meticulosity. When all such variations and inaccuracies
are taken at their utmost, they no more lessen the spiritual
value of the whole, than a mole upon a mother's face
makes her less lovable to her children.

(iii) The very severity and thoroughness of modern
Biblical criticism gives us greater confidence than ever
in the reliability of our sacred writings. The things
which could be shaken are removed, so that the things
which could not be shaken remain more firmly and
clearly than ever. Those who have little or no time or
capacity for exact study may now assure themselves,
as never before (sic), that they ' have not followed
cunningly devised fables,' but are basing their faith upon
the rock of truth. And this especially in regard to the
most important of all matters, namely the crucial question
as to whether the Gospels can be relied on concerning
the historic Jesus. Such reliability is now guaranteed
to us, by their having passed through such a crucible
of exact scrutiny as no other ancient writings have ever
known. So that unmeasured force has been added to the

[1] When the Revised Version was published in 1884, I published
in a volume entitled *Which Bible to Read,* more than 1,000 instances
in which the Version of 1611 needed correction. Recently in another book, *Reality in Bible Reading,* I have given many other
illustrations.

query propounded by the well-known and distinguished sceptic in the 19th century, John Stuart Mill, who wrote :

> Whatever else may be taken away from us by rational criticism, Christ is still left—a unique figure, not more unlike all his precursors than all his followers; even those who had the direct benefit of his personal teaching. It is of no use to say that Christ, as exhibited in the Gospels, is not historical, and that we know not how much of what is admirable has been superadded by the tradition of his followers. Who among his disciples, or among their proselytes, was capable of inventing the sayings ascribed to Jesus, or of imagining the life and character revealed in the Gospels? Certainly not the fishermen of Galilee—still less the early Christian writers.

It is not the task of these pages to show in detail how the rest of the New Testament is similarly made more credible for ordinary Christian faith. That is fully done in numbers of modern monographs. The great, plain, and precious truth is that, thanks to the unflinching and ceaseless scrutiny of modern criticism, the New Testament, taken as a whole and fairly interpreted by itself, is absolutely unique among the sacred writings of the world's religions. There is nothing like it for simplicity, sublimity, moral loftiness, and spiritual inspiration.

(III)

The summary of the whole case must be mostly practical. The main fact to be faced is the same for the Bible as it is for nature. The cheap and easy superficiality sometimes called the 'rule of thumb,' is worse than useless. But the demand for utmost pains and care, thoroughness and exactness, brings correspondingly valuable results. Our daily life supplies abundant illustrations. What is known as the national health—that is, freedom from dire epidemics, reduction of infant mortality, better treatment of disease, and prolongation of human life—is vastly better than ever

before.   But why and how?   Certainly not because of
such pious short cuts as ' faith healing,' or the Eddyism
which falsely calls itself ' Christian Science,' with its
ignorant contempt for the marvels of the human body.
Rather, by the very opposite of these.   Namely, the most
thorough-going, minute, exact, ceaseless investigation,
in physiology, chemistry, and bacteriology, along with
reverent recognition of and obedience to natural law.
History yields only too terrible records of what happens
when these are ignored.   Plague and pestilence, black
death and epidemics, typhus and typhoid, diptheria
and small-pox, have been the scourges which have driven
men to think more carefully and act more wisely.

Scarcely less solemn have been the dire results from
thoughtless, superstitious, bigoted treatment of the
Bible.   Sometimes on its behalf—as in the harsh rigidities
of Puritanism, or the cruelties of a Fundamentalism
which could burn alive in one century 100,000 innocent
women, because the Bible said somewhere : ' Thou shalt
not suffer a witch to live'—a murderous principle approved
even by John Wesley; at another time, through Romish
dread of the Bible, as the main support of Protestantism.
Whence all the devilries of the Inquisition. These horrors
are happily now impossible.   Yet there remain many
possibilities of costly mistake and painful misleading,
in the common indiscriminate reference to the Bible as
' The Word of God.'[1]   For that phrase is just as false in
some respects, as it may, when rightly understood, be
truthfully employed.   But it is better not used at all.
Nothing has given the enemies of Christian faith more
opportunity to blaspheme, than the reckless reference
to the Old Testament as the ' Word of God.' Many years
ago the late Dean Farrar, an accomplished scholar,

[1] Up to quite recent years it was legally criminal and ecclesiastically wicked for a man to marry his deceased wife's sister—because
of some references in Leviticus. As if that ancient Jewish ideal had
anything whatever to do with modern Christian behaviour!

5

pointed out that the phrase 'the word of God' occurs
some 400 times in the Old Testament, and 100 in the New,
but not in any one of them does it refer to the Bible.[1]
The dogged obscurantist persistence of the 'Bible League,'
or 'Wesley Bible Union,' is beyond appeal, and for
sheer assumption of infallibility surpasses the dogmatism
of Rome.   It is as really waste of time and strength
to-day to discuss with such zealots, as the Apostle found
it at Rome (Acts xxviii. 24-28) with many of the Jews.
All who are not blinded with pre-determined Bibliolatry,
will see how much truer it is to say that the Bible contains
the word of God.   For that estimate both sets the
ordinary believer free from former Biblical difficulties,
and puts on him his proper responsibility to follow, in
this as in other matters, the Apostolic ideal—'Test all
things, hold fast that which is good.'

Most of all does this need for careful discrimination
in Bible reading apply to Sunday School work. The
least that can be said hereupon, is that there is both
greater need and larger opportunity for such work than
ever before.   But here again mere superficial routine
is useless.   In these days, just to be content to keep
children in order and 'read round' from the Old Version,
without discrimination or modern and practical application, is sheer waste of time. Whilst in all other directions
education is being continually 'graded up,' if Christian
instruction does not proportionately improve, the faith

[1] A writer named Philip Mauro, in a small volume entitled *The
World and its God,* declares, with overwhelming assurance, that
'This Book bases its claim to acceptance entirely upon the oft-
repeated declaration—"Thus saith Jehovah."   The very nature of
the Book requires that, if we be logical, we either accept it because,
"the mouth of Jehovah hath spoken it"—or that we cast it aside
as the greatest of all human impostures.' And this rhodomontade,
in face of the fact that not once throughout the whole Bible does
the phrase quoted refer to the 'Book' at all. In the New Testament it never occurs.   It is small wonder that such false and
foolish Fundamentalism as this, should alienate men from religion
altogether.

of our young people will be rudely shaken into disbelief and irreligion, as soon as they pass out into their later every-day environment.[1]

(IV)

General conclusion. It is still true that for old and young alike, Christian faith may be all the more 'simple,' and real, for being intelligent. In modern light the true appreciation of the Bible is not lessened but vastly increased. Only two main principles must be observed, with special reference to the Bible and its treatment.

(1) On the part of the average Christian believer there must be a willingness to be taught more clearly and fully what is really true, instead of the all too prevalent assumption that all is known that needs to be known, and anything beyond that is dangerous. The Apostolic word must be reiterated for ever, as the Christian law— 'Finally brethren, whatsoever things are true.' (2) On the part of Christian preachers there must be corresponding competence and readiness to teach. It is no longer enough to 'proclaim the Gospel.' It is truth to the utmost which in our time is the prime necessity. And the truth is, as Jesus said, a 'pearl of great price,' to gain which a man must be ready to give all that he has. The best must always be costly; whereas the tragedy is that

[1] Mr. Stanley de Brath has not spoken too strongly in his impressive volume on *Psychical Research, Science, and Religion,* when he says, 'Plain speaking is required here. It is impossible to exaggerate the harm done by the teaching all but universal in schools of every class. Children are taught that man was created perfect, put in a garden, expelled for eating a fruit, that God drowned the world, and started afresh with Noah, that languages originated at the Tower of Babel because men were building a tower to reach up to heaven—followed by all the myths of the Pentateuch. The ideas thus implanted are on the level of negro fetish. Boys very soon throw all this overboard, and know that clergy teach them what no rational man believes. This is the frequent cause of complete rejection of religion in after life—it is associated with ideas that are historically and ethically false' (p. 182).

ordinary Bible reading costs nothing, either in public or private. Hence it is almost wholly profitless. It is an irksome duty, rather than a constant comfort and inspiration; a mechanical performance, rather than a quickening enjoyment. The pious practice, for instance, of reading the Bible 'right through,' so many chapters at a time, is sheer childish delusion. There are parts of the Old Testament which the ordinary Christian need never touch. Just as in the New, there are portions to which he may turn every day with growing stimulus. All Bible reading is to be measured as to its value, by quality, not quantity. Chapters and verses, in general, are much more hindrances than helps, in regard to personal profit through understanding.

But when the habit of reading regularly, thoughtfully, sincerely, and prayerfully—with the best of modern helps, as in all other subjects—has been formed, its influence for good cannot be over-estimated. The Old Testament is undoubtedly required for the proper understanding and appreciation of the New. Many portions of it are, moreover, full of deep spiritual significance. But it is, after all, by the New Testament that Christianity stands or falls, and Christian faith is established. The writings of the early Fathers and the interpretations of bygone ages, may be left to students, for what they are worth. But each age must form its own estimate and act upon its own interpretation. So, too, in this age must every section of the Catholic Church, and every individual Christian. But when that is done, sincerely and earnestly, with an open mind as well as a pure heart, the Bible remains not only the true foundation and standard of Christian belief, but the exhaustless source of comfort, inspiration, duty, peace, and hope for all who have learned to understand and love it. The proof of this is beyond words, not in argument but in experience.

(5) SIN

It would certainly seem from a careful estimate, extending over many years, of ordinary sermons, hymns, prayers, and homilies, in connexion with Christian churches, as well as from many volumes upon evangelical religion, that the fundamental concern of Christianity is sin. As a synonym of all moral evil, it is taken for the starting point of all else in the Christian faith. Until recent times, the general conception of the salvation of which the New Testament says so much, was, to be saved from an eternal hell of torment which was the inevitable result of unforgiven sin. During the last century, however, a great change has come over Christendom in this respect. The change has been gradual, partial, and silent, rather than open and complete. There are only too many evidences that the former cruelly false and misleading notions have by no means wholly passed away. There are still places and occasions when certain types of ' evangelical ' preachers loudly declare that eternal torment will be the irrevocable fate of all who do not ' accept Christ,' in the way they prescribe. And yet, in spite of all the fulminations of ecclesiastics, and the pleadings of ' mission preachers,' the modern world is manifestly less and less concerned, in the way they so seek to bring about. Sir Oliver Lodge declared, not long since, that ' the higher man to-day is not worrying about his sins, much less about their punishment.' Much criticism has been poured upon that sentence; but it is not disproved by theological frowns. It is as largely true to fact, as it is ultimately contrary to Christian principles. The whole question must turn upon what is really meant by ' sin '; and the briefest attempt to answer that, involves four distinct lines of thought. Namely (I) Acknowledgement of facts; (II) Protests that must be made; (III) Plain principles; and (IV) The outlook at the present time.

(I) It must be acknowledged that there is something terribly wrong with mankind, without at all underestimating the good which is also happily manifest. All history, as well as present-day observation, testifies to the fearful amount of suffering and misery which afflicts humanity. In our own time, the horrors of the late war have been followed not only by national conflicts of all kinds, but by a dire anxiety, in spite of the League of Nations, lest further war should arise, still more horrible in its threat of wholesale destruction. Meanwhile, all our cities contain plague-spots of poverty and vice, where it seems impossible to make life worth living, and social strife is embittered by class hatred. But all this need not be, and ought not be. It is, in a word, the result of sin. So that even if Agnosticism were accepted, and God left out of account, it becomes overwhelmingly manifest that humanity needs nothing so much as to be saved from ' sin '—this being but a short term for moral evil—the doing of what ought not to be done, the being of what men and women ought not to be. The ancient terrible list of the Apostle in his letter to the Galatians (v. 19), can be expressed in modern terms. If we say that drink, lust, greed, gambling, cruelty, selfishness, are still rampant in every nation and manifest in every city, we do but confess that sin is the real cause of human misery.

(II) But so far as the Christian doctrine of salvation from sin is concerned, there is pressing need for a double protest. To an immeasurable extent the aversion of modern men and women, alike intelligent and sincere, to the ordinary preaching about sin, comes to pass through two causes. (i) Sin is falsely conceived and misrepresented. It is traced back to the ' Fall,' Genesis iii.

being treated as an exact historical statement of fact. All there recorded happened so literally, that ever since ' the whole human race has been totally depraved through original sin, and doomed to eternal punishment by the wrath of God.' That this is no cartoon, is witnessed by the following extract from a publication which is now being circulated by thousands, and accepted as Christian truth by myriads.

It is fundamental and vital that we should understand that every part of man fell—man became ' flesh,' fleshly in every part and in every relationship of life. The poison of the Serpent entered the first Adamic race at the Fall, and the whole human race has inherited the utter depravity and corruption of original sin. Six thousand years of trial has proved man to be desperately wicked through and through.

Until quite recently, and in many pulpits even yet, this has been definitely accepted as the Christian origin and significance of sin. But all the vehemence and dogged persistence with which it has been promulgated, cannot make it true. It never was true. The time has come to say so plainly. It needs to be reiterated that Genesis iii. is not history, but allegory; human total depravity is as false in fact as in doctrine; original sin is unthinkable, being a contradiction in terms. The true Christian doctrine of sin has nothing to do with the ' Fall ' story; even as, in all the Gospels, Jesus Himself never once referred to it. (ii) Moreover, the real mission of His Gospel is not to threaten mankind with awful penalties because of evil, but to reveal the love of a Heavenly Father so really and impressively in Jesus, that the sinfulness of sin cannot but speak for itself. The darkest shadows are cast by the brightest light, and need no painting.

(III) The truth concerning sin, from the Christian standpoint, must be stated both negatively and positively.

(i) Negatively. As just pointed out, it is independent of any interpretation of the opening chapters of Genesis. There were no ' first parents,' in the sense usually asserted. We know really nothing about either the origin of the human race, or the beginning of sin. The general truth that humanity emerged gradually from pre-human anthropoidal ancestors, may be regarded—in spite of all obscurantism—as unmistakably established. But the laws of heredity neither cause sin nor account for it. The very essence of sin is the definite volition of a moral personality, which cannot under any circumstances be transmitted. The plain statement of Jesus that ' out of the heart proceed evil thoughts and the things that defile a man ' is not only psychologically true, but doctrinally sufficient. Furthermore, the sinfulness of personal volition, from the Christian standpoint, does not consist in the violation of the ' Ten Commandments ' associated with the Mosaic dispensation. Those commands were wise, and good, and necessary, for the slave rabble which escaped from Egypt. But they no more represent the Christian standard than the multiplication table suffices for the advanced mathematician. They are only partly applicable to modern civilization, and though they need not be contradicted, they must be greatly exceeded if they are to represent the Christian attitude.

(ii) Thus, positively, the whole conception of sin depends upon the thought of God. The Old Testament, for all its value, does not give the Christian thought of God. Not from ancient Jewish kings, prophets, psalmists, seers, but from Jesus Christ alone, comes that revealing of God as Father, who is Spirit, light, and love—which determines clearly, fully, and finally, the Christian doctrine concerning sin. Jesus assumed the Old Testament, as it was current in His day, but expressly refused to take the laws of Moses as the rules for His Kingdom.

He 'came not to destroy, but to complete.'[1] His method was spiritual evolution. Out of nine negatives and one limited positive, He formed two all embracing positives. Taking them out of their original setting in Leviticus and Deuteronomy, He so enlarged and intensified them as to make 'Thou shalt love' the categorical imperative of His whole message to humanity.

From this 'royal command,' as it refers both to God and man, is derived the Christian conception of sin, and the measure of its sinfulness. All the teaching of Christ and all the doctrine of the Apostles throughout the whole New Testament amount to the acceptance, application, and enforcement of His two Great Commands, in all the workings of the human heart, and all the relations of human life. Thus, ultimately, from Christ's standpoint, sin is the scorn of love. It is indeed the 'transgression of the law.' But not the law of Moses. It is the law of Christ which is test and estimate of sin. The sin of sins is, first, the scorn of the Father's love, as revealed in all that Jesus was, and taught, and did. Then, all too surely and easily, from the scorn of the First Great Command follows contempt for the Second. In the degree in which the Father's love is rejected, ignored, despised, the love of our fellow-man becomes only a matter for contemptuous disdain. Under the influence of that disdain, whether deliberate or passionate, are developed all those degrees of selfishness which constitute moral evil and curse humanity, from the nursery to the field of battle. Professor McDougall declares that 'The basis of all thought of and preparation for war is fear. What is needed for peace, is a sense of

---

[1] The commonly accepted rendering here of $\pi\lambda\eta\rho\hat{\omega}\sigma\alpha\iota$ is, in spite of Dr. Moffatt's adoption of it in his new translation, quite misleading. 'Fulfil' has become a technical term for the coming to pass of some prediction. Which is certainly not what Jesus meant. Dr. Weymouth's phrase is quite justified—'I have not come to abrogate them, but to give them their completion.'

security.' That is, the real danger of war is sin. For if only the First and Second commands were accepted and obeyed, there would be absolute security, and no fear at all. But these commands are so inseparable, that he who does not keep them both, keeps neither. For the first is the dynamic of the second, and the second is the necessary result of the first. The dreadful list of the 'works of the flesh' given in Paul's letter to the Galatians, above mentioned, is just the expression of what follows when both are trampled on by human self-will.

What truth, then, is there in the common avowal that this age is losing its sense of sin, and consequently its regard for Christian 'salvation'? There is only too much reason for such a suggestion. Besides the immeasurable changes which have come to pass in the intellectual world through the development of education, the plain fact that nine adults out of every ten in Great Britain—to say nothing of the Continent—are conspicuous by their absence from public worship, speaks for itself. Can it be explained? I fear it can; only too easily. The following summary simply states the facts.

(i) To a tragic extent, all anxiety about sin is just crowded out of thought by the increasing intensity of the fight of life, in the case of the vast majority of our modern populations. Millions of unemployed, besides other millions that are too much employed, are entirely engrossed with the difficulties of sheer bodily existence.

(ii) Where there is time, means, and opportunity for thought, all sense of sin is dismissed through the development of a double determinism. (a) Theoretic determinism, which views every individual as the mere product of his heredity and environment, declaring that no man can help anything he does, so that moral responsibility is nothing but a pious fiction. (b) Practical determinism, which may truly be termed animal sensationalism, in that it puts personal enjoyment, whether coarse or refined, above everything else.

(iii) During recent years, there has been a great and growing reaction against the wild exaggerations and repulsive assertions that used to be made in Christian pulpits and publications, in regard to sin and sinners. Especially also in the hymns which were used in public-worship. Audiences of sincere and morally well-behaved people were called upon to sing such as the following—

> Me, the vilest of the race,
>   Most unholy, most unclean;
> Me, the farthest from Thy face,
>   Full of misery and sin.

> I have spilt His precious blood,
> Trampled on the Son of God,
> Filled with pangs unspeakable,
> I, who yet am not in hell!

> Thou God of glorious majesty,
> To Thee, against myself, to Thee,
>   A worm of earth I cry;
> A half awakened child of man;
> An heir of endless bliss or pain
>   A sinner born to die!

Whilst even children were expected also to sing:

> I lay my sins on Jesus,
>   The spotless Lamb of God;
> He bears them all, and frees us
>   From the accursèd load.
> I bring my guilt to Jesus,
>   To wash my crimson stains
> White in His blood most precious,
>   Till not a spot remains.

It was inevitable that common sense, as well as clearer perception, should revolt against such suggestions—of which the above are only very mild specimens. So the pendulum of thought has swung from belief in original sin and total depravity, to the opposite extreme. All men are declared to be fairly good, and the moral evil which cannot be wholly denied, is regarded as a transient trifle. Omar Khayyám is quoted with relish :

> Said one—Folks of a surly Tapster tell,
> And daub his Visage with the smoke of Hell;
> They talk of some strict Testing of us—Pish!
> He's a good Fellow, and 'twill all be well.

(iv) Undoubtedly, also, the former stern conception of the severity of God which was the main tenet of the prevalent Calvinism, has given way to a wider and tenderer belief in a divine Fatherhood, as applying to all men, and not merely to a few ' converted ' who were attached to churches. This has in some quarters been misunderstood as meaning that sin does not matter; so that repentance, faith, and holiness need not be considered.

(v) It cannot, however, be denied that the sinfulness of minor failures, such as may daily occur in the lives of ordinary people and normal children, has been greatly exaggerated. The development of modern science has so enlarged man's conception of the universe, that all former thoughts of God as an Eastern Despot getting angry over human trifles of thought, or speech, or act, are no longer credible. If there be one great good God over and through such a universe, He must be far too great, as well as too good, to get angry over children's peccadillos, or make mountains of wrath out of human molehills of wrong.

(vi) The development of psychology has also shown that human nature and human life are so complex, and exhibit such admixture of good and evil, that it is utterly untrue as well as unjust, to classify all men alike as sinners, or roughly divide them into sheep and goats.

(vii) The modification of what was formerly preached and taught and threatened hereupon, has been gradually and silently but really proceeding, so that it is no longer taken seriously. All future punishment, in particular, is now set aside as a fanatic delusion.

(viii) The wholesale rejection of former eschatology has created an atmosphere of doubt and uncertainty, not only in regard to the truth concerning the distant future, but as to the entire system of Christian doctrine. (ix) For vast numbers in our modern populations, it is also plain that the authority of the Bible, as the arbiter of human character and conduct, is seriously shaken. It is no longer enough to declare that ' the Bible says so,' in regard to any estimate of human behaviour. (x) The increasing absence from church services cannot but tend to increase modern indifference to the actuality and solemnity of sin. Practical agnosticism prevails on all hands. It is too true that in very many, if not most, churches, there is little clear and impressive teaching concerning sin. But when people are repelled by pious piffle in pulpits, they will certainly not learn Christian truth by wandering about in the fields, or playing Sunday golf and tennis, or poring over Sunday newspapers. Nor will they by spending hours ' listening in ' to a wireless programme which grows so increasingly Godless, that out of seven hours spent on indiscriminate and superficial music, less than one hour is given to anything approaching Christian sanctions on that day.

(IV) In view of all these estimates, which might truthfully be emphasized, the situation to-day, from the Christian standpoint, is confessedly serious. ' Revival Missions,' however largely attended and wisely conducted, do not and cannot stem the tide of modern religious indifference. Nor do they touch or prevent the definite and dogged opposition which is always being maintained by ' Rationalists,' and underrated by the churches. The passing of years compels a watchful student to make some affirmations which are as true as comprehensive, and as sincerely modest as seemingly dogmatic.

(1) It is certain that there will have to be a re-statement of Christian 'fundamentals,' beginning with and determined by the truer understanding of the nature and significance and use of the Bible. The sincere but fanatic outcry against this will doubtless persist. But the false theory of inspiration has led to almost all the other delusions which have misrepresented Christianity, and driven men away from Christ. All that has been outlined above on this theme here applies with emphasis.

(2) Sin can only be rightly understood in the light of a larger, worthier conception of God; drawn not from the Bible as a whole, but from the New Testament revelation which Jesus brings, interpreted in the light of our modern knowledge.

(3) Equally necessary is a truer estimate of human nature, as against the former notions of total depravity, election, and predestination, which were due to Calvinism; and the scarcely less false estimate of extreme 'evangelism,' especially as represented in the popular hymnology which talks of men as 'senseless stones,' 'worthless worms,' 'moral corpses,' 'poor nothings,' 'dust and ashes,' and the like. All such bathos is as mischievous as false.

(4) Upon these two altered conceptions—a worthier estimate of both God and man—the true Christian doctrine of sin will have to be based. The 'Ten Commandments' must no longer be written up in Christian churches as the Christian law. For this they certainly are not; and never could be. Jesus Himself made that plain enough. They are no more sufficient for His Kingdom, than the child's spelling book and multiplication table suffice for the scholarship of his older years. Christ's two Great Commands were indeed taken from

the Old Testament, but were transfigured in His hands, and become in their far greater intensity and comprehensiveness, the only true Christian standard of sin.

(5) It is also of the greatest importance that there should be a clearer understanding and plainer statement of the real mind and spirit of Jesus, as distinct alike from Paul's Rabbinism and from sacerdotal clericalism. For the things which constitute so large a part of Christian worship, and count for righteousness to so many—such as rites and ceremonies, rubrics and liturgies, ornate dresses and formularies—Jesus never showed the slightest regard. The unmistakable characteristics of His teaching and example were simplicity, naturalness, humility, unselfishness, impartial loving-kindness. These, proceeding from reverent love to God and practical love to all men, constitute the veritable heart of His message and the law of His Kingdom, whence comes the true estimate of sin from the Christian standpoint. How much more this estimate involves than obtains from ordinary morality, or Jewish righteousness, or ecclesiastical conventions, is too plain to be misunderstood.

Summaries of any vast subject are useful or useless, just in the degree to which they are expanded by further thought, or dismissed. Erudite volumes like those of Dr. Tennant, and Dr. Orchard, in recent times and others preceding too numerous to mention, have appeared on the subject of sin. But all that is here attempted is such a statement as the most ordinary man or woman can appreciate. In conclusion, therefore, and for the sake of emphasis, the following may be repeated, as the main, unmistakable, and changeless elements in the doctrine of Jesus concerning sin. He assumed without argument the reality of the personality of God, as witnessed in all the Old Testament and accepted by the Jews of His day. But He transformed and transfigured that conception into the personality of a tender

and loving Father, and never-absent Friend. Modern
knowledge has only made explicit what to Him was
always implicit, in regard to the majesty of the divine
nature which we now try to express in such terms as
infinite, immanent, transcendent. But the majesty of
the Father's love is never represented as the meticulous
fault-finding of some despot. ' He knows our frame
and remembers that we are frail,' becomes ' The Father
Himself loves you '; and constitutes the very soul and
substance of Christ's Gospel for humanity. Sin, in all
its forms, degrees, and results, is the scorn of that love.
But there is no 'wrath' of God which is not the expression
of His love. The only condemnation of sin, even in its
severest expression, is the protest of love against the
loss and injury which the sinner inflicts upon himself
and causes others to share. There is nothing in the
' anger ' of God towards sin and sinners, according to
the revelation of Jesus, answering to the offended pride
or jealous resentment of an earthly despot, or the
malignity of an ordinary angry man. The ' wrath of
God ' is, only and always, the grief of a loving Father
over loveless and rebellious children. The punishment of
sin does not consist, nor ever will consist, in externally
inflicted pain, but in its inevitable consequences. To the
persistently impenitent there comes, (i) in greater or less
degree, here and now, alienation from the eternal love
which is the source of all truest happiness and noblest
development. Then (ii) the multiplication of such
individuals in human society, gives rise to the frightful
amount of suffering which otherwise would never be,
in this life. Whilst (iii) in the life to come which follows
upon death, there is, so far as our vision can discern, only
the continuation and intensification of the misery which
here the sinner inflicts upon himself and others. These
three woes are partially represented in words, but in their
dire reality they are beyond expression, for the solemn

emphasis they put upon the overwhelming truth, that the greatest of all human needs, alike for the individual and the race, is salvation from sin.

(6) SALVATION

'Salvation' is undoubtedly the commonest commonplace of Christianity. Apart from references to God, it is the greatest term in all the Bible. It expresses the whole significance, purpose, and worth, of the Gospel of Christ. It has always been, and still is, the ceaseless, all-embracing theme of Christian Churches, in all their services, sermons, hymns, prayers, and homilies. It is the sum and substance of all the dissertations of theology. What is it all about? What does 'salvation' really mean? What is it to be 'saved'? No inquiry in the whole realm of religion can be more pressing than this. The word occurs 160 times in the Bible—in the Old Testament referring mostly to physical or national deliverance—whilst the cognate term to be 'saved,' is found more than 100 times, with definite spiritual significance. Hence, 'salvation' has become the watchword of all Christian churches, though in widely different senses. In the past, the main reference of the term has been to a *post mortem* future. Speaking generally, this was its almost exclusive meaning, until the 'evangelical revival' in the 18th century. Human life was but a guilty, miserable, transient trifle, and the one great matter for concern was how to escape 'eternal damnation.' Thus in the Methodist services, audiences were quite content to sing:

> Nothing is worth a thought beneath
> But how I may escape the death
>   That never, never dies;
> How make my own election sure,
> And when I fail on earth, secure
> A mansion in the skies.

6

Even after the tireless labours of Wesley and Whitefield, that remained the ordinary conception of salvation, and it is still to be found in some popular hymns. The general attitude, yet maintained by Fundamentalists and others, was, as stated above, that the opening chapters of Genesis were literal history, so that through the sin of Adam and Eve all mankind became totally depraved, and in peril of eternal perdition. From this they could only be saved by definite personal faith in Jesus Christ, as represented either by Romanism or Protestantism. There was, however, in and after the evangelical revival, an added sense of forgiven sin which led on to peace and gladness through communion with God, and found expression specially in Charles Wesley's hymns. Such as this:

> My God is reconciled,
>   His pardoning voice I hear,
> He owns me for His child,
>   I can no longer fear,
> With confidence I now draw nigh,
>   And Father, Abba, Father! cry.

But even that sentiment is falsely based, for it assumes all that has just been mentioned, as well as a limitation of the divine Fatherhood, of which Jesus knew nothing. During the last fifty years, however, of which I here speak, a great change has come to pass, gradual indeed, but unmistakable and undeniable, over all that is preached and printed and sung in most Christian churches. There is either no reference at all to hell hereafter, or it is represented in very different fashion from the lurid pictures of the past. Whilst 'eternal punishment' is either definitely dismissed as an old-time fiction, or left as one of the insoluble mysteries of eschatology. Salvation is now generally preached as a present, distinct, personal experience, with a necessary ethical accompaniment— 'things that accompany salvation' (Heb. vi. 9)—and a significance after death, beyond present expression.

Even the Romish Church, which definitely and doggedly maintains its doctrine of a physical, gruesome hell, with a corresponding Purgatory, yet also has in its fold numbers of devout souls whose present experience of salvation is found in such hymns as Faber's :

> For the love of God is broader
> Than the measures of man's mind,
> And the heart of the Eternal
> Is most wonderfully kind.

> If our love were but more simple,
> We should take Him at His word,
> And our lives would be all sunshine,
> In the sweetness of our Lord.

> Do more than pardon : give us joy,
> Sweet fear, and sober liberty,
> And loving hearts without alloy,
> That only long to be like Thee.
> Through life's long day and death's dark night,
> O gentle Jesus, be our light.

In what may be called spiritual ethics, nothing more true and deep and practical can be found that Thomas à Kempis' *Imitatio Christi*. Amongst myriads of other devout believers, alike in all the sections of the Anglican church, and in all the Free churches which used to be called 'Nonconformists,' the same present appreciation of salvation has been felt and shown. And yet it would be difficult indeed to say what the average church-member or church-goer really means by ' salvation.' Some genuine benediction undoubtedly, but enshrouded in a nebulosity of thought and speech which greatly needs to be cleared away, if the 'Lord's Prayer' is ever to be answered. If there be any meaning at all in the ' salvation ' of the New Testament, it is, beyond all controversy, a matter which concerns the many, and not merely the few. It is said to be a ' salvation for all men.' But people generally, whether within or without the churches, know nothing, and care less, about all the erudite theological dissertations which are found in such numbers on library shelves. Yet we are told in the Gospels that ' the common people heard Him gladly.' Why?—but because His teaching was so different from the learned dogmas of His day, in its homeliness and simplicity. Even so in our own time, what the world of mankind needs now more than ever, is not an academic, philosophical, theological salvation, but something equally real and simple, capable of universal application and manifest proof, in the humblest of ordinary human lives. From this standpoint, therefore, we are concerned not with the details of church history, or the decrees of ancient councils, or the trust deeds of churches, or the disquisitions of theologians; but with those great features of the teaching of Jesus, which are too plain to be misunderstood by any open-minded student of the New Testament. There can be no doubt that the final purpose of the whole Gospel of Jesus is that men may be ' saved.' But all that is meant by such salvation, cannot be learned from a few picked passages. The whole of what He was, and did, and taught, must be taken into account, in the light thrown upon it by the rest of the New Testament, and interpreted by all our latest knowledge. It becomes necessary, therefore, to think of ' salvation ' first negatively; that is, to apprehend what, according to the New Testament, it does not mean; and then, positively, to appreciate what it does mean, and ought to mean increasingly for all mankind.

(I) Negatively.

(1) It does not refer, primarily, or above all else, to the future after death. Jesus did, indeed, assume the reality of a life beyond the grave. Also, that the results of this present life would inevitably make themselves felt in that great hereafter. But He never represented salvation as mere escape from the far-off infliction of an

angry God. Nor, certainly, as simply deliverance from a
doom of everlasting suffering. No passage in all the New
Testament has been more misquoted, in this regard, than
Matt. xxv. 31-46, as a careful exegesis soon shows.

(2) For long ages, thanks mainly to Calvinism,
salvation was inseparably bound up with predestination;
that is, the election of some to be saved, and the ' repro-
bation ' of others to be ' damned '—without any reason
beyond the ' divine decrees.' It is difficult in these days
to realize the awful hold which this monstrous misrepresentation had upon the popular mind. Nor can one
understand how cultured theologians like Jonathan
Edwards, and other Puritans divines could ever maintain
it. For in spite of all picked passages in the Bible, it is
as false to the nature of the Heavenly Father whom
Jesus reveals, as it is to the nature of man as a moral
being, and to the whole trend of the New Testament.

(3) According to Christ's Gospel, salvation certainly
does not consist in church membership. Still less is it
punctilious and continual observance of the rites and
forms, ceremonies and sacraments, which have been so
often declared to be essential by sacerdotal ecclesiastics.
The dogmatic avowals of Rome, and Anglo-Romanists,
that there is no salvation outside their pale, are but a
pitiful exhibition of clerical conceit and bigotry, for which
there is not the least New Testament warrant or excuse.
Rather, in such utterances as John x. 16, Acts x. 34, and
Romans ii., there is the unmistakable assurance that
a real salvation is quite possible, apart from any church
association whatever.

(4) It is equally plain that Christian salvation does
not depend upon the exact acceptance of some definite
creed, or the precise definition of any theological doctrine.
As pointed out above, the ' damnatory ' clauses of the
' Athanasian creed ' are much more akin to blasphemy
than the mind of Christ. The dogged defence of them

by some ecclesiastics only serves to show how narrow the clerical mind can become. The greatest discussions in Christian history, from the fourth century onwards, have related to the person of Jesus; and the great division which yet remains has been between the Trinitarian and Unitarian conceptions of God. To a large extent the Trinitarian view has prevailed. So that what is termed 'orthodoxy' has not only opposed the Unitarian view but contemned as well as condemned it. But there is no Christian warrant for such an attitude. Jesus Himself rebuked such a spirit (Luke ix. 49 to 55; Mark ix. 38). And when we call to mind some leaders of Unitarian thought and life, such as Channing, Martineau, Drummond, Jacks, and a host of others, it is certain that many of these have been nearer to Christ and all that His Gospel means by salvation, than can be found in the realm of ecclesiastical dogma, pomp, and bigotry. Christ's own word—'Not every one that saith unto Me, Lord, Lord, will enter into the Kingdom of Heaven, but he that doeth the will of My Father'—is sufficient assurance that no man ever was, or will be, 'saved,' by, or for, the accuracy of his beliefs.

(5) Nor is there any more warrant for the ultra-evangelical representation of salvation as something magically accomplished, once for all, in a moment, through faith. The reference here is not to what was termed 'final perseverence'—once in grace always in grace—for that Calvinistic doctrine is only held now by a few 'particular' Baptists, and smaller sects. But rather to the sincere though mistaken estimate of what takes place at the beginning of real Christian life, when, at some definite time, a man is said to be 'converted.' The common assertion is that then, through repentance and faith, he is 'saved.' Thus at the close of some special 'revival mission' the statement is often made that so many were saved. It is never really true; though there

are numbers of good Christians in the Free Churches
—and especially in the 'Salvation Army'—who would
be ready to testify that at such a time and place they
were saved. It is quite sincere; but seriously untrue.
They may, indeed, sing quite truthfully

> Saved from the fear of hell and death,
>   With joy we seek the things above;
> And all Thy saints the spirit breathe
>   Of power, sobriety, and love.

But it is the latter part of this verse, much more than
the first line, which needs to be emphasized, if the New
Testament truth about salvation is to be understood and
made known. What really happens in all such cases
of conviction or conversion, is a more or less sudden
moral crisis, in which a real change begins in the whole
inner life. In a word, there is morally and spiritually
a new birth—the 'birth from above' of which Jesus
spoke to Nicodemus. But that is not salvation, any more
than birth is life. To be born is one thing; to live is
another. Salvation is a life, not a mere birth. That is
why the entirely wrong rendering of the Old Version in
Acts ii. 47, is so seriously misleading, that it ought never
to be read in public—especially when the Revised Version
which is accurate, is always at hand. Salvation, in the
truly Christian sense, is not an event, but a process of
spiritual development. It is no more a sudden and
definite act, than is education in general. True education,
as a momentary crisis, in unthinkable; but not more
so than salvation. This becomes all the more manifest
when we pass to consider what, positively, salvation does
connote.

(II) Positively.

(1) First, and above all else, according to the
teaching of Christ and the whole New Testament, salvation means something here and now. It is, in some way,

an unmistakable and immeasurable benediction, which is to come to pass through human appreciation of divine grace. Here the first great truth to be apprehended is that 'salvation' and 'eternal life' are synonyms. Also, that 'eternal life,' in Christ's sense, is not something to be known only after death, but is a very present reality. Until the Fourth Gospel is shown to be unworthy of regard, the words of Jesus in chapter xvii. 2 are unmistakable, and are endorsed by the rest of the New Testament—especially in the first of the three Johannine letters. That there is also in this phrase a future reference, is manifest in many passages; but the great truth that must not be overlooked is that the primary significance of 'eternal' is not quantitative but qualitative. It is, in one word, the embodiment of what Jesus said elsewhere—'I am come that men may have life, and may have it in surpassing measure.' It is the surpassing quality of life in fullest, deepest, highest experience, that constitutes real salvation.

(2) To this conscious benediction there must be as real and definite a beginning as there is to physical life. But as no one remembers being born, so may there be an entrance into the spiritual life which salvation means, gradual enough to lack any conscious starting point. In other cases, 'conversion'—which we will consider presently—may be startling in suddenness. The whole case is included in what Jesus said to Nicodemus—'The wind blows how it will, you hear its sound, but you do not know whence it comes, or whither it goes. It is just so with one who is born of the Spirit.' The time or manner of such 'new birth' matters nothing. That which matters everything, is the definite personal appreciation and reciprocation of the love of the Heavenly Father whom Jesus makes real for humanity.

(3) The actual experience of this 'eternal life' cannot be put into words. Even our ordinary physical

life is beyond science to define. Much less can that higher surpassing life, which connotes communion with the living God, be put into human speech. It is as Paul said an ' unspeakable ' gift.[1] But two aspects of it may be recognized.

(i)   In regard to God; the recognition and appreciation by all the powers of mind and heart, of the love of the divine Fatherhood, from which all the rest follows— the development of reverent reciprocating love; the consequent sense of sin as the grieving of love, much more than rebellion against law; the deep appreciation of forgiveness through right understanding of Christ's reconciling self-sacrifice; following upon that, the abiding sense of divine love and care and sympathy.   Such communion with God becomes the source of all that is purest, happiest, noblest, most potent for good, in this life; with the highest hopes for all the future.

(ii)   The God of whom Jesus speaks is, as Paul expressed it in his letter to the Ephesians—' one God and Father of all, who is over all, and through all, and in all.'[2]   Hence salvation, to be real, must include love of all men for the Father's sake.   Concerning this, John uses very strong language—' If a man say I love God, and hates his brother, he is a liar.'   Not too strong, when viewed in the light of Christ's story of the unforgiving though forgiven debtor.   If ' salvation ' does not bring brotherly love, it is counterfeit.   The double benediction of real salvation consists not only in internal peace and comfort and hope, but equally in sharing these with others.   The stress so often laid upon the common rendering of Luke xvii. 21 is quite misleading.   The context shows plainly that the significance of ἐντὸς here, is not

---

[1] The word ἀνεκδιηγήτῳ, which he employed, means even more, signifying that which is equally beyond analysis or description.

[2] Chapter iv. 6, where the word ' you ' of the old Version, is out of place, being the interpolation of a copyist, as textual scrutiny shows—with all respect to Dr. Moffatt's translation.

'within,' but 'in your midst.'[1] The 'you' is plural
not singular. The Kingdom of God cannot, indeed,
be 'within' any man. For it rests upon *two* great
commands, and cannot be established upon either alone.
Salvation, to be real, must be both individual and social.
If what is desired is an end to the sorrows, and sufferings,
the cruelties, and shames, the wars, and fears of wars,
which mar civilization, then real salvation would accom-
plish all this, as surely as the incandescent filament in
our lamps puts an end to darkness. The man who is
'being saved,' cannot but be the saviour of others.

(4) Really, all this goes into one word. Salvation
is character. No more, no less. Whether towards God
or man, now or hereafter. A man's character is the
man himself, in all his relations, including all his
thoughts, feelings, volitions, words, and deeds. Human
characters differ immeasurably in moral quality, ranging
from angel to devil. But the distinctive mark of the
character which is 'being saved,' is its response to Christ's
own test—'What *extra* do ye?' (Matt. v. 47). Not mere
goodness, but the Christ-likeness which answers to his
appeal—'Come unto Me, and learn of Me.' This is
indeed the truth of truths for the Christian faith. It
cannot be stated too clearly or emphatically. All else
is subservient to this end, and must face this test. Everything in doctrine or worship, ritual or sacrament, form
or ceremony, religious convention or ecclesiastical rubric,
is only valuable in the degree in which it leads on to
Christ-like character. The New Testament term for this
is 'holiness'—never better interpreted than by Prof.
Seeley (in *Ecce Homo*)—as 'that higher-toned goodness
which not only abstains from vice, but regards even a
vicious thought with horror.' All else is, as Paul so
plainly said, comparatively 'nothing.'[2] The everlasting

---

[1] See Dr. Moffatt's rendering—as against both A.V. and R.V.
[2] 1 Cor. xiii. 1, 2, 3.

hall-mark of salvation is—'He who in these respects serves Christ, is accepted of God and approved of men.' That the character which such an ideal betokens, is the final test of the value of Christian faith, does not rest upon any selected passages, but is the unmistakable declaration of the whole New Testament. By such Christ-like character Christianity must be for ever tested, and either saves or mocks humanity.

(5) We are driven to ask, how does this Christian doctrine of salvation apply to all men? They cannot be left out of thought. Salvation cannot be confined to an esoteric society, such as Anglicanism or Methodism. That the 'Gospel of Christ' is intended for all men in its proclamation of salvation, is beyond question. But a few moments' impartial thought makes such a suggestion appear quixotic and unthinkable. We need not agree with Kipling that

> East is East, and West is West,
> And never the twain shall meet.

But at least the characteristics of East and West are indescribably different. Europe, Asia, Africa, and America, are easily mentioned; but no words can do justice to the differences in race, colour, temperament, idiosyncrasy, and environment, which are connoted. Even in Europe alone, the unlikenesses between the various nations amount to antagonisms in thought, feeling, ideals, customs, beliefs, which are beyond measure.

Moreover, in this country, scarcely less differences exist, between all the various classes of men and women, from slum dwellers to the 'aristocracy.' They live, to an immeasurable extent, in different worlds. Christianity is pledged to the avowal that they all need salvation. But nine tenths of them pay no regard to it whatever. In the theological sense, they are not and never will be 'saved.' Are these then all doomed to irreversible and everlasting punishment, after death sweeps them off the present plane of life? The bare suggestion shocks the moral sense intolerably. It would make God to be an infinite monster, and the ' love ' of God a contemptible mockery.

Must then salvation, on the world scale, be dismissed as a delusion? No. All these and all humanity may be divided into two great classes. (i) Those who have, and (ii) Those who have not, heard and known the truth concerning Jesus and His Gospel.

As to (i), there are confessedly millions, even in this country, who have nothing whatever to do with Christian churches. But their moral responsibility for what they might know and appreciate concerning Christian truth, is beyond any man to determine. Each of us has to make his own character, and the real question upon which ' soul-saving ' turns, is how far that character fulfils or ignores Christ's two great commands. So far as regards national environment, there are, happily, thousands of converts through Foreign Missions in all parts of the world, who illustrate this, and show how, amid all the differences of clime and circumstance and temperament, this ' new creation ' of character is what ' being saved ' really means.

(ii) The vast majority of mankind have, however, never really heard of Jesus. Even if the 580 millions of nominal Christians could all be accounted real, there are yet some 1,200 millions of other religions, or no religions, to whom Christ and His message are nothing. All the wonderful work of Foreign Missions does but little to alter this disproportion. But they are all included in the Apostle's summary (Rom. ii); which makes plain that character is the test by which men and women are and will be judged, irrespective of creed or circumstance. There is no limitation to the divine sympathy which this includes, and the one absolute certainty is that ' the Judge of all the earth will do right.'

(6) Let us then try once more, because of the unspeakable importance of the theme, to state succinctly and carefully why this salvation—which consists in attaining through the grace of God which Jesus reveals and embodies, a character true to Him and worthy of Him—is the only salvation which now, more than ever, humanity needs or can appreciate.

(i) Whatever becomes of theological systems, orthodox or heterodox, it is as certain as our life, that men will no more agree in the future concerning religion than they have done in the past. This is sufficiently illustrated in Christendom to-day. The differences in religious conviction between the churches—Greek, Roman, Anglo-Roman, Anglican, Free Church, Unitarian —are quite irreconcilable. Besides which, however wonderful is the history and influence of Christianity, the total number of those who have in any true sense been accounted Christ's disciples, has been and is but a mere fraction of the millions that have constituted humanity.

(ii) It is no less plain that amongst those who have heard and have rejected Christ's Gospel, must be included vast numbers of men and women whose moral characters have been unimpeachable. All these must be reckoned amongst the unsaved—the ' lost,' according to Romish and Protestant theology alike. Are we then to conclude that such men as Strauss, Renan, Lecky, J. S. Mill, Charles Bradlaugh, G. J. Holyoake, John Morley, William Archer, and the like, are to be cast into an eternal hell of suffering? To prove that from the New Testament, would simply mean the dismissal of the Christian Scriptures from all further notice.

(iii) Yet for all these, as for all moral beings, in some degree, there is one inevitable and final test. All these differences of creed—or no creed—based upon differences of knowledge and opportunity, of heredity and

environment, the wide world over, do afford both opportunity and necessity for the formation of character.
Character is all that matters. This, both Jesus and the
Apostles have made plain for evermore. The hosts of
those who have never heard of Christ, are in the Father's
hands quite as tenderly as those who have. The Apostolic
summary in Romans ii. 6 to 11, covers the whole world,
and extends unto the end of time—' Wrath and indigna-
tion, tribulation and anguish, upon every soul of man that
worketh evil—glory, honour, and peace, to every man
that worketh good—for there is no respect of persons
with God.' Whilst within the pale of Christendom,
amid the whole indescribable conflict of convictions,
creeds, standards, ritual, and church government, the
words of Christ ring on through the ages—' He who has
My commands and obeys them, he it is that loves Me.'
All else is, in comparison with that, a trifle.

(iv)   Moreover, it must never be forgotten that the
character which alone deserves to be called Christian, is
not ordinary goodness, but something more, answering
to Christ's question—' What *extra* do ye? ' (Matt. v. 47).
The point to be repeated here, is that it is just this
distinctive ' higher-toned goodness which we call holiness,' which constitutes salvation, and makes the greatest
impression upon humanity. It marks out the man who
is ' being saved,' as different from all others. The form
of doctrine or church association through which it comes
to pass, matters no more than the shape of the vessel
matters to the parched traveller who is saved through
the water it contains. Consider but a few modern names,
taken at random, of those who differed in almost everything but this, that for them all salvation consisted in
ceaseless endeavour to be true to Christ's ideal of character. Luther, Calvin, Wesley, Whitefield, Moffatt,
Livingstone, Gladstone, Father Damien, Bp. Hannington,
Dr. A. Schweitzer, Henry Martyn, David Hill, Cardinal

Newman, Charles Kingsley, Dr. Martineau, Alexander
Maclaren. These are they whose influence for good upon
humanity will continue, more than that of all those whose
names are extolled so highly on Empire Day.

(v) But there is a far greater host of unknown
Christians, who are true to the same ideal; and it is
through their character and influence, not through any
one section of the Catholic church, nor through any creed,
or ritual, or theological dogma, that Christ's Kingdom
on earth will ever come. Through saints, not through
systems, will that Kingdom—which ' is not eating and
drinking, but righteousness and peace and joy '—ever
prevail in human society. It is said that the work and
influence of John Wesley and his helpers, was the salvation of England in the 18th century. Assuredly it was
not the preaching alone, which accomplished so much.
It was the multiplication of individuals who were ' being
saved,' and so illustrated the prayer they learned from
their Saviour—' Thy Kingdom come, Thy will be done,
on earth as in heaven.'

(vi) But He made it plain beyond doubt, that His
Kingdom does not end with death. For the moment we
assume it—Christian eschatology will be considered
presently. It is enough here to call to mind that the
nature of the great hereafter, its joy or pain, must and
will, for every human being, turn upon character. Not
upon creed, or association with any church, but upon
the use made of whatever truth has been known, under
any circumstances of heredity or environment. There
is no possibility of mistaking the mind of Christ herein
—or the doctrine of the Apostles—' So then form no
premature judgement, until the Lord comes. For He
will bring hidden secrets to light, and show plainly
each heart's intentions. Then will the approval come
to every one from God Himself ' (1 Cor. iv. 5). The
Christian hope of heaven is indeed a blessed hope of

salvation in the world to come, as really as in this life. But that salvation will only be the perpetuation and development of the character that has here and now been begun. Release from the limitations of the body, and deliverance from the hindrances, conflicts, and burdens of physical existence, will open the door to boundless possibilities of growth in knowledge, and capacity, and opportunity, which are now beyond all our thought. Whilst the corresponding increase in communion with God, connotes the certainty that salvation will include blessing beyond present expression, without measure or end.

(7)   ATONEMENT

Of all the main elements of Christian faith, none has been as much discussed, or has given rise to so much controversy, as that theological estimate of the death of Christ which is generally known as 'The Atonement.' There is no theme upon which all Christians, of all Churches, so agree to differ. There is no probability now of any nearer approach to unanimity, than centuries ago. It is certain that no statement, however carefully worded, could be formulated, which would be acceptable to all believers, let alone to all theologians. Why did Jesus die? What is the real significance of His death? Was it absolutely necessary, and divinely intended—or only the natural consequence of His teaching, and His attitude towards His environment? These and other inevitable questions are answered in numberless different ways by Christians equally sincere, intelligent, and devoted. What is the ordinary man to think and feel? If right thinking and feeling are essential to a valid and potent Christian faith, how is he to come to such with anything like assurance? In view of all the ensuing

confusion and perplexity which yet prevail, and in the
light of fifty years of honest and careful scrutiny, let me
here give—not a summary of all the theological logomachies hereupon, for that would be as profitless as
impossible—a brief outline of what seems finally to be
the real, necessary, impressive, and hopeful truth. Three
main lines of thought open out for consideration. (I) The
plain facts of the case as recorded in the Gospels. (II) The
estimate of these facts in the rest of the New Testament.
(III) The true statement and appreciation of the whole,
in the light of present-day knowledge and experience.

(I)   The plain facts.   The modern attempt to call in
question the historicity of Jesus and so reduce His death
as well as life to a mere myth, only merits the dismissal
accorded to it above.   Thanks to the Biblical criticism
which ' Fundamentalists ' so despise, the Gospel narrative
is to-day substantially more reliable than ever before,
and the main features of the narrative stand out with
vivid verisimilitude.   We have there set before us a
Jewish peasant with a wonderful boyhood, becoming the
itinerant teacher of a new type of religion, distinguished
from the Judaism of scribes and Pharisees, and making
special appeal to the ' common people.'   But their
sympathy and expectation are turned to disappointment
and hatred, by the envy and malice of the orthodox
teachers who, through persistent bitterness and intrigue,
at last compelled the Roman authorities to treat Him
as a criminal, and crucify Him as a traitor.   He submitted
to all their insults and cruelty without resistance or
reproach, and died as a malefactor.   But He assured
His disciples that that death would not be the end.   That
after three days He would rise again to a fuller and
higher life.   The Gospels all affirm that this prediction
was fulfilled, and that Christianity sprang from that
triumph over death.

7

Those are the simple facts. So far as Christ's death is concerned, it is only what might be expected from human nature. History supplies numberless analogous cases. And yet—in all the world's history, there has been but one Calvary. Modern knowledge of comparative religion has called up many names of leaders or saviours connected with other religions, and laid great stress upon the likeness between what is recorded concerning them and the Gospel narrative. There is thus much talk about Krishna, Buddha, Osiris, Horus, Mithras, Attis, Tammuz, Prometheus, Dionysius, Quatzalcoatl; and it is undeniable that many events related in connexion with their worship, seem to be similar to those narrated in the Gospels concerning Christ. But however interesting and significant these may be, honest and thorough scrutiny proves two things. (i) That it is simply impossible to regard the Christ of the Gospels as in any sense derived from them. His character towers above them all in its sublime purity and nobility as unmistakably as Mont Blanc above the surrounding valleys of Switzerland. To take but one typical example—His keenest critics, or bitterest opponents, cannot even imagine anything in the life of Jesus, approaching the amours of Krishna with Radha. (ii) The whole truth concerning the death and resurrection of Jesus, is as distinct from these myths and fables, as the warmth of summer is from the chills of winter. The strong words of the great sceptic J. S. Mill, above quoted, in the middle of the last century, have only gained emphasis through the intervening years. They remain alike unanswerable and conclusive.

The mystery which above all staggers and indeed overwhelms every thoughtful mind which has not committed itself to atheism, is that God, to whom Jesus always referred as His near and loving Father, should leave Him to be done to death in all His innocence by a pagan tyrant, egged on by a brutal mob, under the influence of religious fanatics, many of whom were also hypocrites. He being what He was, makes the tragedy of His murder as insoluble from the divine standpoint, as explicable from the human. For indeed what was He? There is no critical reason for doubting the truthfulness of that record concerning His character, as portrayed in the Gospels, which led J. S. Mill and a host of other sincere and cultured unbelievers such as Strauss, Rénan, Lecky, Goethe, to acknowledge its peerless nobility and beneficent influence. In His whole teaching and deportment there was nothing that His bitterest enemies could fix upon to His discredit. They had no answer to His modest but unhesitating challenge, 'Which of you convicts Me of wrong doing?' whilst the Roman governor, in spite of the howling mob, declared that he could find no fault with their victim. But all His moral and spiritual excellence, together with the protests of Pilate, availed nothing against the virulence and cunning of His enemies. So they hounded Him to a shameful death. That is a succinct but true and sufficient summary of the facts, as we have received them.

But there is also one other fact of immeasurable significance. There have been thousands of such murders in human history? Why has Calvary become so unique? There has been nothing like it for influence upon humanity. None of the age-long and vehement oppositions to Christianity, no cynical scorn for modern Christendom, no sadly justified denunciations of Church history, lessen the truth that the cross of Christ has moved the world through nearly two millenniums, and moves mankind still, more than all the tragedies that have happened before or since. More indeed than any other event in human history. That is the incontrovertible fact for which in its vast scope there must be some adequate cause. What is it?

(II)   The New Testament estimate. The history of the early Christian Church, and of the various portions of our Testament, must be sought elsewhere. Our modern appreciation of all the facts is no more necessarily the same as that of the first believers, than is our expectation of Christ's 'second coming.' But there is nothing to unlearn in regard to the reality and sublimity of the effects of that tragedy upon Calvary. Its world-wide and age-long results must be ascribed to the blending of two causes—the tragedy itself, and its aftermath. In other words, the special significance of Christ's crucifixion, and the even greater significance of His resurrection.

These are for ever inseparable. The resurrection is unthinkable without the preceding death. The death is a pitiful and meaningless collapse, without the resurrection. One of the greatest mistakes of evangelical Christianity has been, and yet is, the separation of these two, and the general ignoring of the resurrection in the constant reference to the cross of Christ as the 'central truth of Christianity.' For as surely as no one-sided arch is safe, or even imaginable, so, as Paul emphatically wrote (1 Cor. xv. 14, 17) is the cross of Christ of no avail in isolation. However much popular theology may protest, it is true, as pointed out above, that the cross of Christ is *not* 'the central doctrine' of Christianity. It is no more central than in the human body any one vital organ is central. As the Apostle truly said (1 Cor. xii. 12 to 25) several organs in the human frame are absolutely essential to life, and all are mutually dependent. So is it in Christian faith. On several occasions Paul made his convictions plain—'It is Christ who died, yea, *rather*, that was raised from the dead.' Whilst it is manifest beyond words that neither death nor resurrection would be of any avail, without the preceding life and character of Jesus.

His resurrection is here, with sufficient reason,

assumed. Not indeed the physical revival of the body
which hung upon the cross, as some still sincerely but
unwarrantedly assert. For that is sufficiently contradicted
by all the recorded events of the following forty days.
But there are overwhelming reasons for accepting as true
the transformation of the ' natural body ' of Jesus, after
His death, into the ' spiritual body ' of the risen Lord.
That is enough for Christian thought and life; and
it warrants all the triumphant assurance of the Apostle
in his letter to the Corinthians. But that unmistakable
triumph over death, reflects back upon the cross the light
which transforms that death from an ordinary brutal
murder, into something unspeakably more significant
and truly sublime.

There are three great distinguishing characteristics
of the death of Jesus. (i) It was absolutely undeserved.
For His life had been without blemish, and His character
beautiful beyond compare. The alleged voice from heaven
was certainly justified in Him—' This is My beloved
Son.' (ii) His sufferings and death were wholly voluntary. Indeed doubly so. For He well knew to what His
teachings and appeals and general attitude would lead,
and yet He maintained unflinchingly what He declared
to be the Father's will. But also, when the foreseen
avalanche of bigotry and hatred broke upon Him, if He
had so willed—so He solemnly declared—the Father
whom He revealed would have intervened to save Him
from His murderers. But He chose rather to endure to
the uttermost, knowingly and deliberately.

(iii) Yet in that endurance of suffering there was
unmistakably something more than physical pain, or
even soul disappointment at the scornful rejection by the
people whom He had loved. Thousands of martyrs have
endured all that with perfect calm, or even with triumphant joy. Why did He so quail at the prospect? Why
pray so intensely that ' if possible ' the ' cup ' might pass

from Him? What did that cup portend? Why did not
the Father answer His agonized plea? The attempts to
solve such questions as these have occupied theologians
from the first century until now. Interminable controversies have arisen, and whole libraries have been written
by way of exposition. How intense and prolonged have
been the efforts of Christian teachers to fathom this
mystery, is witnessed in a host of familiar names. In his
own weird way Studdert Kennedy puts it thus :

> There you see the spectacle of men—good and holy men, and
> very brainy men too—wrestling to express what the life and death
> of Jesus meant to them, in terms of their knowledge and their
> thought, and you get up with a sigh muttering to yourself—Good
> Lord, what a business this Christianity is! It is impossible to
> make a seamless robe out of the patchwork quilt of Christian
> theology; impossible to make a consistent whole of the conflicting
> theories.[1]

A few years since a notable symposium was published
by James Clarke & Co., containing the deliberate and
careful statements of seventeen of the ablest and most
representative of Protestant divines. But what does it
all come to? Merely a partial negative agreement.
A few ancient monstrosities are dismissed, but beyond
that, there is mutual contradiction and confusion. But
assuredly Studdert Kennedy is right when he declares
that—' The time has now come when we should lift from
our people the load of misunderstanding that arises
from our tangle of outworn metaphors ' (p. 226). Let
us at least try so to do.[2]

(III) The truly Christian attitude to-day. The endeavour to state afresh, in the light of to-day, what is the

[1] *Food for the Fed Up*, p. 209.

[2] In my volume entitled, *Christian Essentials*, I have given one
whole chapter to this same theme. I see nothing now to retract
from that statement; but what follows may be regarded as additional—in a case in which repetition is pardonable for the truth's
sake.

essential and needed truth concerning the death of Christ, falls necessarily into two portions, negative and positive.

(1) Negatively, there are certain departures from past conceptions which are as necessary and indeed inevitable, as they will by many be deemed subversive.

(i) In general, Dr. Munger's summary is entirely warranted.

The Atonement as a dogma, in all its various theories, rests upon a basis of other dogmas that are fast disappearing. Indeed, these fading dogmas created the various theories. The fall of Adam, federal headship, total depravity, and guilt of all minkind, the curse of God pronounced upon all; election to salvation or eternal destruction; these dogmas demanded and shaped the Atonement according to the way in which they were interpreted. The dominating factor was not the Atonement, but some dogma of depravity, or Divine sovereignty, or justice, or sacrifice; and as there were always changing, the Atonement was refined in order to secure harmony in the system.

All such basic conceptions must now be as definitely set aside, as the Ptolemaic system of astronomy.

(ii) There need be in Christian doctrine hereupon, no more reference to the ' fall of Adam ' than Jesus Himself made, that is, none at all. The hymn of which Mr. Gladstone was said to be so fond, is thus misleading.

O loving wisdom of our God!
   When all was sin and shame,
A second Adam to the fight
   And to the rescue came.

O wisest love! that flesh and blood
   Which did in Adam fail,
Should strive afresh against the foe,
   Should strive and should prevail.

Congregations which substitute emotion for truth, may go on to sing such words; but they do not alter the certainty that the representations in the opening chapters of Genesis are allegorical not historical, and as such cannot form the valid basis for a definite theological system.

(iii) There is neither need nor warrant for the gross exaggeration of personal wrong-doing, in which popular evangelical theology so often indulges. The Fundamentalist slogan—'We deserved eternal death'—is not justified. Nor many of the strong expressions found in some 'Gospel' hymns—such as

> O Jesus, my hope!
> For me offered up,
> Who with clamour pursued Thee to Calvary's top.

> I have spilt His precious blood,
> Trampled on the Son of God,
> Filled with pangs unspeakable,
> I, who yet am not in hell!

(iv) There is no more warrant for the constant reference to the 'wrath of God,' as in such hymns as this :

> For what you have done
> His blood must atone;
> The Father hath stricken for you His dear Son.
> The Lord, in the day
> Of His anger, did lay
> Your sins on the Lamb, and He bore them away.

Not because of divine indifference to moral evil, but because that word, in ordinary usage, conveys a false impression. There is no 'wrath of God' which is not in perfect harmony with the love of God. So that there never was any need of anything to reconcile God to man, but always and only, something to make men see and feel the holy love from which they turn, and in that sense be reconciled to Him.

(v) The employment of the word 'atone' must drop out altogether, by reason of its untrue implications. Thus such verses as these,

> For every sinful action
> Thou hast atonement made;
> The perfect satisfaction,
> Thy precious blood has paid.

> He dies to atone
> For sins not His own;
> Your debt He hath paid, and your work He hath done,

are not true Christian doctrine, but the strained imagination of a certain school of theologians. The older version of our English Bible has led many astray by its rendering of Rom. v. 11. But the correction in the Revised Version, is still flouted in public, as well as ignored in private. The Greek word, however, is unmistakable.

(vi) Popular Hymns do undoubtedly convey the beliefs of myriads of sincere Christians, especially as regards the element of substitution in Christ's self-sacrifice. Thus

> The blood Thou hast shed
> For me let it plead,
> And declare Thou hast died in Thy murderers' stead.

or

> He purchased the grace
> Which now I embrace;
> O Father, Thou know'st He hath died in my place.

Thus Dr. Machen, in his recent much discussed book on *What is Faith?* says definitely (p. 164)—'We deserved eternal death : but the Lord Jesus took upon Himself all the guilt of our sins and died instead of us on the cross.' The sufferings of Jesus were vicarious indeed, for they were endured on behalf of humanity, in order to demonstrate as nothing else could do, the holy patient love of God for sinful men. But to say that He died instead of the human race, is pure theological fiction.

(vii) There was thus no 'satisfaction' to divine justice, ever paid, or contemplated. The Prayer Book phrase—'a full, perfect, and sufficient sacrifice, oblation, and satisfaction, for the sins of the whole world,' is but theological invention.   It finds embodiment indeed in many hymns.   Such as

> Rejoice and be glad! for the blood hath been shed;
> Redemption is finished, the price hath been paid.

> There was no other good enough
>   To pay the price of sin;
> He only could unlock the gate
>   Of heaven, and let us in.

But such suggestions are contrary to the whole representation of God as a Father, upon which Jesus laid such stress.   The only 'satisfaction' concerning Christ's self-sacrifice ever contemplated in the Gospel, is that illustrated in the parable—'while the prodigal was yet a great way off, the father saw him, and was moved with compassion.'

(viii)   Certainly also the term 'punishment' has no place in Christian thought concerning Calvary.   Jesus was never punished, for any one, or anything.   The hymn above quoted used to run

> For what you have done
>   His blood must atone:
> The Father hath punished for you His dear Son.

But that false word, at least, has been now removed. The substitution of 'stricken' for punished, is doubtless taken from Isaiah lxiii., where no mention or thought of punishment is found.   Yet it is only too true that in the minds of great numbers of Christians, the idea that Jesus was punished instead of 'the guilty race' still remains.

(ix)   There must be great reduction, if not entire cessation, in the ceaseless references to 'blood' which occur in 'evangelical' preaching and singing.   The frequent mentions of blood in the New Testament were inevitable, since all the first converts were Jews who had been brought up under the Old Testament system of animal sacrifices. But the writer of the letter to the **Hebrews** emphatically declared that that ancient system was superseded in Christ's death; so that there was no further necessity for any appeal to blood. No passage in the whole Bible has been more often misquoted than (Heb. ix. *22*)—'without shedding of blood there is no remission '—as if it were a Christian principle! Whereas the context shows, beyond all question, that the writer was only referring to what had once obtained, but was now for ever set aside.

There is also another consideration. We are living now in the twentieth century, not the first, or even the eighteenth. Modes of speech which were once inoffensive or even useful, are so no longer. There are not a few passages in the ' Authorized ' Version of the Bible, though it is only three centuries old, which cannot be decently read in public to-day, owing to the development of a keener mental and moral sensitiveness. Even so, in these days, the reference to ' blood ' is only tolerable when it is not thought about. Such expressions as these are less and less desired, or warranted.

> There is a fountain filled with blood
> Drawn from Immanuel's veins;
> And sinners, plunged beneath that flood,
> Lose all their guilty stains.

In plain truth, that is but ghastly imagery, calculated much more to alienate than to impress every thoughtful man, woman, or child. So too are the following.

> Jesu, Thy blood and righteousness
> My beauty are, my glorious dress;
> Midst flaming worlds, in these arrayed,
> With joy shall I lift up my head.

> His blood demands the purchased grace;
> His blood's availing plea
> Obtained the help for all our race,
> And sends it down to me.

> Take the dear purchase of Thy blood.
> Thy blood shall wash us white as snow.
> That blood which cleanses from all sin,
> That efficacious blood apply.

Whilst even children are called upon to sing about such as themselves :

> Because the Saviour shed His blood,
> To wash away their sin;
> Bathed in that pure and precious flood,
> Behold them white and clean.

Careless preachers and conventional congregations may go on to employ such phrases, and certain theologians to defend them; but they leave no room for wonder at half empty churches. In reference to the greatest of all earth's tragedies, there is neither need nor room for such gruesome realism. ' Blood,' in this most sacred of all references, means the life and love, as well as death of Christ. The mere repetition of a word whose very sound has become repulsive, does less than nothing to bring home to the men and women of this age, the tender, solemn, precious realities of Calvary. Even the well-known hymn of Dr. Watts, which is perhaps the best and utmost that language can express, is marred by the second verse,—

> Forbid it, Lord, that I should boast,
> Save in the death of Christ, my God;
> All the vain things that charm me most,
> I sacrifice them to His blood,—

where the last line is meaningless, even if the theology of the second line is allowed to pass. If only, instead of that meaningless last line, he had written

> All the vain things that charm me most,
> I scorn them, for the path He trod,

the sense would have been as much more appropriate, as the rhythm would have been improved. But conventional sounds too often trample truth underfoot.

(2) Positively, in the light of plain facts, apart from
Biblical misrepresentations, theological assumptions and
ecclesiastical superstitions, there are four main features
of this immeasurable tragedy which cannot be mistaken,
namely, obedience, love, sorrow, assurance. If, as seems
probable, the word 'atonement' is retained in the future
by reason of its sound, rather than at-one-ment, which
alone is true—it must at least be understood that the
four elements just mentioned express and exhaust the real
significance of the death of Jesus on the cross.

(i) The whole tragedy, all the anguish and bitterness of those last hours, was the result, voluntarily and
deliberately endured, of His utmost obedience to the
highest ideal, that is, His Father's will—'The cup which
My Father hath given Me, shall I not drink it?' His
commission was to reveal to human nature the true nature
and attitude of God, as the heavenly Father. Had He
been less true to that, He would not have stirred up the
envy, hatred, and malice, which compassed His death.
His voluntary endurance of Jewish maledictions, even
unto death, was the completion of His revelation and the
consummation of His obedience, which led to His
significant cry—'It is finished!'

(ii) Inseparable from that obedience was His unmeasured love, both for the Father and for mankind,
whom the Father through Him sought to win into real,
holy, happy allegiance. For that love, which bound Him
equally to the Father and to mankind, there are no
words, nor does human thought conceive it. Many
notable instances of vicarious devotion may indeed be
cited. Such names as Leonidas, Arnold von Winkelried,
Father Damien, Bishop Hannington, Henry Martyn,
Mary Slessor, and a host of others, spring into recollection. There is also a noble army of unknown martyrs
who, for others' sakes, have 'not counted their lives dear
to them,' but have literally died for their fellows. And

yet, in the love-tragedy of Calvary, there is something
more than in any or all of these. Something which the
writers of the New Testament strive in vain to express,
though their phrases transcend criticism and baffle
exegesis. Once more Dr. Watts' immortal verse comes
as near to reality as language can—

> See, from His head, His hands, His feet,
> Sorrow and love flow mingled down:
> Did e'er such love and sorrow meet,
> Or thorns compose so rich a crown?

(iii)   For in that blending of love and sorrow lies
the very heart of the meaning of the cross of Christ. Not
in any ' satisfaction' to divine justice; nor any punishing of innocence instead of guilt; but in the bearing, for
love's sake, of such sorrow as only love when wounded
and scorned, can know. The sorrow was manifold.

(a)   For the persistent malice and wickedness of
His human environment, and all the moral evil which it
represented, which may truly be called the sin of the
world.

(b)   The pain of sharing the Father's sorrow, as the
only anger of which love is capable. Of the sorrow of
God, indeed, the churches say little. But it is beyond
words to portray the reality of the divine sorrow, at the
utter rejection of that revelation of holy love which
was incarnate in Jesus Christ.

(c)   The pained sorrow at the knowledge of His own
failure to win men to the Fatherhood which He made
so real to them. He said indeed—'If I am lifted up
from the earth, I will draw all men unto Me.' That
has been overwhelmingly fulfilled. But to draw is not
necessarily to win. His tears over Jerusalem were
typical of His heart-ache for humanity.

(d)   There was also the sorrow of knowing what
would be the inevitable result of their rejection of His
whole mission and message. The threatening shadow of

the fate of the city was already creeping on. To which must be added the awful pain of the vision of all the suffering and wrong, the cruelty and wickedness, the horror and misery, of the centuries to follow, from that day to this—the pitiful history of both the church and the world, wherein He would be 'crucified afresh, and put to open shame.'

(e) Inseparable from all this was also the physical agony associated with a tortured body, leading only too easily into the mental anguish which extorted from Him the cry of heart-broken loneliness, as if forsaken by the Father whom He had so trusted and obeyed. All that such quotation from the Psalm meant to Him, we shall never know. Its very difference from the triumph-songs of so many martyrs, fills us with humble awe. It enshrouds Calvary with impenetrable mystery.

(iv) Yet along with all this, there is the assurance which both preceded His dark hour, and in the end dispelled all His grief and pain. 'After three days he will rise again.' His seeming end was to be but the beginning of a new Kingdom of Heaven on earth, and the pledge of a yet more glorious realm of diviner life beyond the grave. It was the knowledge and appreciation of this assurance of the risen life, as inseparable from the tragic death, that made the Apostle so bold to declare—what evangelical theology still hesitates to endorse—that the resurrection was of even greater import than the crucifixion, and the triumph more to humanity than the tragedy. 'It is Christ that died— yet *rather* that was raised from the dead.'

These four then—obedient fulfilment of His whole sublime commission; love for the Father and for all humanity; pain and grief beyond utterance; assurance that in spite of all His 'finished' travail, He would triumph over death and evil;—these were the real constituents of the cross of Christ. All else is but human

invention. In face of the certain and virulent denunciations of 'Fundamentalists' and others, who by the
very bitterness of their anathemas show that the real
heart of the meaning of Christ's cross is unknown to
them, it may be well to repeat this summary.

In the whole mystery of Christ's last earthly hours,
there is no reference at all to any fallen humanity as
doomed to eternal death through the sin of Adam. There
is no reference to the former Jewish ritual of blood-
shedding.[1] 'No mysterious necessity; no governmental
exigency; no expiation of guilt, or propitiation of wrath;
no satisfaction of justice, can be found in it—unless
found in the heart of Fatherhood and in the relation of
father and son. Everything is simple, natural, universal.
If this confounds accepted theological distinctions, so
be it.'[2]

Thus far it has been assumed that Jesus was really
human. That does not preclude the question was He only
human? Was He *a* Son of God only as every other man
may be, or *the* Son of God who could say, in an un-
approachably unique sense, 'I and My Father are
one'? After what has been said in a previous section,
the latter cannot be denied or evaded. His own avowal
that He was one with the Father 'before the world was,'
must be taken into full account. What light does this
throw upon the darkness which enshrouds Calvary?
There are two great truths to be faced, and it must be
confessed that in neither of these do words help much
to express the inexpressible.

(i) The reality of His divine nature does not lessen
the actuality of His humanity. How the divine can so
co-exist with a human personality we shall never know
—though for that matter we are equally unable to under-

---

[1] Matt. xxvi. 28 is clearly explained by Exod. xxiv. 8. It is the
blood of a covenant of love, not a sacrifice for sin; see Mark xiv. 24.
[2] Dr. Munger—*Symposium* mentioned above, pp. 363, 366.

stand how brain and mind co-exist and co-operate in ourselves. But the humanity of Jesus remains here the unmistakable starting point for all the rest. And it was that humanity which suffered physically on the cross. The devout believer may doubtless sing sincerely,

> Forbid it, Lord, that I should boast
> Save in the death of Christ, my God.

But that comma after ' Christ,' represents an abyss which can only be viewed with reverent awe. Such phrases as these—

> Sins that sacrificed my God,
> My God for me resigned His breath,
> The immortal God for me hath died,

ought never to be either sung or printed. The rhapsody of devotion does not cover up the intolerable contradiction in terms which the ' death of God ' conveys.

(2) But, indirectly, the truly divine-human personality of Jesus does add measureless significance to His death. He suffered, indeed, as ' the son of man,' in the whole realm of physical being. But He never ceased to be, in the supremest sense, the Son of God. The ' rulers of this world ' in their ignorance did crucify ' the Lord of glory.' The reverent analysis of the Apostle in Phil ii. 5 to 11, was not just an echo of unmistakable words in the fourth Gospel, for it was written earlier. But it incalculably enhances the awe-inspiring tragedy of the Cross, to think of Christ's humanity as being the voluntary laying aside of essential Deity, in order to become veritably a man amongst men. All theological attempts to express such incarnation, are as vain as seeking to put earth's oceans into the cup of a little child. At least it compels us to think of Calvary as something inexpressibly more than a judicial murder, or the martyrdom of a saint. Instead of being the very core of the mystery of evil, the cross of Christ becomes the

8

incandescent focus of love divine. By His unspeakable but real oneness with the Father, the suffering Son of God exhibited, first to His mockers and murderers, then beyond them to all the ever-widening circles of humanity, the real attitude of the one, only, and infinite God, towards mankind. That, when appreciated, is the greatest truth that can impress the human mind. It is also the uttermost appeal to the human heart.

If one may dare, in a last word, to attempt to summarize such tremendous truth, then thus.

The Gospel of Christ does not—as is the custom to say—'start with the fact of sin,' but with the overwhelming actuality of that love divine which is really, though on a scale that transcends all our thought, exhibited in evolution. The beginning and end of Christ's significance and appeal to humanity, is His revelation that God, the one and only God of the universe, is love; love from everlasting to everlasting; love beyond speech or thought; but coming nearest to expression in the one great, tender, only name, which Jesus substituted for the Jahveh of the Old Testament—'The Father Himself loves you'—'God is love.' That is the Alpha and Omega of Christian faith. Creation by evolution is the expression of the eternal purpose of love divine —beyond human comprehension truly, in its vastness and complexity, but culminating in that which Jesus makes both real and appreciable. Because God is love, He cannot but desire to be loved. On this planet, man, after long ages of preparation, is the only creature capable of reciprocating divine love. But in order to be capable of reciprocating, he must be also capable of rejecting. Compelled love is a contradiction in terms. That rejection, possibly only since the dawn of manhood, is sin in all its myriad forms and degrees. But sinners cannot be compulsorily transformed into saints. They cannot be compelled to love. So that the 'wrath' of God is but the sorrow of a Father over a rebellious child. On a measureless scale, the Prophet's representation holds good—' I have nourished and brought up children, and they have rebelled against me.' That is the true history of a ' sinful world.'

Since forced repentance is out of question, only appeal is left. There are, indeed, to an observant human eye and a sensitive human heart, numberless divine appeals in nature and in experience. But their tragic failure to move men is manifest, alike in history and in to-day's environment. Hence, ' in the fulness of time' the Father comes Himself, in the person of the eternal Son, to make this tenderest, mightiest, final appeal to the human soul—the father's appeal to the prodigal to come back from sin and shame and suffering, to love and happiness and home and hope. From such response to Christ's First Great Command, would undoubtedly follow that keeping of the Second which would redeem civilization from all its troubles. But Dr. Munger is certainly right in his avowal that

Christianity will not evangelize the nations on the strength of a verbally inspired Bible, and a doctrine of the Atonement struck through with Hebrew ritualism and construed by mediaeval logic from facts that have turned out to be composite legends. But Father, Son and Holy Spirit; Love, Forgiveness, Righteousness— these, in their simple and direct form, are at home all the world over, and are full of God's power, because ' He hath made of one blood all nations of men '—and is the Father of all.[1]

(8) SACRAMENTS

One of the strangest things in the whole history of religion is the part that ' sacraments ' have come to take in Christianity. With the sole exception of the Society

[1] *Symposium,* p. 376.

of Friends and the Salvation Army, all the varied sections of the Christian Church regard sacraments with extreme reverence.   In some cases that reverence is not only deepened into solemn awe, but the sacraments are regarded as absolutely essential, alike to the faith of the individual and the doctrine of the church.   Endless controversies hereupon have arisen in the past, but the present attitude of Christendom may be expressed in a few sentences. The Greek and Roman churches insist upon seven sacraments, whilst magnifying one above all.   Anglo-Catholics do not acknowledge seven, but otherwise follow Rome.   The Anglican church, in general, acknowledges only two sacraments, Baptism and the Lord's Supper, but lays greatest stress upon the latter.   The Free Churches are somewhat divided.   One large section puts greatest importance upon Baptism; others regard both sacraments as equally obligatory.   Whilst very many, probably the majority, although avowedly accepting both sacraments, pay utmost regard to the Lord's Supper, and much less to Baptism.   The one question concerning all these differences is whether the supreme authority for guidance is to come from the New Testament, or from the blending of tradition with church history and the writings of the early 'fathers.'   This, at least, seems undeniable —that our New Testament records are the basis of all else, and that whatever comments upon them may have been made in the past, we have now to interpret them in the light of our modern knowledge.   In such light several questions press for careful answer.   (1) ' Sacrament,' not being a New Testament word, what does it really mean?   (2) How many sacraments are there?   (3) Are sacraments essential to Christian faith and life? (4) What is their true significance and value?   (5) What methods in their observance are necessary or desirable?

(1) The term ' sacrament,' we know, originally meant a pledge, whether civil or military.   It was the accepted

equivalent of μυστήριον, and so came to signify a solemn
mystery of Christian faith. It applied at first to any
sacred thing, and in that wide sense, sacraments were
common to all ethnic religions. But it was also closely
connected with sacrifice in Pagan religions, and came,
in Christian usage, to have special reference to the self-
sacrifice of Christ, regarded, according to the Epistle
to the Hebrews, as the culmination and fulfilment of the
Jewish sacrificial system. But there is, in all the New
Testament, no warrant whatever for regarding the Lord's
Supper—or as it has come to be called, the Christian
' Eucharist '—as in any sense a sacrifice. It is always
represented as a reverent and tender memorial service,
and thus a special means of grace. In the words of the
Westminster Shorter Catechism it is—' A holy ordinance
instituted by Christ, wherein by sensible signs, Christ
Himself and the benefits of the new Covenant, are
represented and applied to the believer.'

(2) As to the number of sacraments, it was only in
the 12th century that Peter Lombard clearly stated
the Romish list of seven—Baptism, Confirmation,
Extreme Unction, Penance, Eucharist, Orders, and
Matrimony. From that time, the number seven held
until the Reformation, when, under the influence of
Luther, five were dismissed. From that date, in all
the Protestant churches, only two are recognized, Baptism
and the Lord's Supper. There is no likelihood of any
change; although no Protestant would deny the sacred
associations of marriage, or the Christian Ministry.

(3) But are sacraments essential to Christian faith
and life? A good succinct answer is given by Dr.
Stalker :

The necessity is what is called *necessitas praecepti*—the use of
sacraments is necessary because commanded by Christ Himself.
But it is not a *sine quâ non*, because the same blessings which are
communicated through the sacraments, can be obtained without

as amongst the Methodists. Which of these forms is
adopted, or by what method, matters nothing spiritually,
even as the Apostle so strongly declared in regard to
circumcision, in his letter to the Galatians (v. 6, vi. 15).
So that there is ample room for differences of conviction,
or environment.

(iii) In other countries, where the Christian Gospel
is preached to non-Christians, it is in perfect accord
with Christ's own command, and the whole attitude of
the New Testament, as well as most fitting and helpful
in the nature of the case, that new converts should be
baptized, to signify the reality of their entry into a new
spiritual life. For thereby they pass from the former
darkness into the new light of Christ's revelation, and
pledge themselves to live according to His commands.
It is not necessary here to enter further into the prolonged
controversy concerning the time and manner of baptism.
The preceding cases will cover all, and answer to Paul's
judgement in his letter to the Romans (chapter xiv.).

(II) So we come to the Lord's Supper, which, alas,
has been the subject of more pronounced and bitter
controversy even than Baptism. These pitiful logomachies
cannot be summarized. It is only too clear that keen
divisions of opinion still separate those who should be
one, and there is no prospect of unanimity. In this
country there are three distinct attitudes in Christian
Churches, which can neither be mistaken nor blended,
in regard to what is variously termed the Lord's Supper,
or the Eucharist, or Holy Communion.

(1) Two definite and important sections of modern
Christianity, as above named, do not recognize the
necessity of any sacraments. This may seem an extreme
attitude in face of the many references to them in the
New Testament. But the Friends, or Quakers, subject
everything to their special doctrine of the ' inner light,'

which virtually makes all Christian faith and life one
continual sacrament.

Practical rather than doctrinal reasons led General
Booth and his co-workers to leave sacraments out of their
categories of doctrine and service. The special nature
of their appeals throughout the country rendered the
regular observance of sacraments impracticable. Meanwhile their fearless, tireless, self-denying devotion to
preaching the Gospel, as they understand it, together
with the supplementing social work which has developed
throughout the world by means of the Salvation Army,
entitle them to a very high place in the ranks of Christ's
loyal disciples. Judged by His own words—' If you
know these things, blessed are you if you do them '—
they have not now, nor ever will have, cause to be
ashamed.

(2) A very large number of real and devoted
Christians, including many on the Continent and in
America, and almost all the Free Churches throughout
Great Britain, whilst accepting the sacred obligation of
the Lord's Supper as a sacrament, yet regard it simply as
a tender and solemn memorial service. They acknowledge
its deep spiritual significance; but hold that it requires
nothing more than genuine faith and reverent love on the
believer's part, to make it all that Christ Himself intended
it to be. The Continental name for this view is Zwinglian.
Since it is sometimes described as superficial, or as tending
to belittle the spiritual worth of this sacrament, it may
be well to quote an authoritative statement.'[1]

(i) The Eucharist is not a repetition of the sacrifice of Christ,
but a commemoration of that sacrifice. (ii) The bread and wine
are signs or symbols of the broken body and shed blood of Christ;
(iii) The reference of the Eucharist is, therefore, rather, to Christ
crucified than to Christ glorified. (iv) In the Eucharist, Christ is
truly our food, and through Him our spiritual life is nourished,

[1] See *Encyclopaedia of Religion and Ethics,* vol. 10, p. 914.

but He is appropriated by faith alone. (v) The Eucharist, as a true communion of the body of Christ, is specially significant for the life of the church community, being the sign and pledge of united allegiance to Christ and membership in Him.

Such an attitude is as far from superficial as it is true to the New Testament. The name 'Eucharist' has become ecclesiastically fashionable, but the plain term 'Lord's Supper' answers every purpose, and runs no risk of being entangled in sacerdotal sophistries.

(3) 'Sacerdotal sophistries' seems perhaps a hard term to employ, concerning a doctrine and practice of the Lord's Supper which has for centuries been continuously held by the great Greek and Roman churches, and still obtains throughout a large section of the Anglican church in this country, as well as amongst not a few in the Free Churches. The real question, however, is not what the churches have done, or the early fathers thought; but what, with the New Testament before us, we cannot but discern to be Christ's own intention, and the true interpretation of Apostolic teaching and practice. To put it in clear brevity, the alternative is between the view just described as Zwinglian, and that which is conveniently summed up as 'sacerdotal.'

For what does this latter doctrine involve? The main items are as follows. (i) The Lord's Supper—always called the 'Holy Eucharist'—is singled out from all other Christian doctrines or acts of worship, as being 'The Sacrament' which, in its inscrutable mystery, is above all else, central in significance, and absolutely essential to 'salvation.' (ii) It can, however, only be valid as a sacrament, when 'admininstered' by a special class of men named 'priests,' who have special powers committed to them by episcopal ordination. (iii) But this episcopal ordination must be guaranteed by Apostolical succession. How far this obsession may go, is illustrated in the published attitude of Rev. R. J. Campbell, for many years a prominent Congregationalist minister, who now declares that

Anglo-Catholics may be right in what they say, about the necessity of making sure that only a *validly ordained priesthood* should be allowed to consecrate the sacred elements. To admit a counter principle, would be to run *the risk of profaning the most solemn of all mysteries.*[1]

(iv) Then the self-sacrifice of Christ on Calvary is said to be repeated in the order of service known as ' High Mass ' amongst Romanists, which is largely copied by Anglo-Romanists—commonly called Anglo-Catholics. (v) The Anglican Prayer Book, in its Communion service, rules out some of these conceptions, but still leaves much which shows the same leaning towards Sacramentarianism.

At the time when this page is written, the Bishops are meeting in solemn conclave, to consider the revision of the Prayer Book, which is declared to be ' the most insistent crisis that the Anglican Church has experienced since the Reformation.' The burning question which involves a ' threatened break-away of 700,000 Anglo-Catholics,' is whether it shall be legal—' to reserve the Sacrament, for the purpose of the Communion of the sick and other persons, unable to attend at the Church.' This plainly involves two things. First, that in order to all that ' salvation ' means, it is absolutely necessay to ' receive the sacrament.' Secondly, that some such magical change, indefinable either theologically or scientifically, has been wrought in the bread and wine, through the words of consecration uttered by the ' celebrant,' that they have become 'sacred elements'—without which ' Holy Communion ' is worth nothing ! How far this Pagan superstition is from the New Testament, is plain to every open mind.

[1] *A Spiritual Pilgrimage,* p. 320. The italics are mine, and speak for themselves as to how far from the mind of Christ the sacerdotal obsession can lead some men.

But amongst the Free Churches of this country—
with the exception of Wesleyan Methodists, who in this
service employ the Anglican Prayer Book—this whole
sacerdotal attitude is repudiated.   In order to appreciate
their positive doctrine it is specially necessary to
emphasize certain uncompromising negatives. The New
Testament, fairly interpreted by itself in modern light, is
the sole and sufficient authority for these.[1]

(i)   In His last tender behest, Jesus never intended
any such thing as a repetition of His own self-sacrifice;
or any offering for sin; or anything approaching the
gorgeous ceremony and stilted pomp of ' High Mass '
and its Anglican imitation. These are purely ecclesiastical
inventions.

(ii)   In obeying His behest, there is neither need
nor room for the intervention of any ' priest.' Of such
priesthood the New Testament knows absolutely
nothing.

(iii)   There is, in all the New Testament, no mention
whatever, nor even suggestion, of any ' administration '
of the Lord's Supper. This term, in spite of its common
and thoughtless adoption, even by the Free Churches,
is but a misleading appendage of sacerdotalism.

(iv)   There is no warrant whatever for laying
supreme and incomparable emphasis upon the Lord's
Supper, as ' The ' Sacrament, to the disparagement of
all else.

(v)   Nor is there for so continually extolling it; or
insisting upon it as superior to all the other means of
grace; or proclaiming it the ' central act ' of Christian
worship, and teaching.

(vi)   There is no warrant whatever, either in the
words of Jesus Himself, or any others in the New Testa-

[1] The whole case is succinctly but carefully and sufficiently
stated in my booklet entitled, *Christian Truth Concerning the Lord's
Supper,* published by the Epworth Press.

ment, for supposing any change at all in the nature or substance of the plain elements of bread and wine used in the Comunion service.

(vii) There is no warrant whatever for speaking of the bread and wine, in their whole connexion with this service, as 'mysteries.' The words of 'consecration' do nothing to differentiate them from the food used at any ordinary meal. There is no more 'mystery' in this service than in every heartfelt prayer; or in all the spiritual fellowship with Christ and with each other which constitutes Christian reality. The talk about 'profaning the sacred mysteries' by the touch of any devout Christian man or woman, because not episcopally ordained, is sheer Pagan superstition, contrary to the whole tenor of the Gospel of Jesus Christ.

(viii) There is no necessity whatever that the Communion service should be conducted by any special class of men. It was natural that the Apostles and Elders—for the New Testament knows nothing about either Bishops or Priests, in the modern sense—should conduct such a service. Just as to-day the custom that the Pastor of a Church should do so, rests upon respect for his work, enhanced by personal regard. The protest of the writer of 1 Peter v. 3, against 'lording it over the charge allotted,' is but an echo of the stronger words of Jesus Himself in Matt. xxv. 20 to 28. Whenever special occasion should arise, any truly Christian man, or woman, is just as qualified to conduct this service, as any Bishop or Archbishop that ever was or will be.

(ix) Finally, there is no use or merit whatever in this 'Holy Communion' service *ex opere operato*—that is, apart from the personal faith and devotion of the believer. The mere attendance at such a service is of no more avail than the turning of a Tibetan prayer-wheel. As long as the New Testament lasts, these words of the Westminster Shorter Catechism will hold good,

to the human mind. As Sir James Frazer has said in his
notable volume hereupon—' What we all want to know is
whether death is the end of all things for the individual,
whether our conscious personality perishes with the
body, or survives it for a time, or for eternity?' The
question is as old as humanity. Its antiquity has been
recently emphasized by the remarkable discoveries in
the tomb of Tutankhamen. It is beyond controversy
that ' the whole of Egyptian religion was based upon a
conviction of personal inmmortality.' But in some form
or other, similiar convictions have obtained in all nations,
even amongst those which are deemed the ' lowest.'
In his second volume, Sir J. Frazer investigates this belief
amongst the Maoris, Tongans, Samoans, Hervey
Islanders, Society Islanders, Marquesans, Hawaiians, and
others, and finds it to be, in all these cases, both real and
influential. All life is endowed with an instinct for
continuance. All living creatures flee from, or fight
against, anything which threatens to end their life. But
it is the specific human faculty to conceive of a future
beyond the grave which will mean not merely the continuance of our present faculties, but their enlargement,
either for joy or sorrow, to an immeasurable extent.

On Christian principles, this human anticipation is
both confirmed and endorsed. It is true that the early
Jews did not accept the beliefs which surrounded them in
Egypt; nor is there in the Old Testament any reference
to an after life, save the dim notion of a gloomy ' Sheol '
for departed mortals. It was not until the time of the
Maccabees, and not even then by all the Jews, that
individual survival after death became the national faith.
But in Christ's time, by all save the Sadducees, it was
generally accepted. He not only assumed but endorsed
and emphasized it.

But it is necessary to make a clear distinction between
two senses which attach to the word ' immortality.'

Primarily, it stands for the simple survival of the human personality, after the body is broken down by death. But it may also convey the meaning of endless existence —the continuance of the new life after death for ever and ever. This is indeed, when truly contemplated, an overwhelming conception. So that there are, herein, two great questions to be faced. (I) Does the human soul, or self, survive the collapse of the body? (II) Is there to be somehow, somewhen, a second death which will end all—or will the soul go on, and on, and on, to exist for evermore?

(II) It will be best to take first the latter of these queries, because be can say so little about it. The most earnest and careful thought can only bring us to inconclusive conclusions. (1) No human being can form any rational idea of what is meant by 'eternity.' No mortal brain can grasp the idea of everlastingness. The more we try to conceive it, the farther it recedes from us. (2) All, therefore, that we can say, or think, is that when once the human soul has been freed by death from its bodily limitation, we know of nothing that can destroy it. Its annihilation is as unthinkable as its endless continuance. We know nothing of any second death. The phrase which occurs in Rev. xx. 14, is pure imagery, as the context shows.

(3) It is not true that the human soul which has a beginning must of necessity have an end. Whether the human personality arises by creation or evolution—by what is technically termed Creationism or Traducianism —is quite irrelevant. The same divine power which brought it into existence, can maintain it. There is nothing save that divine will, to prevent its continuance. (4) But if God be the loving universal Father such as Jesus represents, every human being is His child. We cannot conceive of the loving Father destroying His own

9

children—however little some of them seem to us to be worthy of His love. (5) No final dogmatism is possible in face of the inevitable antinomies. (i) We cannot conceive of the Father destroying His own children. (ii) Nor can we conceive of His approval of any who are content with evil. (iii) Nor can He compel any such to turn to good. That would be self-contradiction. (iv) Furthermore He could not, being Love, ignore the indescribable difficulties, and often tragic circumstances, under which myriads of human beings are driven by heredity or environment to spend their earthly lives. In view of all these considerations, the truly Christian conclusion would seem to be to regard human beings, in the light of the revelation of Jesus, as the children of God whom death does not destroy, but ushers into a larger life to which we know no end. The rest is in the Father's hands.

(I)   As to simple survival. It would be wasted time to consider how long a human personality may survive, unless there is valid evidence for the fact of survival. Dr. W. N. Clarke, in his excellent *Outline of Theology,* has truly summed up the vast literature of the subject in saying that

> The best human thought, springing from the best experience, recognizes more and more the intrinsic value of man, and tends constantly to the assertion of immortality as a universal human endowment. (p. 452.)

For such an avowal, reasons may be alleged on four distinct lines, Scriptural, Scientific, Moral, and Actual.

(1)   As already intimated, Scriptural reasons for life after death are not found in the Old Testament until the times of the Apocrypha; but the New Testament everywhere assumes it. Jesus Himself offered no more proofs of human survival after death, than He did concerning the being of God. He assumed both, without

hesitation or equivocation. His strongest words of contradiction—' you, therefore, are greatly mistaken '—were addressed to those Sadducees who raised difficulties, with a view to rejecting altogether the after-life. His definite dismissal of their attitude was accompanied by an unmistakably positive assertion—' God is not the God of the dead, but of the living, for in His sight all are living.' (Luke xx. 38.) Everywhere and always He treated men and women as those who through death would enter upon another life. For all who have any Christian faith, His testimony is sufficient.

(2) But for others, valid appeal may be made to science. Quite apart from the remarkable phenomena associated with psychical research during recent years, three allegations may be made on scientific grounds.

(i) The human instinct hinted at above, has first to be accounted for; and then its demand for satisfaction fairly estimated. The human recoil from extinction at death is almost universal. It is strongest in noblest characters, and as in the case of Prof. Huxley—witness his letter to Lord Morley—is deeply felt by many who have no religious bias. Tennyson's oft quoted protest only puts scientific truth into poetic form.

> My own dim life should teach me this,
>   That life shall live for evermore;
>   Else earth is darkness at the core,
> And dust and ashes all that is.

(ii) The witness of modern psychology in this direction is becoming more and more pronounced. Materialism indeed is not dead; but it certainly is moribund. Both biological and psychological scrutiny lead to the conclusion that the body is not the man, any more than the brain is the mind. The 10,000,000,000 cerebral cells cannot of themselves create one single thought, or feel even the smallest desire. The self is much more than an inert ' epi-phenomenon.' A man is not a ' cunning cast in clay ; nor a ' magnetic mockery ' ; but an inscrutable combination of the physical and the spiritual. The death which breaks down the former, does not necessarily touch the latter.

(iii) The modern doctrine of evolution supplies additional reason for believing that death does not end all for human beings. Scientific authorities tell us that it has taken 100,000,000 years to produce a human being. If that be so, and after life's fitful moment nothing is left but a handful of ashes, then Fiske and Tennyson are both right. The philosopher truly says :

The more thoroughly we comprehend that process of evolution by which things have come to be what they are, the more we are likely to feel that to deny the everlasting persistence of the spiritual element in man, is to rob the whole process of its meaning. It goes far toward putting us to permanent intellectual confusion. For my own part, therefore, I believe in the immortality of the soul, not in the sense in which I accept the demonstrable truths of science, but as a supreme act of faith in the reasonableness of God's work.[1]

Whilst the poet makes it vivid, in declaring that if man is only destined at the last to be

> Blown about the desert dust
> Or sealed within the iron hills;
>
> No more? A monster then, a dream,
> A discord. Dragons of the prime,
> That tear each other in their slime,
> Were mellow music matched with him.

If a modern organ with five manuals, 100 stops, and 10,000 pipes, took ten years to build, and then, after being used for five minutes, were broken up, every sane man would say that it represented lunacy. But all the organs ever made, or most complex machines invented by the brain of man, are clumsy nothings compared with the marvellous complexity of the human body,[2] to say nothing

[1] *Destiny of Man*, p. 116.
[2] For further statement of this see my booklet, *The Mystery of Painlessness*, Epworth Press.

of its inscrutable interblending with mind and soul. All the marvels of modern anatomy, physiology, and psychology, combined, serve to show that the suggestion of annihilation at death for human beings, is as unscientific and irrational, as it is to normal minds unwelcome.

(3) But in addition to the above, there are definite moral reasons which nothing but sheer atheism can set aside, for believing in human survival after death. On the Theistic assumption—justified elsewhere—four suggestions appear to be both inevitable and irresistible.

(i) In the minds and hearts of all those who deserve to be accounted the best specimens of humanity, there is a sense of imperfection and failure, with a longing for further opportunties of development, which cannot be quenched, any more than the marvellous instincts of insects, fishes, and birds. If Jesus meant the benediction —' Blessed are they that hunger and thirst for goodness, for they shall be satisfied '—then there is good ground for the presumption that He who is Himself the Infinite Good, will not suffer His children's noblest craving to be quenched in the hour and article of death.

(ii) On the assumption that God is such as Jesus declares Him to be, it cannot be denied that this life abounds, throughout human society as we know it, with direct, flagrant, immeasurable, contradiction to all that is right in His sight. Ages ago Prophets and Psalmists[1] voiced the perplexity of myriads of other thoughtful observers. If this life were all, then in numberless cases evil triumphs over good, man sets God at defiance, and the kosmos becomes a moral chaos.

(iii) So far as our knowledge extends, and our power avails, it is impossible either to put an end now to all moral wrong, or cherish any rational hope of its being ended on the human plane, in the course of the ages. Even when the very best and utmost are made of all the

[1] See Psalm lxxiii; Jeremiah xii; Job, passim, &c.

moral advance which in some respects distinguishes this present age from the past, there is no ground whatever for anticipating the final victory of good over evil, or right over wrong, in the prospects of modern civilization.

(iv) It comes, therefore, to this, that the belief in God as revealed in Jesus, and the hope of a future life in which justice, truth, and love shall prevail, stand or fall together. If there is nothing but extinction at death for human beings, then on any principles of justice or mercy, it were far better that millions upon millions of mortals had never been born. So many, so terrible, so inexplicable have been, and still are, the cases of absolutely innocent suffering, undeserved sorrow, cruel bereavement, premature death, that if there be not for all such some real hope of comfort and compensation hereafter, as is hinted at in the parable of Dives and Lazarus—'now, here, he is being comforted'—they have simply been the helpless victims of unjustifiable malignity, through the mindless and heartless working of brute forces. A good God becomes as unthinkable as Sir Francis Younghusband has declared, in his pathetic volume entitled *Within*. If this life be all, then truly God is but 'the baseless shadow of a wistful human dream,' and man becomes the mere incarnation of mystery and misery.

(4) But this is not the whole case. Faith and hope are good, and are well buttressed by the above suggestions. The witness of Christ's own triumph over death, in accordance with all His teaching, cannot be overestimated. The reality of His resurrection has been so thoroughly demonstrated by Christian scholars, in full view of all modern criticism, that it may here be assumed.[1]

But in these materialistic and spiritually callous days,

---

[1] No better statement can be found than that of Dr. Sparrow Simpson, entitled, *The Resurrection and Modern Thought*. Published by Longmans. Though I find nothing to alter in chapter v. of my *Miracles of Unbelief*, written a quarter of a century ago, pp. 135-173.

there is room for more. It may and must now be said with all deliberation, that the above conclusions are substantiated by facts. More will be said hereupon in the section given to Spiritualism. Here it is enough to affirm that testimonies to actual communication with the departed, showing that they still live, and possess all the faculties of personality, are multiplied. They are, moreover, of such a character,[1] that to reject them off-hand, or dismiss them as unworthy of regard, is to give up utterly and for ever all value in human testimony. In which case, manifestly, Christianity becomes an utter delusion. But when justice is done to such testimony, it is not enough to say that we believe, on good grounds, that death does not end all, for men and women. We *know* that it does not.

(*ii*) *Resurrection*

If it is assumed that death does not end all, the immediate and inevitable question arises—in the Apostle's words—'with what manner of body do they come?' The article in the Creed which is so often repeated— 'I believe in the resurrection of the body,'—has, until quite recently, conveyed two things to the ordinary mind. (1) That after death there would be a long interval of unconscious 'sleeping,' until some far-off literal 'Day of Judgement.' Then (2) the former physical body would be reconstituted, so as to make the entire man exactly what he was before death. The utter impossibility of this latter notion is, however, now manifest. But one must own that it is by no means generally dismissed. Yet it is impossible to mistake the teaching of the Apostle Paul as to the 'resurrection body'—'there is a natural body and there is a spiritual body'—for which the modern

[1] Out of a host let the reader consider only these two plain and careful volumes—*Man's Survival after Death* by C. L. Tweedale, (Grant Richards); and *After Death* by Camille Flammarion, the well-known astronomer (Fisher Unwin).

term is coming to be the 'etheric' body. In any case, the risen body of Christ Himself exhibited a transformation into what was so manifestly ultra-physical, that the popular notion specified above ought never to have arisen.

But the question as to when this spiritual body is to be inhabited, has yet to be faced; and it must be acknowledged that the frequent recurrence of the term 'resurrection,' together with a few isolated passages—such as John vi. 40, 54, v. 28—make it difficult to understand that when 'the earthly house of our tabernacle is dissolved,' we shall be at once 'clothed upon with our habitation which is from heaven.' But Canon Streeter has said with truthful emphasis,[1] 'The belief in a long interval between death and resurrection, cannot claim to have behind it the authority of our Lord's own teaching.' Nor indeed that of the Apostle, whose expression of desire—'Not that we would be unclothed, but that we would be clothed upon, that what is mortal may be swallowed up of life'—cannot, by any honest exegesis, be postponed to some far distant future. When all the New Testament is taken into full account, it becomes manifest that the term 'resurrection' really conveys all that we now mean by the survival of the conscious personality, and its immediate clothing with a spiritual body fitted for its new sphere of being. Less than this cannot be understood from the words of Jesus to the dying robber; or His lesson concerning Dives and Lazarus. Nor is there any room whatever for prolonged unconsciousness in Paul's yearning—'to depart and be with Christ, for it is very much better.'

Thus these other words of Canon Streeter are, to an open mind, entirely warranted.

If we affirm that we too, at once and without any interval of

[1] In his volume on *Immortality,* p. 118.

waiting, shall take on our new celestial bodies, we affirm exactly what the Apostles taught would happen to themselves, and to every member of the Church they knew. The notion of an age-long interval between death and resurrection, is an inheritance from the letter of Jewish apokalyptic, which the actual belief of the first generations of Christians had in practice, though not in theory, already discarded. Hence although we may recognize some elements of truth in the expectation of a 'last day,' I would urge that Christian teaching would do well to surrender, openly and completely, the belief that the resurrection, that is, the assumption by the spirit of its celestial body, is postponed to a distant future.

(iii) Judgement

When it is understood that 'resurrection' in the New Testament signifies, not the physical reassembling of human bodies at some distant date, but the immediate continuity of conscious personality after death, we have still to face with reverent honesty the meaning of such words as the Fourth Gospel records (v. 28).

Marvel not at this; for the hour cometh in which all that are in the tombs shall hear His voice, and shall come forth; they that have done good unto the resurrection of life; and they that have done ill unto the resurrection of judgement.

It is small wonder that such words have led to a popular theology which more careful thought cannot but reject. Canon Streeter has well said that

If we get rid of the supposed interval between death and resurrection, we dispose at the same time of the interval between death and judgement. For each man, the day after death is also the 'day of judgement.'

But this, again, is in manifest opposition to the traditional and ecclesiastical notion of some 'intermediate state,' to be followed by a far distant terrestrial day when, in overwhelming spectacular and material fashion, all the human beings who have ever lived on this planet, are to be assembled and judged according to their doings in this life. From that judgement they are to be dismissed, either to everlasting happiness, or everlasting misery. This doctrine has for centuries past, been preached in sermons and printed in books. But its most common and influential statement has been in hymns which are yet sung—though not as much as formerly—by ordinary Christian congregations. Take but one or two specimens which are typical of many more.

> Before me place, in dread array,
> The pomp of that tremendous day,
>   When Thou with clouds shalt come
> To judge the nations at Thy bar;
> And tell me, Lord, shall I be there
>   To meet a joyful doom?

Two of the best known hymns in church use, are 'Luther's' and the 'Dies Irae.' They do not need quotation—consider only these verses:

> The ungodly, filled with guilty fears,
>   Behold His wrath prevailing;
> In woe they rise, but all their tears
>   And sighs are unavailing;
> The day of grace is past and gone;
> Trembling they stand before His throne,
>   All unprepared to meet Him.
>
> When the Judge His seat attaineth
> And each hidden deed arraigneth,
> Nothing unavenged remaineth.
>
> Ah, that day of tears and mourning!
> From the dust of earth returning,
> Man for judgement must prepare him.

Such hymns would still be sung without hesitation by most Christian congregations. But the time has certainly come to say, unhesitatingly and unequivocally, that this whole representation is untrue. Unfortunately, it is deeply rooted in the popular mind, though seldom heard now in sermons. In the interests of Christian truth it would be, however, vast gain, if many such hymns as those indicated, could be burnt and forgotten. In our time, the mere marshalling of selected passages from the New Testament has ceased to be effective, even when endorsed by ecclesiastical authority and orthodox convention. If half-empty churches are to be filled, and the outsiders gathered in, there will have to be reality of thought and speech which will bear the fierce light of modern knowledge, whether historical, or critical, or scientific.

In the great matter here considered, and with the whole New Testament before us, there is no question as to the reality of judgement to come. All our difficulty is as to its time, and manner, and result. To take literally such a parabolic isolated uterance as—' before Him shall be gathered all nations '—is shown by a moment's real thought, to be sheer childishness. Whilst to suppose all humanity, through all the ages, with its incalculable grades of moral merit or demerit, simply separated as ' sheep from goats,' in irreversible judgement, is to treat a figurative fraction in a parable as the actual sum of Christ's teaching, and so to misrepresent His whole Gospel.

The plain truth may be thus summarized. There is no question as to the moral quality of the personal continuity which resurrection involves. For all men, though in infinitely varied degrees, there is in this life not only opportunity but responsibility for making character. This is manifest in all history, as well as in observation and experience. That character each human soul takes with it, necessarily, into the hereafter, when death breaks down the mortal body. But death is a purely physical event, which no more touches character than a tunnel does the train that passes through it. No L.M.S. train entering a tunnel, emerges a L.N.E.R. train. Even so, the truth concerning judgement is well expressed in such words as Matt. vii. 21; John v. 29; Gal. v. 6 and vi.

15; together with such other unmistakable utterances as Rom. ii. and 1 Cor. xiii.   There is neither need nor New Testament warrant for any such 'intermediate state' as has occupied the ingenuity of many theologians in bygone days.   Its usual reference to 1 Pet. iii. 17 for Scriptural basis is not warranted.   The rendering of that passage by Dr. Moffatt and Dr. Rendel Harris, is textually justified, and points to an entirely different exegesis.   Judgement begins to operate as soon as our personality passes out of this sphere of being, with its limitations, into another which is as real as it is beyond our present powers of apprehension.

(iv)   Hell

The inevitable accompaniment of popular Christian belief concerning judgement, is the further conception of Heaven and Hell.   Until quite recent times, the great end of Christian faith was thought and said to be to 'escape Hell,' and 'go to Heaven.'   But in the closer consideration which is now forced upon us, four questions demand plain answer.   (i) As to localization.   Is Hell a place?   There is both room and need even yet to say definitely, it is not.   To preach, or sing, or pray, about 'going' to either Heaven or Hell, is but childish prattle. Doubtless some sincere believers are quite content to read and take literally the utterly misleading word in the English versions of John xiv. 2, 3.   But the intelligence as well as scholarship of to-day knows better.[1] We know that 'when the earthly house of this tabernacle is dissolved' the 'house not made with hands' awaiting us, has nothing to do with any local or material environment.   Here again, the mischief of popular hymnology is measureless.   Grown people in Christian congregations are still asked and content to sing:

[1] For fuller exposition, see my *Reality in Bible Reading,* p. 136.

> Lo! on a narrow neck of land,
> 'Twixt two unbounded seas I stand,
>   Secure, insensible;
> A point of time, a moment's space,
> Removes me to that heavenly place,
>   Or shuts me up in hell.

Or this :

> Sweet place; sweet place alone!
>   The court of God most High,
> The heaven of heavens, the throne
>   Of spotless majesty!
> O happy place! when shall I be,
> My God, with Thee, to see Thy face?

Whilst many sing with rapture such hymns as

> Jerusalem the golden,
>   With milk and honey blessed,

and would by no means refuse to join in this :

> When, shrivelling like a parchèd scroll,
> The flaming heavens together roll,
> And louder yet, and yet more dread,
> Swells the high trump that wakes the dead;
>
> O, on that day, that awful day,
> When man to judgement wakes from clay,
> Be Thou, O Christ, the sinner's stay,
> Though heaven and earth shall pass away!

But when everything has been said concerning poetic imagery, it should be enough to reply that these representations are untrue, and therefore unworthy.

(2) Until recent years there has been almost universally, the associated notion that hell was a place of 'torment.' Dante's *Inferno*, for all its poetic genius, has done immeasurable harm, in seeming to support the monstrosities of the Romish Church herein, as well as of some sections of Protestantism. A few years ago these gruesome representations were quite common in preaching which was called 'evangelical.' Some of Mr. Spurgeon's famous sermons bear lurid witness to this;

though they are outdone by the Romish catechism—which is still taught. Seeing, however, that the physical body is unquestionably disintegrated at death, this notion means that countless millions of human bodies would have to be re-created, on purpose to subject them to endless physical agonies. No wonder that such a ghastly conception has been scornfully rejected by the modern mind.

Such repulsive notions have, indeed, dropped out of reference in most churches; but there is still left an obscurantist relic, in the conception that future punishment must at all events mean something painful, inflicted *ab extra,* by an angry God. This also is false; and is not justified by such a word as John iii. 36, when interpreted in the light of the whole New Testament. All real punishment is self-punishment; not an infliction, but a natural and necessary result of character. Even here and now, it is matter for plain observation and experience that the most real hell for men and women, is of their own creation. It is character, not environment; our own behaviour, not the treatment by others; that make only too many houses that should be homes, veritable hells. That will be intensified beyond expression, when the delusions and limitations of the present are removed by death. There is no other hell; nor ever will be. 'Which way I turn, myself am hell,' is reality dark enough, and sad enough, without any addition of lurid mediaeval superstitions. All the figurative language of the New Testament such as, 'There shall be the weeping and gnashing of teeth,' expresses no other, no more, no less.

(3) But the greatest horror of popular theology and the keenest theological controversies, have been related even more to the duration of 'future punishment' than to its nature. Whatever kind of suffering may be implied in being 'lost,' the doctrine of the Christian church has long been that it is 'eternal.' That is to say, it is

to go on helplessly, hopelessly, for ever and for ever.
All the 'orthodox' churches have, indeed, in days gone
by, laid great stress upon it. It is now seldom, if ever,
heard in sermons, or found in print. But these churches
have never openly disowned it; and in many hymns it is
still retained, and emphasized.

> When we came, and whither, wending,
>   Soon we must through darkness go,
> To inherit bliss unending
>   Or eternity of woe.
>
> O Thou who wouldst not have
>   One wretched sinner die,
> Who diedst Thyself my soul to save
>   From endless misery;
> Show me the way to shun
>   Thy dreadful wrath severe.

Whilst in the Anglican church, the Athanasian creed
unequivocally declares, twice over, that—'unless a man
thus think of the Trinity, without doubt he shall perish
everlastingly.' And highly placed clerics demand that
this shall be read in public! It is small wonder that
thoughtful minds to-day regard such utterances with
utter revulsion. For it is quadruply false. (i) No
mortal being has ever grasped, or ever will grasp, the
idea of endlessness. Those who have talked most about
it, have least known what they were saying.

(ii) The attempts to derive this terrible doctrine
from the New Testament, do not by any means yield, to
modern minds, the unequivocal conclusions which were
formerly drawn from them. The horror of the 'orthodox'
doctrine has driven many thoughtful Christians to find
refuge in the notions of 'Conditional Immortality,' and
'Annihilation.' But careful consideration shows that such
suggestions are neither in harmony with the character
of God, as Jesus reveals Him, nor can they be derived,
by fair and full exegesis, from the New Testament

passages usually alleged on their behalf. It must suffice here to consider the one instance which has so often been quoted as most pronounced and final. Matt. xxv. 46, in the 'Authorized' Version, reads—'These shall go away into everlasting punishment.' But really, it has nothing to do with the doctrine in question. For (a) the word rendered 'everlasting' is quite unjustified. The Revised Version substitutes 'eternal' which—as John xvii. 2 and the whole of John's first Epistle show—is primarily qualitative. In this parable it says nothing whatever as to duration. But also (b) even if it did— there is no reference at all to the 'saved,' or 'lost,' as these terms are understood in 'Gospel preaching,' or theological discussion. If 'blessed' were taken to mean all that is generally implied in 'salvation' after death, it would unmistakably contradict the rest of the New Testament. For most assuredly, some of the greatest unbelievers and strongest opponents of Christian faith have embodied in their lives all that is here pronounced 'blessed,' and so find rightful place with the 'sheep' on the right hand. The whole story is but an instructive comment on the Second Great Command, and an emphatic lesson in Christian philanthropy.

Thus (iii) when the suggestion of absolutely endless suffering is at all realized, its usual dogmatic statement is seen to be altogether irreconcilable with the character of God as revealed in Jesus Christ. One cannot wonder that in days when men are driven to think as never before, this awful doctrine has driven more away from Christian faith than all other difficulties combined. In the degree in which it is realized, it is only compatible with blank atheism.

(iv) Moreover, in its exclusion of the possibility of repentance hereafter, it is manifestly contrary to the truth concerning the continuity of human personality after death. For it is part of the very essence of person-

ality to be free to choose. If that which survives death
has no such moral freedom, then it is not the man at all,
but his mocking automaton, which has survived. All due
regard may be paid to the representations of this life as
a time of responsibile probation. But the fact that we are
here to make character, and undoubtedly do make it,
and take it with us through death's tunnel, does not
warrant the conclusion that thereafter there shall be
no possibility of alteration. If, as is generally assumed,
the ' saved ' are to progress in all goodness, there must be
corresponding possibility of moral change for the ' lost.'
What influences for good may be hereafter brought to
bear upon a personality which has here persisted in
known evil, we do not know. But we do know that a
moral being cannot be compelled to love, on either side
the grave; for that were a contradiction in terms. That
is why what is known as Universalism cannot be preached
either Scripturally or logically. It can never be anything
more than a faint hope. Its utmost significance is voiced
by Tennyson.

> Behold, I know not anything,
>   I can but trust that good shall fall,
>   At last, far off, at last, to all;
>   And every winter change to spring.

But for a free personality, love can no more be prevented
than compelled—hereafter any more than here. That
which is not revealed in Christ's Gospel hereupon, may
well be left in His hands whose love cannot but mean that
He will do all the best that can be done, for every soul,
now, and evermore.

(v) Heaven

In some form or other the hope of a better, happier,
larger life beyond the grave has always appealed to
human hearts. It has brought comfort, strength, stimulus,
in varied degrees, to untold millions, as they have passed

10

through this vale of tears, often crushed under a burden
of unexpected and inexplicable sorrows. The claim of
the Christian faith above all other religions, is that it
brings the brightest and noblest hope, on the surest
guarantees. This finds its supreme expression in the
words of Jesus recorded in the Fourth Gospel—which
have brought more comfort to human hearts than any
ever uttered. The faulty English Version of 1611,
mentioned above, is, we know, sacredly enshrined in
myriads of memories.

> Let not your heart be troubled; ye believe in God, believe
> also in me. In my Father's house are many mansions; if it were
> not so I would have told you; for I go to prepare a place for you.

But they suggest a great question, namely, whether,
in Christian thought and teaching, old association, which
is often misleading, is to triumph over truth, which is
always best. In this case, although the Greek word for
'believe' serves to express either the indicative or
imperative mood, the whole context shows that here it
is an exhortation, not an assumption. Jesus did not
take their faith for granted; but bade them have faith
both in the Father whom He revealed, and in Himself.
Then, too, the word 'mansions,' to which so many
blindly cling, is to-day most misleading, and entirely
contrary to the true significance of the word which
Jesus employed. The Latin 'mansiones,' taken from the
Vulgate, really means a halting place on a journey, and
this corresponds truly to the word μοναί in the Greek.
But the resistless flux of speech has made 'mansions,'
to-day, mean just the opposite—a permanent and exclusive abode—very far removed from the intention of
Jesus, and the Christian hope of Heaven.

The word 'Heaven,' and the phrase 'going to
Heaven,' though deeply entrenched in popular usage, have
become so entangled with ecclesiastical misrepresentation
and ignorant imagining, that they yield little real comfort

for this generation; whilst the symbolic imagery of the last portion of the New Testament has been seized upon by popular preachers and hymn writers, as the literal realities in store for the ' saved.' But the prospect of being dressed in white and crowned, singing psalms for ever amid palm branches, only nauseates thoughtful minds, and makes Heaven contemptible. True, a great change has come over Christian pulpits in this regard. But the repellent hymns still remain in use. To say that they are only poetic imagery, does not make them harmless. Consider only one or two typical specimens.

> Lift your eyes of faith, and see
>   Saints and angels joined in one;
> What a countless company
>   Stand before yon dazzling throne!
> Each before his Saviour stands
>   All in milk-white robes arrayed,
> Palms they carry in their hands,
>   Crowns of glory on their heads.

Such foolish rhapsody may have suited the time of Charles Wesley, but it is worse than useless now—though it may be heard in any church on any Sunday. Or consider Faber's verse

> Father of Jesus, love's reward,
>   What rapture will it be
> Prostrate before Thy throne to lie,
>   And ever gaze on Thee!

Jesus Himself never used, or suggested, such mocking sentimentalism.

Or take the hymn above mentioned, beginning,

> Jerusalem the golden,
>   With milk and honey blessed,

and go through it thoughtfully. It may have served the mysticism of Bernard of Cluny, but it is pious piffle to this generation. The same must be said in simple truth about Dean Alford's verses beginning,

> Ten thousand times ten thousand,
>   In sparkling raiment bright,
> The armies of the ransomed saints
>   Throng up the steeps of light.

Alas, there are not a few of such productions in actual use, and the very least that can be said of their mischief is that they do definitely train Christian congregations to thoughtless unreality—which is the dry rot of public worship.

Only a few years ago, it was the regular custom to train the children in Sunday Schools to sing continually about dying and 'going to heaven'; and although, happily, a real change is coming to pass in this respect, the old morbid sensationalism dies hard. Our little ones are still too often bidden sing :

> Around the throne of God in heaven
>   Thousands of children stand,
> Children whose sins are all forgiven,
>   A holy, happy band,
>   Singing, Glory, glory, glory!
>
> In flowing robes of spotless white,
>   See every one arrayed;
> Dwelling in everlasting light
>   And joys that never fade,
>   Singing, Glory, glory, glory!

What impression is that likely to create in the minds of scores of healthy sensible boys and girls? Is it any wonder that as they grow older they wander away? Or this :

> There is a better world, they say,
>   O so bright!
> Where sin and woe are done away,
>   O so bright!
> And music fills the balmy aid,
> And angels with bright wings are there,
> And harps of gold and mansions fair;
>   O so bright!

The marvel is—and the deep regret—that educated men,

in these days, should put such mischievous doggerel into hymn-books, which thus revolt where they ought to attract.

Hence the whole conception of the beautiful and inspiring side of the life to come, has been made incredible, undesirable, contemptible. This does immeasurable injustice to the Christian hope. Meanwhile, but little is said, with any note of certainty, as to the naturalness, the applicableness, the inspiration, of the Christian promise, in view of all our deepest needs and noblest desires. But good Dr. Watts put into his verse both reality and attraction immeasurable, when he wrote concerning the Christian hope :

> Then shall I see, and hear, and know
> All I desired and wished below;
> And every power find sweet employ,
> In that eternal world of joy.

Dr. Pringle-Pattison puts it into more technical expression, when he says that

We ought to think of immortal life not as the simple continuance of a being in existence at the same level of his powers and attainments, but as progress, or advance, in the most real sense; a continuous growth towards the stature of a perfect humanity.

All that such suggestions convey, and much more, is pledged to those who here, in the strength of grace ' seek for glory, and honour, and freedom from corruption ' as Paul set forth in his letter to the Romans (ch. ii.). Whilst the ' eternal life ' of which Jesus spoke and John wrote as a present experience, will be in the Heaven of the New Testament deepened, and intensified beyond mortal thought. It will, indeed, be a new, larger, fuller life, quite as really, and as immeasurably, as our present every-day experience is an unspeakable enlargement and enrichment of our pre-natal existence. In the Apostle's great and all inclusive word—' To be with Christ is

very much better ' than all the best we now know, or
can desire.

(vi) *The Second Coming*

From the very beginning of the Christian era until
now, the subject of the return, or ' second coming,' of
Christ, has occasioned much difficulty and endless discussion.   In recent years, numbers of volumes have
appeared vehemently declaring that the spectacular
return of Christ, with indescribable pomp and splendour,
may be expected now at any time.   According to some,
who are known as Pre-Millennialists, this will be followed
by a thousand years of Christ's visible reign on earth.
Others, with equal dogmatism, insist that the Millennium
is to precede the coming, so that this view is known as
Post-Millennialism.   If for nothing else, this whole
school of thought is discredited by its utter confusion.
Repeated attempts to fix a date for the great spectacle,
have proved as futile as the expectations of the first
Christians, or those which moved the world to frenzy in
the year A.D. 999.   The amount of sincere Bible study
occasioned has been admirable, but unfortunately based
upon an exploded theory of inspiration, which has led
to misunderstanding and misinterpretation.   So has it
come to pass that vast numbers not only in the ' evangelical ' churches, but in the other sections known as
Plymouth Brethren, Christadelphians, Seventh Day
Adventists, and Russellites, maintain the Pre-Millennial
expectation with undiminished persistence and propagandism.

None the less it becomes increasingly manifest to all
who have an open mind, that this whole attitude is as
unwarranted as it is sincere, and as untrue as it is dogmatic.   The best, that is truest, statement of the whole
matter, in my judgement, is that found in Dr. W. N.
Clarke's most valuable *Outline of Christian Theology;*

where, in Part vi, he discusses ' Things to come.' To that I must refer the reader for fuller detail than need here be given. We will briefly mention first, negatively, a few reasons for dismissing this whole temporal spectacular conception; and then, positively, the true New Testament doctrine.

(1) This whole spectacular interpretation makes Jesus definitely contradict Himself, in saying at one time that His coming would be immediate, at another that it would be long deferred, and at another that it would be a gradual, long-continued process.

(2) If a spectacular and cataclysmic coming were to be understood, there is a direct contradiction to Christ's own words in Luke xvii. 20, and Matt. xiii. 33.

(3) The whole notion of a not-far-distant coming Millennium is contrary to a right understanding of the New Testament in general, and some portions in particular. The only reference to it is in Rev. xx. 1 to 10. But that whole book was written for the immediate cheering of Christians, then undergoing great trials, and its predictions are declared to be near their fulfilment (Rev. i. 3; xxii. 10). As Dr. Clarke says—' It was by no means intended to describe Christ's victories in detail, or to enable its readers to foretell the future. There is no question as to a pre-millennial or post-millennial advent.'

(4) Millennialism misrepresents the nature and spirit of Christ's Kingdom—as shown in Matt. xviii. 20; xxviii. 20; also throughout the Gospel of John, specially chs. xiv. to xvii.

(5) It is definitely misleading in its treatment of the Books of Daniel and Revelation—the wrong date being ascribed to the former, and the meticulous interpretations of their symbolism being unjustified.

(6) It ignores the prevalent influence of Jewish expectation in Christ's day, and that of the writer in

Revelation (i. 7). The appeal of the penitent robber on the cross, and the triumphant entry into Jerusalem, show what was then the general belief which coloured early Christian expectation.

(7) It ignores the significance of the mistake of Paul and the early Christians, with its following correction. (Acts iii. 19 to 21, [R.V.]; 1 Thess. iv. 13 to 17; 2 Thess. ii. 2.)

(8) The reality of their mistake is seen in the fact that what they so ardently looked for, never came. All subsequent history has also contradicted it. All modern expectations have likewise ended in disappointment. Dr. Clarke well says :

> So numerous have been these failures, as to suggest the real cause of them. The entire labour of forecasting is misplaced.

(9) The whole Millennial scheme is self-contradictory, seeing that there is no possible reconciliation between the two main contentions. Neither does justice to the whole New Testament.

(10) In any case, such a millennium, whether pre- or post-, is practically unthinkable. Such a literal coming and spectacular judgement, were only conceivable in the time of the Ptolemaic astronomy, or when the flat earth theory prevailed.

(11) It rashly attempts what is definitely forbidden, as in Acts i. 6; and contradicts Christ's words in Matt. xiii. 31, 32, 33, and xxiv. 36.

(12) The whole conception of Christ's so coming, to overcome all evil by force, is equally unthinkable in itself, and contrary to all we know of the divine procedure both in the physical and moral realms. The method of creation is unquestionably that of evolution, not sudden creation. A thoughtful writer has well said :

> Nothing can I fancy more horribly incongruous with all I know of Christ, than the belief that some day He will return to earth with

love for only a few, to emulate the deeds of a Napoleon or a Genghis Khan.[1]

(13) It misrepresents the whole nature of His Kingdom and its methods. As to its nature, the prayer —' Thy will be done on earth, as it is in heaven '—should suffice. Whilst as to its development—' The Kingdom of God is in your very midst '[2]—speaks for itself.

(14) Millennialism is a doctrine of spiritual despair. It ignores all the reality of the work of the Holy Spirit in and through the Christian Church; besides undervaluing the present power of Christ in the hearts of myriads of devoted disciples, together with the potency of a living Christianity in the midst of modern humanity. On the whole, therefore, the estimate of Dr. David Smith is well warranted.

With these facts before us, it is hardly necessary to say that the idea of the Millennium is nothing more than an old Jewish fancy. It was a mere allegory, and while its perversion was excusable in the ignorance of the Middle Ages, it is deplorable that, at this late day of grace, the radiant vision should be so abused by coarse and stupil obscurantism.

Positively, it remans to try to apprehend the true meaning of the many references to this subject in the New Testament. The whole question is one of interpretation. When it is made plain that Christ's ' second coming ' is not, and cannot be, a sudden, physical, spectacular, cataclysm, what is left? At least four distinct conceptions. The real second coming is (i) spiritual and symbolic; (ii) invisible to bodily vision; (iii) gradual in its methods; and (iv) now still proceeding.

(i) The language of the Books of Daniel and Revelation is not only symbolic, but finds its fulfilment in the times when these portions of the Bible were written. The most careful modern scholarship is agreed that the

[1] *Methodist Recorder,* August 14, 1919.
[2] Not—' Within you,' as is so commonly quoted—see p. 86.

true date of Daniel is about A.D. 160. Its predictions have nothing to do with a distant millennium, but with the events soon following upon the Maccabean revolt. Whilst the figures and visions of Revelation also relate, as the letters to the seven churches plainly show, to current events, and their immediate consequences in the persecutions and trials of the second century Christians. The spiritual nature of Christ's kingdom could not be more emphatically stated than by the Apostle Paul—' The Kingdom of God is not eating and drinking '—that is, anything material—' but righteousness, and peace, and joy in the Holy Spirit.'

(ii)   The unmeasured stress laid upon the words—' In like manner' in Acts i. 11, is as unwarranted as misleading. If those three words are to be taken as crass literalness, so must all the rest of the narrative. That is to say, the Ascension was (a) manifest only to a select few as chosen witnesses, with no reference whatever to a multitude. (b) It was an utterly quiet and retired spot. A greater contrast to the imagined scenes of the millennial advent cannot be conceived. (c) There was an utter absence of all pomp and splendour. (d) The phrase ' a cloud received Him out of their sight,' is nothing more than a figurative way of saying that He vanished, just as He had done from the supper table at Emmaus.

(iii)   Although neither what happened at Pentecost, nor at the destruction of Jerusalem, was regarded by the early Christians as the expected Parousia, yet both events did really fulfil Christ's own emphatic words. The fate of the holy city, as the centre of the old dispensation, opened the door wide for the development of that spiritual beginning which came at Pentecost. No ' coming ' could be more in harmony with the words of Jesus.

(iv)   From that time to this, the prayer that Jesus taught—' Thy Kingdom come '—has been on the lips

and in the hearts and lives of all His true disciples, and
becomes, in spite of all that seems to the contrary, more
influential every generation. It is simply true that
Christ is coming now every day. Dr. Clarke says, as
truthfully as succinctly,

No visible return of Christ to the earth is to be expected, but
rather the long and steady advance of His spiritual kingdom. The
expectation of a single dramatic advent corresponds to the Jewish
doctrine of the nature of the kingdom, but not to the Christian.
His coming is not an event, it is a process that includes innumerable
events, a perpetual advance of Christ in the activity of His
Kingdom. It has continued until now, and is still moving on.
Christ came long ago, but He is truly the coming One, for He is
still coming, and is yet to come (p. 444).

So that, finally, the most important consideration of all
is found in the Revised rendering of Acts iii. 19, as
against the older Version, which is definitely wrong. The
Apostles did not say—' when the times of refreshing shall
come '—but ' Repent and change your ways, that your
sins may be blotted out, *that so there may come* seasons
of refreshing.' Manifestly, the false rendering represents
the better times as waiting for God to do something marvellous. Whereas the truth, as shown in the accurate
rendering, is that it is rather God who is waiting for
human repentance and obedience. Whence the plain and
impressive conclusion emerges, that the only Millennium
worth thinking about by Christ's disciples, is that which
He calls upon them to be continually helping to bring
to pass. And with this all the New Testament agrees.

(10) SPIRITUALISM

A brief consideration of the modern movement known
as Spiritualism, necessarily follows Eschatology, because
it relates so definitely to the belief in a future life and

in the possible proximity of discarnate human spirits. In some form or other, this belief has been held by all grades of humanity, as far as our knowledge of history extends. How greatly that knowledge has been increased in recent times, such works as those of Sir J. Frazer testify. But the special development of those beliefs which go now by the name of Spiritualism, began about the middle of the 19th century, and has steadily grown until in this country alone, there are some 600 societies or Lyceums, with probably 100,000 members. In America there are very many more, so that the world total of two millions is claimed with some reason. Its influence is by no means confined to the avowed adherents, for in all ranks of society as well as throughout the churches, there is a growing number who more or less fully acknowledge its phenomena, and sympathize with its main principles. It was at first, like the Salvation Army, only an occasion for derision. But that stage is now definitely past. The irresistible testimony borne to the frequent occurence of remarkable phenomena, led, in 1882, to the formation of the Society for Psychical Research, under the guidance of Messrs. Myers, Sidgwick, Lodge, Gurney, Barrett, and Podmore. The publication of the *Proceedings* of this Society, along with the two volumes by Myers on *Human Personality,* and two others upon *Phantasms of the Living,* did much to break down the stone wall of ignorant prejudice, and prepare modern minds for further revelations. All kinds of opposition still abound; but a movement which in its main features is supported by such men as Sir Wm. Crookes, W. T. Stead, Sir Wm. Barrett, Sir Oliver Lodge, Sir E. Marshall Hall, Prof. C. Richet, and others of high rank, can no longer be treated as mere absurdity or fraud. The strongest opposition, alike from men of science and religion, issues from quarters where there has manifestly been no careful and thorough examination, but mere superficial acquaintance, allied with prejudice and stereotyped ecclesiastical convention. After forty years careful watching, I am convinced that this whole movement merits much more serious regard. There are really four matters for consideration. (I) Physical Research—which has been compelled to acknowledge the reality of phenomena inexplicable on ordinary scientific lines. (II) Spiritism —which not only endorses the facts, but definitely ascribes them to the agency of departed human spirits. (III) Spiritualism—which on this Spiritistic basis constructs a religion. (IV) Christian Spiritualism—which accepts the facts of Spiritism, but cannot endorse the religious attitude of ordinary Spiritualism.

(I) It is unnecessary to dwell upon the reality of the marvellous phenomena which occur in the realm of Psychical Research. In regard to numberless instances of actual happenings of which science can give no account, where fraud or self-delusion were equally impossible, the testimony of such a volume as Prof. Richet's *Thirty Years of Psychical Research*, is final—seeing that that author himself, in the very front rank of science, does not accept the Spiritistic explanation of the facts which he so emphatically endorses. His reference to *Cryptesthesia* is a mere confession of scientific despair.

(II) So we come to estimate the Spiritistic explanation. Here there are three things to be considered. (1) The supernormal facts; (2) Their significance; (3) The possible dangers associated with their investigation.

(1) As to the facts themselves. (i) The ignorant abuse with which they are often met, whether by men of science or religion, is as unworthy as it is useless. As the late Sir Wm. Barrett said at the recent Church Congress :

Small wonder that men in all classes have lost respect for the teaching of the Church, when we find such an exhibition of ignorance and intolerance on the part of leading ecclesiastics. If these men had but given as many hours to the subject, as some of us have given years, they would not talk such rubbish.

(ii) It is sheer falsity to ascribe all the phenomena of Spiritism to fraud or trickery. Maskelyne's vaunted exposure only exposes itself. For he dare not even attempt without his most elaborate apparatus, to produce any of the numberless marvels which occur in Spiritism with no apparatus at all. To suggest fraud, in connexion with many of the best investigators, is sheer insult. It would be quite as justifiable to suggest that Dean Inge helps himself to the weekly offertory at St. Paul's.

(iii) It is no more sensible, let alone respectful, to credit such men as those above named, with ignorant or weak-minded self-deception. It would be ridiculous, if it were not so impudent, to suggest, as Dean Inge does, that

A few highly educated men who have long been playing with occultism and gratifying their intellectual curiosity by exploring the dark places of perverted mysticism, have been swept off their feet by it, and their authority as men of science, has dispelled the hesitation of many more, to accept what they dearly wished to believe.[1]

The fact that there have been some fraudulent mediums, and some instances of trickery at séances, is nothing to the point. There have been plenty of rogues and hypocrites and fools in connexion with Christian Churches. Does Dean Inge infer that therefore all Christianity is a delusion? If Christianity is to be judged by its best, not its worst, exponents, so in common fairness must Spiritism.

(iv) For certainly the facts remain. To suggest that any cleric living is more keen or averse to delusion than, say, Prof. Richet, or Sir Oliver Lodge, is but ignorant impertinence. If the testimony borne to the

[1] *Outspoken Essays*, p. 267.

phenomena of Spiritism by such witnesses is to be scorned, then there is an end for ever to all value of human testimony for anything.

(iv) The facts being undeniable, if the Spiritist explanation of them is dismissed, there is no other. Richet's *Cryptesthesia* is but a confession of ignorance. But to acknowledge that the operation of non-human intelligences is demonstrated, and yet refuse to believe it possible that they may be departed human spirits, is mere unscientific prejudice.

(2) As to the significance of the facts, on the assumption that the Spiritistic explanation of them is true, there are at least half a dozen inferences of greatest importance.

(i) We have an actual and unanswerable disproof of the materialism which prevailed during the last half of the nineteenth century, and in some quarters still persists. When Sir E. Ray Lankester endorses Mr. Hugh Elliott's avowal that 'the brain is the mind'; that thought is nothing more than 'cerebral vibration'; that consciousness is mere 'epi-phenomenon'; and the soul nothing more than imagination; it is manifest that argument is useless. But facts are beyond argument. If there is valid reason for acknowledging the reality of but one communication from the departed, Materialism with all its gruesome consequences, is exploded, and finds its proper place alongside the Ptolemaic astronomy.

(ii) There is also a vast and valuable contribution to human psychology. For it is shown that we are much more wonderful than we knew. Hereupon Richet truly says that

What we call human consciousness, human personality, which seems at first quite elementary, is much more complicated than we think. Therefore we must repeat here the Socratic phrase—'Know thyself.' By knowing ourselves, in fact, we shall know the greatest mystery of the universe which is within our reach.

In these days, the vast increase of population and the crush of modern life, along with other depressing influences, greatly tend to belittle human nature. Thus there is unmeasured value in any doctrine which checks this tendency, and puts man upon a higher level than that of a mere animal. It is the 139th Psalm in modern light culminating in the Revised rendering of Psalm viii. 5, or, as Dr. Moffatt puts it—' Thou hast made him little less than divine.'

(iii) As to whether Spiritistic phenomena have really demonstrated human survival after death, at least the same principle should surely prevail in psychical research as in physical. No one thinks of scornfully rejecting the verdict of a specialist, when consulted as to some grave bodily ailment. Why should not the deliberate judgement of such psychical experts as those above named, after thirty or forty years of thorough investigation, be at least of equal value? When from such quarters there comes a definite and unhesitating assurance of actual communing with departed friends, if that is rejected, nothing is left but to pronounce numbers of the ablest and best men living, either fools or liars, or both in one. In such case, why should their critics be accounted intelligent and truthful?

(iv) The demonstration—which is more than belief —of a world of spiritual existence so real and so near that anywhere and everywhere and always, as Tennyson says,

> Yet there may be those about us,
> Whom we neither see nor name,

is a matter of unspeakable significance. It adds a new atmosphere to our whole existence, and cannot but exercise a profound influence upon all our deeds and words, as well as thoughts and feelings.

(v) Moreover, in some cases, amid the never ceasing removal of loved ones from our present sphere, there are special circumstances where, not seldom, the grief and loss of bereavement make a definite and reliable assurance of their well-being, to be comfort beyond expression; whatever else a well-grounded Christian faith may bring. Sir Oliver Lodge gives one pathetic instance of this, in a letter of thanks he received from a sorely distressed widow, who wrote—

With all my heart, I thank you. From my childhood I have been brought up to follow the Church teaching, but in my awful sorrow, I needed something beyond it. I wanted to know, and to realize, that what my husband so ardently believed, was true, and that death did not destroy more than the body. I thank God you have so helped me.

(vi) The reality of a life to come is confessedly asserted by all the churches, and formally stated in creeds. But in the rush and crush of modern life, together with the prevalence of animal indifference to higher things, sensational excitement, and reckless frivolity, it is easily overlooked, and generally crowded out of thought, or dismissed as mere speculation. So that there is ample room and real need for some influence to put emphasis upon the truth that death does not end all, and that this life however wonderful and valuable, is but an introduction to another, greater and still more important.

(vii) There is yet another consideration of utmost importance. If the cultivation of modern Spiritism, with its development into Spiritualism, did nothing else, its contribution to Christian reality would be valuable beyond expression. Even in this, that it is helping, almost more than any other influence, to compel Christian churches to revise their eschatology. The doctrines which until recently have ruled in Christendom, have been sufficiently outlined above. They have always alienated thoughtful men and women, but have now become simply intolerable. But there is no frank and open acknowledgement of mistake, as there ought to be. When, however, communica-

11

tions come from the other side, which, after the severest testing, are accepted as genuine by those most competent to judge, they do so manifestly contradict the ecclesiastical traditions and dogmas of the past, that some very real modifications must be made in Christian eschatology, if the churches are to retain any hold upon the modern mind.   Slowly, indeed, such modifications are taking place.   But they are half concealed by a timid conventionalism, or denounced by a raucous obscurantism.   So that there is great need for the clearing of the mental atmosphere.

(3)   But it is now necessary to point out the dangers which may be associated with Spiritism, and at least demand that the whole matter should be handled with the greatest care.   The words which are so familiar in the usual marriage service, find here most forceful application.   All such investigation is—' not to be taken in hand unadvisedly, lightly, or wantonly; but reverently, discreetly, soberly, and in the fear of God,'—as well as with all possible scientific caution.   The reasons for this are manifest.

(i)   It is undeniable that there is ample scope in séances, and other methods of investigation, for fraud and trickery.   In too many cases, these have been definitely demonstrated.   The fact that some mediums are paid, does not of necessity involve that they are any more dishonest than doctors or clergymen, who also receive fees.   But it does suggest that the utmost precaution must always be taken, when there is any possibility of deception.

(ii)   It must also be acknowledged that even when fraud is unthinkable because of the known character of the medium, there is yet left the possibility of honest self-deception on his or her part.   The most sincere and honourable medium may be led astray by mere imagining.   Some telepathic communication, or the uprising of that sub-consciousness which is now shown to be so real, may be mistaken for a message from the world of departed spirits.

(iii) In some cases the usual methods adopted, as at séances or in trance mediumship, may be fraught with real danger, or may be positively harmful, whether physically, mentally, or morally. The suggestion of Sir Conan Doyle that every woman should cultivate mediumship is most unwise; especially as coming from a medical man. No one with a neurotic temperament or hysterical tendency should ever attempt it. For although the wildly reckless assertions of opponents in regard to frequent developments of lunacy amongst Spiritists, have been shown to be utterly false, there is a residuum of truth in the suggestion, which needs to be always borne in mind.

(iv) It comes indeed to this, as a general principle, that only those who possess a sound mind in a sound body, are really qualified to touch this vast and complex subject at all. Again, Tennyson gives a worthy suggestion,

> How pure at heart, how sound in head,
>   With what divine affections bold,
>   Must be the man whose thought would hold
> An hour's communion with the dead.

Even amongst such, there is still room for selection. Because a man is healthy, strong-minded, and pure-hearted, it does not follow that he is capable of giving the best medical advice to an invalid. But if, to make the opinion of a physical specialist worth having, long and severe training, with years of experience, are accounted absolutely necessary, it should be even more so when the questions to be answered belong to the psychical realm. For that is after all, yet more complex, and wonderful, and difficult, than all the affairs of the body.

(III)   So much for Spiritism, as the only true and sufficient explanation of the unquestionable phenomena which have been witnessed, and found to be otherwise inexplicable, in the course of psychical research. If it may be assumed, from all the facts and reasons for believing, that these phenomena do definitely prove intelligent communications to have been received from our known and loved ones who have passed beyond the veil, what are we to think of the Spiritualism which, on this basis, claims to be the only true and sufficient religion? Much may truly be said as to the goodness of its general principles.   Its representation by some clerics and obscurantists as a deadly enemy to Christianity, is but a display of ignorant bigotry.   Its reverent theism, its stress on moral character, its emphasis upon the Apostolic warning that ' whatsoever a man sows that shall he also reap,' together with its distinctive aim to comfort those who mourn, and invest the life to come with reality and hope—these all are in perfect harmony with Christian doctrine. And yet, when utmost allowance is made for all these, there are not a few plain respects in which, from the Christian standpoint, it cannot be regarded as either sufficient or final. Such as these.

(1)   Spiritualism has no definite creed, or doctrine, beyond the seven elementary principles which are already acknowledged as Christian. The one doctrine of human survival upon which its utmost stress is laid, is undoubtedly of great value as a foundation for religious belief. But it is certainly not enough to constitute a religion for humanity, or a substitute for Christianity. Sir Conan Doyle's avowal that if only men can be made to realize that death does not end all, then everything that is wrong will be righted, is pitifully as well as emphatically untrue.

(2)   What approach to a creed there is in Spiritualism, according to most of its avowed representatives, is

definitely Unitarian. This, to say the least, and with all respect to many noble men who bear that name, is not the Christianity of the New Testament. A lofty theism is undoubtedly a good foundation, but does not constitute the Christian religion.

(3) The Spiritualist treatment of Jesus Christ, and estimate of Him as merely a psychic medium, however specially endowed, is neither true nor worthy, so long as any regard is paid to our Christian Scriptures. How definitely the higher and truer estimates of Christ's person and work are set aside, is seen in the official Spiritualist Hymn Books, one containing 170 hymns, the other 600. These both not only never once mention the name of Christ, but in several of the best known hymns in ordinary use, where He is reverently referred to, His name is actually removed, and some other substituted! Whatever else this kind of religion may be, certainly it is not Christianity. It is, however, only fair to add that there is a special section of Spiritualists—known as the ' Society of Communion '—who do not endorse this attitude, but share the usual reverent evangelical faith.

(4) But taken as a whole, Spiritualism's estimate of the mission and work of Jesus, including His teaching and character, His life and death, is superficial, and untrue to the Gospel narratives. These all are, assuredly, not truthfully summarized in saying that He was ' an exalted medium.' Whatever theological confusion there may be concerning His death on the cross, at least it is so unique that to ignore its whole significance, is to make Him either deceiver or deceived, to such an extent as to destroy Christianity. There may be many facets to a diamond, each when in the light emitting its own distinct flash of colour. But their very differences at least show that the diamond is not an ordinary piece of glass. It is no less true that all the varying views concerning the ' atonement,' conspire to show that such a death,

after such a life, is unparalleled in human history, and cannot truthfully be treated as a trifle.

(5)   Much the same, though in lesser degree, applies to the Spiritualist view of the Apostles and their labours, as narrated in the Acts and Epistles of our New Testament.   Psychic research has indeed thrown real light upon some of the events recorded; but to represent the Apostles and their co-workers as merely clairvoyant, or clairaudient, or mediumistic, is to falsify their whole attitude, and give the lie direct to their most definite and outspoken convictions concerning Jesus and His Gospel.

(6)   Furthermore, Spiritualism, as a religion, can never suffice for the world as we know it, by reason of its superficial and off-handed treatment of the great problem of moral evil.   It may be true that some theologians have made a kind of fetish of sin, by one-sided exaggeration.   But that is no reason whatever for treating it as a trifle, and ignoring altogether the dire reality, prevalence, and significance of wrong doing.   Sir Conan Doyle's declaration that men and women are almost all good, and that by and by everybody will be perfectly happy—together with Dr. Ellis Powell's assertion that ' sin is a mere theological fiction,'—combine to represent God after the fashion of Omar Khayyám, quoted above.

> They talk of some strict testing of us—pish!
> He's a good fellow and it will all be well.

But such, assuredly, is neither the God of whom Jesus spoke, nor the safe foundation for any helpful or hopeful religion.

(7)   On the other hand, that which the true Gospel of Christ, as represented throughout the New Testament, puts above all else—and that deservedly, for in plain truth it is humanity's only hope—Spiritualism treats with complete indifference, as being not worth notice. We have seen that the phrase ' eternal life ' in New Testament usage is primarily qualitative, and refers not

to mere duration hereafter, but to a distinctive type of human character, here and now. The true name for this special character is 'holiness.' Unfortunately that term has taken on an unattractive sound, and is alike misunderstood and misrepresented. Here all that need be said is that it constitutes the very essence of the meaning and worth of the Christian religion, and stands for very much more than the mere knowledge that the human personality will survive death.

(8) The fact that such a main element in Christianity and important an ideal in Christian life, can be wholly ignored by almost all Spiritualists, shows how very partial and superficial is their treatment of the New Testament generally. They seem to have no eyes for anything save that which appears to favour their explanation of Spiritistic phenomena. That is, however, only to repeat on a large scale, in the opposite direction, the very mistake of which they so strongly complain in ordinary Christians. It is true that orthodox teachers and conventional believers have to a great extent overlooked the many references with which the Bible abounds, to such occurrences and influences as are now termed 'Spiritistic.' The supreme instance in the New Testament of communion with the departed is, confessedly, the marvellous event known as the Transfiguration. No conventional sophistry can dismiss that as fraud or delusion. There are however many more Biblical witnesses to the actuality of such communing, which are as a rule strangely ignored. But to acknowledge these, and then ignore all else, is even more mistaken and unworthy. In appreciating one aspect of New Testament teaching, there is neither need nor warrant for disowning all the rest.

(IV) So we come to what may be called Christian Spiritualism, that is, the truly Christian attitude towards this whole movement. It may be expressed, fairly, I think, under the following items.

(1)   The Apostolic appeal to the Philippians expresses for evermore the one great principle—purposely reiterated in these pages—which must rule all else, 'Whatsoever things are true.' Ignorance, fear of consequences, prejudice, abuse, can never be Christian, under any circumstances. Christ's own assurance that His disciples should know the truth and so be made free, applies here as fully as in all other respects. So does the wise warning of Gamaliel recorded in Acts v. 38, 39—which merits both quotation and attention.

And now I say to you, Refrain from these men and let them alone, for if this counsel or this work be of men, it will be overthrown; but if it is of God, you will not be able to overthrow them; lest haply you are found to be even fighting against God.

In modern language, therefore, the true Christian attitude is well expressed by Dr. J. Paterson Smyth.

Let us keep an open mind. There are more things in heaven and earth than are dreamed of in our philosophy. The subject deserves more serious scientific investigation than it has received. We need little bands of men scientifically trained in weighing evidence, not prejudiced or indifferent, not credulous or incredulous—men of honest mind, and especially religious men, in the broadest sense of the term, who would face the inquiry earnestly and solemnly, in the name of the God of Truth.

(2)   When, therefore, it is asked if a Christian can be a Spiritist, the answer is emphatically, Yes. For Spiritism really represents the fearless search for truth, along with an avowed finding of such truth as yields most real and timely support to Christian faith in these days. But it is quite another matter to ask if he can be a Spiritualist. For apart from the fact that some Spiritualists are avowed Agnostics, the general attitude of Spiritualism, as above shown, is distinctly Unitarian. 'The Society of Communion' which affirms the contrary, represents only a small minority of Spiritualists, as the two best

known weekly journals of Spiritualism continually illustrate. Until, therefore, the New Testament is shown to be unworthy of regard, Spiritualism as at present constituted, may be treated with all respectful sympathy as a lofty form of theism, with helpful influences. But Christianity it certainly is not.

(3) Some Christian believers, it may be frankly acknowledged, do not need the help of Spiritism. Special training, temperament, and environment, may so combine as to bring them complete satisfaction and comfort in the faith they have, without any extraneous help. It is, however, probable that the number of such grows less with every generation. And the comforting assurance with which they are content, yields no warrant whatever for despising others who lack their confidence and value the confirmation of faith, in some respects, by fact.

(4) For there are very many, quite as sincere as the satisfied believers just mentioned, and generally even more intelligent, to whom such help as Spiritism affords is of peculiar value. The case quoted above from Sir Oliver Lodge is typical of a host. There is no Christian warrant for the harsh or contemptuous treatment some-times accorded them. Christ's own treatment of Thomas, is an example that His avowed disciples to-day would do well to remember and emulate. Instead of scorning His troubled follower for needing something to see and feel, the risen Lord granted him his request, with tender sympathy. A wall that needs no buttress may be strong —but a weaker wall well buttressed may be stronger still.

(5) On the other hand, apart from eschatology, Christian doctrine has nothing to learn or gain from Spiritualism. The vaunted seven principles of the latter are (i) The Fatherhood of God; (ii) the Brotherhood of man; (iii) Continuous existence; (iv) Communion of spirits and ministry of angels; (v) Personal responsi-

that any member of the ordinary churches should forsake his spiritual home. Indeed in so doing, he runs the risk of repeating the experience related in Aesop's fable of the dog crossing the stream with meat in his mouth, and losing the substance by grasping at the shadow. For however much the various sections of the true Catholic Church may differ in their precise views, they all in their thought of and relation to Christ, stand for a great deal more than Spiritualism has to offer them. True Christian faith may well and thankfully embrace all that is demonstrable in Spiritualism; but Spiritualism will have to enlarge and deepen its conception of the Christ of the Gospels immeasurably, and its appreciation of His whole character and work, before it can be either truly Christian, or a sufficient religion for humanity.[1]

[1] As the above is only a summary, and much is assumed for which proof may quite reasonably be asked, the reader is referred to the list of publications on this whole vast theme which can be obtained on application at the Psychic Bookshop and Library, Abbey House, Victoria Street, Westminster, London, S.W.1.

III
PRACTICAL ISSUES

(1) CONVERSION

Conversion from the scientific or psychological standpoint, is not here under consideration. That theme is receiving plentiful attention at the hands of the new psychology. The reference here, in harmony with the general employment of the word throughout Christendom, is practical rather than theoretic, pragmatic rather than psychological, and theological rather than scientific. Throughout all the Christian world 'conversion' is spoken of, preached about, enshrined in hymns, as an unquestionable necessity. That necessity is based for the most part, on the words of Christ to Nicodemus, which are so well known in the mistranslation of the 'Authorised' Version—'Ye must be born again.' But the notion of repetition which the word 'again' connotes, is entirely unwarranted by the Greek. Nor is the Revised Version much better. Whereas the only true rendering of the word, ($\check{\alpha}\nu\omega\theta\epsilon\nu$,) is perfectly simple, and occurs again in v. 31—namely—'from above.' That is definitely a new birth, as distinct from what has physically preceded. And such is, undoubtedly, what conversion ought to signify. But it has come to mean something very different in its employment by some sections of Christendom. Here, however, we are not concerned with the sacerdotal vagaries of Rome, or their echoes in Anglicanism, but with that attitude of the Free Churches which is generally known as 'evangelical,' and is supposed specially to represent real Christianity. Two main matters call for careful notice. (I) The general significance of Conversion, as taught and accepted. (II) Wherein it is mistaken, and needs re-statement.

(I)   In its usual Protestant employment, conversion is taken to represent a definite crisis of mind and heart, more or less violent, in which a real and great transformation comes to pass, both within and without the individual life.

(1)   Within, the man, or woman, or child, is said to pass from being a ' child of wrath ' through the fall of Adam, and so in danger of eternal damnation, to becoming a child of God through believing that Jesus died for him.   It is implied, if not said, that Jesus paid the penalty of sin by dying instead of him.   So that He is through faith forgiven and thenceforth ' saved,' with a right to special peace and joy in believing and assurance of love divine.   This is, confessedly, a bald statement of the case.   But it is substantially true, and is either assumed or asserted, with all emotional emphais, in special sermons and missions, as well as reiterated in numberless hymns.

(2)   Such an emotional crisis, it is understood, must be accompanied by a corresponding effect on general behaviour.   There must be a turning away from all wrongdoing, in all degrees, and entrance upon a new life of true Christian goodness, that is holiness, in all human relationships.   There can be no question whatever that in myriads of cases, this ethical result has followed the preceding internal crisis.   No one who desires the highest welfare of his fellows, would wish to belittle or prevent such ethical results.   As they are stated impressively in Gal. v. 22, they constitute the only hope for future humanity.   But neither personal experience nor ethical improvement can justify a false theological basis.   The strength of personal conviction does not guarantee the truth of any doctrine.   Vast numbers of Romanists,

Buddhists, Swedenborgians, Agnostics, are as firm, intelligent, and sincere, in their convictions, as any Methodist or Baptist. Lord Morley was quite as honest and intellectual as Mr. Gladstone; Sir F. Younghusband as the President of the Wesleyan Conference; and Leslie Stephen as the Archbishop of Canterbury. All these unbelievers have lived pure and noble lives. So that whilst conversion does indeed rest upon Christian conviction, if it is to be valid as an appeal to the world, it must rest no less upon truth in fact, and accuracy in New Testament interpretation. And this is just where there is great need for closer examination, in view of the whole modern environment.

(II) There is much Christian lamentation, with no little reason, that in these days, conversions in some churches never occur, and in others are much less numerous than formerly. That it is so, cannot be denied. Whence it comes to pass that in this so-called Christian country—to say nothing here about the Continent—seven at least out of every ten adults, are entirely out of touch with all the churches, and are manifestly un-Christian, with an increasing proportion decidedly anti-Christian. Why is this? Unquestionably because of the lack of Christian conviction. Why then is that lacking? Because modern knowledge, whatever name it bears, has shown that the former grounds for such conviction are not true. That plain fact has to be faced. Conversions do still occur throughout the churches, and there are ample reasons social and political, as well as religious, for affirming that the hope of humanity is in their increase. But the convictions which are needed to bring that increase to pass, must rest upon other grounds than those which have hitherto sufficed. In plain speech, that which is not true will have to be given up, in order that what is true may be made clearer and more impressive.

This is a hard lesson for many besides Fundamentalists; but once again, the only real Christian concern is for—' Whatsoever things are true.'

(1) Let us mark, therefore, first, what is not true, as regards the grounds of Christian conversion. For brevity's sake, we will take a recent typical statement of a devoted preacher. It is said concerning him that—' He was very strong and clear on the utter ruin of the human heart by the Fall, and the redemption by the blood of Christ, as our substitute.' By such preaching myriads have been moved. But that does not make the grounds of its appeal true. Millions have been moved by the appeals of Moslem, Buddhistic, Mormon, and Jesuit preachers. Just now, not only at Dayton in Tennessee, but throughout America, and in this country, vast numbers are moved by Fundamentalist appeals. But neither the force nor the persistence of any appeal makes its basis valid. The question must always be, does it rest on truth? Tried by this test, the preacher's appeal above quoted, is not valid. All its echoes, from any and every orthodox quarter, cannot make it valid. For the things which were made so ' clear and strong,' are simply untrue. Let us view them distinctly. (i) As to the Fall. It is assumed that the third chapter of Genesis is literal history in all its detail. But the time has come to say plainly that it is not. There never was such a man, such a woman, such a serpent, such a God. (ii) The utter ruin of the human heart by such a ' Fall,' is doubly untrue. The human heart is not totally depraved; what evil there is, does not come from the Fall. (iii) Redemption by the blood of Christ as our substitute, is also doubly false. The redemption of Christ in the New Testament—as outlined in a previous section, is not by blood—the true significance of which is shown in the Epistle to the Hebrews[1]—but by love. And it is made

1 The usual false quotation of Heb. ix. 22, is dealt with above.

manifest—as has been sufficiently shown in a preceding section—that Jesus was not our substitute in bearing our death penalty, but our Saviour in revealing the uttermost love of God as our Father. It is by no means sufficient, herein, to quote certain expressions of the Apostle Paul. The notions of blood and substitution are partly relics from the Old Testament, and partly importations from the Pagan and Roman blood-religions such as Mithraism, in the midst of which early Christianity was developed. It may be interesting to note here the words of a well-known Theologian and scholar, which endorse the above attitude. Says Dr. A. E. Garvie :

> The theories of original sin and total depravity cannot be defended to-day, and need not be defended, as they are not the foundation on which the evangelical representation of the Christian message needs to be built. The story of the Fall in Gen. iii., is now generally admitted as not literal history. These doctrines have no root in the teaching of Jesus, and even little connexion with the teaching of Paul. Christ never in his teaching alludes to that story. He simply assumes that men are sinful and need forgiveness, lost and need salvation. The view held at the Reformation, and in evangelicalism since, that God imposed on Christ the penalty of sin, and that his death is the penal substitution for ours, cannot now satisfy us. It offends our moral sense. We must start from the revelation of the Fatherhood of God in Christ.[1]

Doubtless many sincere Christians will yet oppose the truth herein, just as the Jews did when Paul first brought them Christ's Gospel, instead of the law of Moses. But it is useless to resist what is true; and to insist upon what is not true, because it is bound up with old association, is just to repeat the wrong which the Apostle so strongly condemned in writing to the Romans (Rom. iii. 8). If it is said that the blood of Christ, in the New Testament, really signifies the love of Christ, the question

[1] The *Evangelical Type of Christianity*, pp. 60, 62, 64, 76, 77, (Epworth Press).

at once inevitably arises why should blood, that is, mortal suffering, be necessary for the demonstration of love? Was it the will of God, or the will of man, that brought Jesus to Calvary? Assuredly it was *not* the former. Why should Christians hesitate to give up the false for the true? Until the 17th century, the Christian church was quite satisfied with the Ptolemaic astronomy—and fought desperately to retain it. But what Christian, what Fundamentalist, wishes or dares to go back to it now? Evolution is passing through a similar stage of opposition; and the time will come when to talk about the 'bankruptcy of evolution' will be met with the same pitiful smile as now greets those who assert—from Scripture—that this is a flat world which was created out of nothing, exactly 6,000 years ago. A man's adult knowledge is always better than his childhood's limitations, and that which is really true, concerning God and man, Christ and the Bible, brings a far better Gospel for humanity than ever came from ecclesiastical systems or theological shibboleths.

(2) So then, in brief but careful outline, what is the truth concerning this whole matter? If the account in Genesis as hitherto understood—and still not seldom maintained—does not give us the valid basis for conversion, what does? No succinct statement can be better or truer than that of Sir Oliver Lodge, in his excellent little book—*The Substance of Faith Allied with Science*.[1] In his 'catechism' it is asked :

What then may be meant by the Fall of man?

At a certain stage of development man became conscious of a difference between right and wrong, so that thereafter when his actions fell below a normal standard of conduct, he felt ashamed and sinful. He thus lost his animal innocency, and entered on a long period of human effort and failure; nevertheless the consciousness of degradation marked a rise in the scale of existence.

[1] Methuen & Co.

Fuller statements will be found in such works as those of Prof. J. A. Thomson—*The Gospel of Evolution* and *Concerning Evolution*—with a host of other able writers. These make it plain that man is not descended from anything, but has ascended, according to the divine principle of creative evolution, from lower forms of life, through innumerable upward stages. When and how the progenitors of mankind became human enough to be moral beings, we shall never know. Nor is it necessary that we should. Any more than we know just when the little animal we call a human babe becomes a child; or a little child becomes morally responsible. It is wasted discussion to ask for the inscrutable. What we do know, is that the child belongs to and is lovingly cared for by its parents, through all the stages of its development, from the pre-natal to the full-grown adult. Even so with the human race. According to the teaching of Jesus and the Apostles, *all* human beings are God's children; as dear to Him as the new-born babe to the mother, or the full-grown son or daughter to the father.

What then is meant by Conversion? At least this. It has nothing to do with Adam and Eve, but everything to do with the Heavenly Father whom Jesus reveals. In that regard it has two distinct aspects. One may truly be said to be normal, or primary, whilst the other is secondary, or abnormal. One or the other is plainly essential to what the Gospel means by ' eternal life.'

(i) The true significance of the term ' conversion,' as generally employed, is really *reversion*. It is illustrated unmistakably in such cases as the prodigal son; Peter, in his bitter repentance; Saul, in his transition to Paul; with numberless other instances such as those narrated by Mr. Harold Begbie in his volume entitled *Broken Earthenware*. Christian history is happily crowded with accounts of such conversions. They are quite undeniable in their nature and effects, as Prof. Wm. James had to acknowledge in his notable book on *The Varieties of Religious Experience*. They deserve to be recognized and appreciated to the uttermost. They represent great part of the work of the Christian church in every age and every nation. And yet—with equal plainness and emphasis—it must also be acknowledged that they do not represent the whole case, nor even the better part, of true Christian conversion. They represent, mercifully, what does happen; but not what ought to happen. If we may judge from what Paul writes in his second letter to Timothy, the latter was never, in this common sense, converted at all. For there was in his case as 2 Tim. i. 3, 4, 5, show, no such reversal as in Paul's own life; no call for such repentance as Peter's; no shameful return home as with the prodigal. His case is certainly typical of what *ought* to be, and *might* be, in every Christian home. For there, certainly no need exists that son or daughter must first forsake their parents and play the prodigal, before they can be sure of a mother's love or a father's blessing. Does any earthly father, worthy of the name, wish his children first to sow their wild oats, and then repent? Or does he regard them as aliens, foul and unworthy, until some strong convulsion or drastic change happens to them? Very much, sometimes too much, has been made of the prodigal in Christ's story. But when all is considered fairly, it is not only clear that the elder brother is far from being as black as preachers generally love to paint him, but in every sense he was the better as well as happier of the two brothers, and worthier of his father.

(ii) So we come to see that the normal and better aspect of conversion—that which ought to happen in every Christian country, and every Christian home—is represented by Timothy rather than by Peter, and stands for *realization*, much more than reversion. It is illus-

trated, happily, in myriads of cases, by that which comes
to pass in homes where Christian truth and love prevail.
In every such case, the child is loved before it is born,
and after birth there are six definite stages which can be
no more denied, than sharply distinguished from each
other. The new-born babe is the incarnation of ignorance
and selfishness. It is none the less beloved by its parents.
Soon there comes the dawning stage of recognition. It
will lie happy in its mother's arms, and nowhere else.
Out of this stage grows the next, slowly but surely,
namely the appreciation, intelligently, of loving tenderness on the parents' part. Soon follows on that the stage
of reciprocation. The child knows that it is loved, and so
loves in return. As that develops, there comes the stage
of willingness, and even anxiety, to serve—to prove the
reciprocated love in action. Then, as the months or years
pass on, there ensues that final stage of perfect loving
trust and confidence between parents and children, which
make the home to be a heaven. This is not fiction, thank
God, nor imagination, but what actually happens in
myriads of Christian homes.

But all these stages are, or ought to be, as real spiritually as domestically. If the doctrine of Jesus respecting
the divine Fatherhood be true, and the estimate of the
Apostle as to its human application—' For this cause
I kneel before the Father—from whom all fatherhood
in heaven and on earth derives its name' [1]—then it is
this normal conversion, by realization, which *ought* to
come to pass in every Christian home and every Christian
church, throughout the land. All other conversions, by
reversion, are abnormal; the second best, but not the
best. Just as in every happy family, it is best and normal
that each child should grow up into love and service.
It is abnormal, and only a second best, that one
should wander away into shame, and then repent and

[1] Eph. iii. 14, *Twentieth Century New Testament.*

be welcomed with forgiveness. Hereupon, doubtless, some queries suggest themselves which must be frankly answered.

(a) What then becomes of ' sin,' and where is the need for forgiveness? For sin as a whole, the previous section thereupon must suffice. How much is said, preached, sung, printed, about sin, by Christian teachers of all kinds, needs no illustration. But it does demand careful estimate, and serious modification. In some cases, alas, only too many, thanks to the evil influences of civilization, it is tragically justified. But on the whole, it is not warranted. In the vast majority of cases it is grossly exaggerated. The average man, or woman, or child, does not deserve the things that are said. At the moment there is before me a Fundamentalist Journal which says, with all possible emphasis, concerning all men indiscriminately—' We all deserved eternal death '— which is simply untrue. Nor is there any warrant for the gruesome and repulsive things which are voiced in so many hymns. A few specimens here represent many more.

> By Thy Spirit, Lord, reprove,
>   All my inmost sins reveal,
> Sins against Thy light and love
>   Let me see, and let me feel;
> Sins that crucified my God,
> Spilt again Thy precious blood.
>
> Thou know'st the baseness of my mind,
> Wayward, and impotent, and blind;
> Thou know'st how unsubdued my will,
> Averse from good and prone to ill;
> Thou know'st how wide my passions rove,
> Nor checked by fear, nor charmed by love.
>
> Me, the vilest of the race,
>   Most unholy, most unclean;
> Me, the farthest from Thy face,
>   Full of misery and sin;
> Me with arms of love receive
> Me, of sinners chief, forgive!

Weary of earth and laden with my sin,
I look at heaven and long to enter in;
So vile I am, how dare I hope to stand
In the pure glory of that holy land?
The while I fain would tread the heavenly way,
Evil is ever with me day by day.

So one might go on. O the pity of it! For myself, I am
sure that I am no better than the average Christian, or
indeed average citizen. But I am equally sure that
these horrid things are not true of me, nor of my children,
nor of those who sing them. The dreadful terrors,
struggles, and agonies, which have been so often thus portrayed, and in some cases are actually endured by peni-
tents, are but theological nightmares. They are a libel on
the character of God whom Jesus reveals as a Father,
whose 'tender mercies are over all His works,' and
whom Paul declared to be 'The Father of mercies, and
God of all comfort.' His description of Himself as the
'chief of sinners' was only a rhetorical figure expressing
His remorse for former mistaken zeal, and has no application to human nature in general. The truth concerning
average human nature is well expressed by one of the
best known Mission preachers [1] concerning his youth—
'Although I was a mischievous boy, I was not really
a bad boy.' And if he, like myriads of others, as a wise
and loving father, in training his children no more
exaggerated their faults than exonerated them from
blame when really wrong, surely the words of Jesus find
truest application here—'The Father Himself loves you.'
For those to whom that was said, were far enough from
being faultless. The reality of sin, and human need of
Christ's redemption, will never be brought home to the
modern mind by pietistic exaggeration, but only by a true
indictment for despising, or ignoring, the Father's love.

(b) If the norm of conversion is realization, not

---

[1] Gipsy Smith—see his Life.

reversion, when and how must it come to pass—even as Jesus said—'You must be born from above'? When a drunkard, or a prodigal, or an agnostic, is 'converted,' there is a manifest crisis, and an explanation as to how it came to pass. But if there is no manifest or necessary reversion, how comes the realization which is essential? The first answer to such a query is that it is quite irrelevant. It does not matter to me when or how I was born, so long as I am alive and well. When or how my children first came to know and love me, really does not matter, so long as they have come to appreciate and reciprocate my love. Surely the words of Jesus to Nicodemus cover the whole case. 'The wind blows as it will, and you hear its sound, but do not know whence it comes or whither it goes—so is every one who is born of the Spirit'—'born from above.' In conversion by realization, there may, or may not, be a crisis—it is irrelevant. In the best of homes, with an atmosphere of mutual love, there may yet be some special occasion, some event, some day or hour, when the child consciousness is quickened, more or less suddenly, into the reciprocation of parental love. But that does not mean, never could mean, that unless a child can point back definitely to some particular hour when such reciprocation happened, it is an alien and not a beloved member of the family. The deepest, sweetest, strongest, realization of the preciousness of a great home love, may come to pass quite gradually and almost unconsciously. Myriads of the best workers in Christian churches have no vivid memory of any crucial hour, when 'a load of guilt' was taken away, and an altogether new life began. It is a plain fact that to-day all the best Christian work is being done, with few exceptions, by those who, like the elder brother in the parable, have not 'wasted their substance in riotous living,' and then crawled home again in shame, but have been faithful to holy duty from the beginning.

The prodigal's case has been much overpreached. It was never intended to be a general representation of human nature. Conversion by reversion is indeed better then impenitence; but conversion by realization, is better still.

(3) In whatever way conversion comes to pass, is it the work of man, or of God? There is here no room for a theological wrangle, for it is both. The Apostolic word is sufficient for all cases and all ages.

So then beloved friends, as you have always been obedient, and not merely when I was actually with you, so now that I am far away, labour all the more earnestly, aye with all reverent anxiety, to complete your own salvation. For it is God who, for loving kindness' sake, is moving within you, both to will and to work (Phil. ii. 12).

One might as well ask which is most necessary for good health, pure air or the use of sound lungs. The analogy holds good. For the air is given independently of man's creation; but certainly it waits for his inhalation. The grace of God is manifest both in the moral capacity of human nature, and in the revelation of real and waiting love in Jesus Christ. The responsibility of the individual is clear. He cannot be compelled to appreciate or reciprocate love. God Himself, in Jesus Christ, can only say ' Come unto Me.' Such a divine appeal may come in a myriad ways. Either as it does to a little child in a happy home, or through the conscience of a guilty wanderer. But that is all. The utmost that God can do for a moral being is to appeal. Conversion is the answer to that appeal, and no words ending in -ation are required to explain or justify it.

(4) In face of all the facts of modern life, the question becomes indeed pressing, what can the churches do to increase the number of conversions? The usual answer to this query, since the days of Wesley, has been what are called ' revival missions.' If we leave out the word

' revival,' much may be said on their behalf. Within the churches as well as round about them, the wave of strong emotion which as a rule accompanies such efforts, is definite gain in moving folk out of sleepy indifference or heartless conventionalism. And from this there need be no reactionary disadvantage. And yet it is only too manifest that the results of such efforts are disappointing, in view of the vast population which is now confessedly outside the churches. What is wanted is a perpetual mission, which shall bring to bear upon the modern mind the very maximum and optimum of Gospel appeal. That will never be accomplished save in one way; namely, the constant preaching, teaching, pressing home of the truth, the whole truth, and nothing but the truth, as it is in Jesus. The main elements of such a perennial mission seem to be these.

(i) The Christian appeal in these days must be based upon what we now know to be true, not upon theological fictions, however venerable. The sincerity and devotion of Fundamentalists are beyond question, but their very zeal alienates where it ought to convince. To tell men that they are all children of the devil, totally depraved, and doomed to everlasting misery, unless they believe certain statements about Christ and the Bible, is simply to drive them to scornful disbelief.

(ii) They must be told the truth concerning themselves, as well as concerning God, for the basis of any appeal to become the disciples of Jesus. That they are children of God as their Heavenly Father; and that therefore the very essence of sin is the scorn of His love —trampling on Christ's First Great Command. From that follows the contempt for the Second, which has filled all history with bloodshed and still tends to make civilization into pandemonium. The evil consequences of sin are manifest enough in hearts and lives, without any lurid threatening. The appeal of the Gospel is to all that is deepest and best in human nature, and brings its own witness as to the reality of salvation here, with valid promise of a greater blessedness hereafter.

(iii) Such truth must be brought home more really to children. First, in the home; where the best means of every kind should be employed to make it attractively plain to them, that they already belong to God as their Heavenly Father, and that the loving service of Christ is the greatest happiness that can come into their lives. It is too true that Romanism, with all its false doctrine, takes more care of its children than Protestants do—and so ensures their conversion—by realization—as they grow older. That is the way in which Rome 'grows.'

(iv) If, as we say, Protestants hold truer doctrine, it assuredly remains for them to prove—whether in the home, or the school, or the pulpit, or daily life—the worth of what they teach, by corresponding behaviour. That is, by being in themselves what the children of a loving Heavenly Father should be. Such a reminder, I know, is a mere platitude. But it is no more a platitude spiritually, than fresh air and sunshine are physically. We live by platitudes. Every medical expert knows that if the nation had more of those two, the standard of health would rise immeasurably. So, too, for this nation as for the world at large, would there come to pass the greatest possible deliverance from evils of all sorts, if the two Great Commands of Jesus were but obeyed. The mighty motives and reasons for such obedience are not 'wrath' and threats, but love and hope. As Dame Mary Scharlieb, the venerable woman doctor (æt 81), has just said to the Institute of Hygiene:

Altruism is the secret. You will not get far in the love of others until you are a lover of God. That is the foundation of the whole thing.

When men have scorned the love and lost the hope, through perversity in known evil, it is salvation to them to be converted by reversion, and brought back to the Father who loves them. But it is far better that they should be converted by realization, that is, by growing up into the understanding, and appreciation, and reciprocation, of that love divine, as surely, and as consciously, and as happily, as the child grows up into all the benediction of a mother's love and a father's care. Even as Timothy had done, according to Paul. And as Jesus did Himself.

(2)   PRAYER

Prayer is a commonplace of all religions, and certainly of Christianity. Leaving its significance for other faiths to a more suitable occasion, we have here to summarize the Christian doctrine of prayer all the more carefully, because it is even yet so much misunderstood and misrepresented. It has become a hackneyed theme to which church-goers listen patiently, as in duty bound, but from which they get little comfort or inspiration. Hence it is so often neglected or ignored. It becomes just a matter of ' saying one's prayer ' perfunctorily, night and morning. Whilst ' only a prayer-meeting,' has become a common phrase in the churches, indicative of the feeling with which an assembly for united devotion is too often regarded. But all this is unmistakably contrary to the estimate of prayer writ large throughout the New Testament. There is, alas, no question that the vast majority of men, women, and children, in this ' Christian ' country to-day are utterly prayerless. Why? There are more reasons than one. But one reason undoubtedly is that prayer is so largely misunderstood. Jesus made prayer natural, easy, comforting and inspiring, helpful and enjoyable. But the churches have made it hard and irksome. So the many remain prayerless. It seems necessary, therefore, in the interests of Christian truth, to think much more carefully on four aspects of the case. For all true prayer there must be (I) A truly Christian conception of God. (II) An equally true estimate of man. (III) A clearer understanding of what prayer itself really means. (IV) An honest facing of the many questions which arise, as to what prayer really does, or fails to do.

(I) Right thoughts of God. In His doctrine of prayer, as witnessed in the Gospels, Jesus everywhere and always assumed the reality of the being and nearness of God, with some of the elements of His character as exhibited in the Old Testament. In nothing is the significance of His ' but I say unto you ' more manifest, or more impressive, than in His unmistakable assertion of the divine Fatherhood. This, in its definiteness and comprehensiveness, not only exceeds all the highest and broadest conceptions of preceding Jewish prophets and psalmists, but supersedes all those lower, narrower, harder thoughts of God which inevitably occurred in the upward evolution of the religion of Israel, from the original worship of a tribal deity to the acknowledgement of one God over all. The sublime truth that the one and only God of all is towards humanity as a father, in the fullest and tenderest as well as holiest sense, is the very heart of the Gospel of Jesus, as has been emphasized above. Science does not contradict but supplement this revelation. The love of ' the Father ' is not altered, or lessened, by our knowledge of the awfulness of the immanent and transcendent God who pervades the universe. The divine goodness of which Jesus Himself is the pledge, is only magnified beyond expression by what we know of the universe as compared with what the Apostles knew. Thus the modern Christian finds more than ample warrant for that blending of utter trust with deepest reverence, which creates the atmosphere for all true prayer. The beginning of all Christian prayer is ' our Father.'

(II) As to man. It is quite as necessary in Christian prayer to have a true conception of human nature, as of the divine. Unfortunately, the estimate of the human in common Christian parlance, is very far from true. Books of devotion, sermons, hymns, abound in utterances which are as false to fact as contrary to the Father's will; besides being quite untrue to the ideals and example of Jesus. The most real reverence does not necessitate abject self-despising. No earthly father, deserving the name, wishes his children to come to him crawling on hands and knees, with groans of self-contempt and moans of self-condemnation. Yet this is the fashion in much that goes by the name of prayer. Its fallacy is twofold. Human nature in general is contemptuously belittled; whilst the moral wrong in human hearts is untruly exaggerated. Wholesale denunciation of human character is a commonplace in public prayer. The much-extolled Anglican prayer-book commits all worshippers, every day of their lives, to the assertion that spiritually—' there is no health in us.' Which is quite untrue, concerning any of them. As for the hymns that are used in such worship, they have been only too truly described above. More might be added. In these hymns, ordinary members of Christian congregations are bidden call themselves ' dust and ashes,' ' worthless worms,' ' senseless stones,' ' poor nothings,' and the like. Even the hymn which appeals to so many hearts—' Jesu lover of my soul '—is marred by similar falsity. As where it says,

> Just and holy is Thy name,
> I am all unrighteousness;
> False and full of sin I am,
> Thou art full of truth and grace.

But these two middle lines are quite false. They are

not true of any one who sings them. If the writer had
been content to say instead,

> Pity my unrighteousness,
>   Weak, and prone to sin I am,
> Thou art full of strength and grace,

that would have been true. The plea for poetic licence
is not here justified. All such talk is not humility. It
is the prostitution of humility; and there is not one word
of Jesus Himself to warrant it. In what is called—as
wrongly as persistently—the 'Lord's Prayer,' there is
no sign of any such abject obsequiousness. Those few
sentences are not indeed a prayer at all, any more than
A, B, C, is the alphabet. They are but the beginning of
a prayer, as a lesson in prayer. In the great Teacher's
own words—'After this manner, pray ye.' But that
lesson has been completely lost in the indolent, mechanical
fashion of 'repeating the Lord's Prayer'—the very
thing, which, at the time, Jesus specially prohibited.
(Matt. vi. 7,) But the simple, trustful, reverence of His
'Our Father who art in Heaven,' is too often miserably
contradicted in the unnatural attitude towards God which
addresses Him rather as an Eastern despot, before whom
His subjects must wallow and cringe, rather than as a
loving Father to whose arms His children may run with
confidence. Some of His children, certainly, may be
worse than others in their behaviour. But if the story of
the prodigal son means anything at all, it is surely that
even at our worst we are all still His children. The
prodigal said truly that he was 'no longer worthy to be
called thy son.' But he did not call himself a pig; either
before his return, or in his father's presence.

   (III) When right thoughts of God and man prevail, it is still necessary to ask what Christian prayer
really means and involves. It may be either individual or

collective. Each of these cases merits careful consideration.

(1) As to individual or private prayer. The conception of prayer which generally prevails, is asking for something. It is closely associated with kneeling, or some bodily posture, as a token of reverence. Mr. R. Blatchford's popular expression—'kneeling and begging,'—is only too true a representation of the ordinary notion concerning prayer. Such a superficial fallacy goes far towards explaining the prayerlessness which in these days is, alas, increasingly prevalent. It would seem as if the best way to correct it, is to emphasize a few negatives.

(i) Of these the first may well be the idea that prayer is a simplicity—the simplicity of begging for something. So far from the truth is this popular notion, and yet so closely bound up with the word prayer, that it would be an immeasurable gain for Christian truth if this word could be dropped out of use entirely, until its misleading narrowness could be ruled out of thought. It is easy enough to sing,

> Prayer is the simplest form of speech
> That infant lips can try,

but those who sing it, forget that they are no longer infants, and ignore the truth that follows,

> Prayer the sublimest strains that reach
> The Majesty on high.

But sublimity is not simplicity. Simplicity may avail for babes, but for those who are older, prayer must mean much more. Childishness is good in a child, but in a man it is pitiful.

In real Christian prayer, there is always a definite seven-fold complexity. Just as there is in the ordinary light of day. To most folk it is just simple white light, no more. But to the student it means that all the seven colours of the solar spectrum are blended into one. Their separate identity can be shown at any moment by a little prism. They are visible enough, and always in one order —red, orange, yellow, green, blue, indigo, violet—in every rainbow. There could be no truer analogy concerning prayer. For it is always complex, with seven distinct elements, in a rightful order, which blend into one. Thus they mean so much more than 'kneeling and begging,' that the only term which does them all justice is communion. Real prayer is *communion* with the Father whom Jesus reveals.

(a) Of these seven elements the first is *adoration,* or reverence. 'Our Father,' indeed, but to-day more than ever, 'hallowed be Thy name.' As pointed out above, the awfulness of the one God of the universe is now unmistakable. So that unless communion with Him begins with reverence, it never begins at all. (b) Next to adoration cannot but come, to every thoughtful mind, the remembrance of that boundless, ceaseless, mystery of good upon which we live from moment to moment. Modern *thankfulness* ought to put unmeasured emphasis upon the Psalmist's words—'Bless the Lord O my soul, and forget not all his benefits '—which, alas, the majority do. (c) But with the thankfulness comes also the recollection of our failures to respond to that goodness. How often in selfish, wilful, misuse of life's blessings, we sin against love. Here is the need for *penitence.* (d) But repentance without *resolution* is mere mockery. 'Make me as one of thy hired servants,' said the prodigal. Words could not better express the penitent's resolve, the soul-determination to lead a new life, and play the wastrel no more. It is mockery to arrange a prayer service in which, every Sunday, the suppliant should be content to say—'we have left undone what we ought to have done.' The twenty times repeated 'I will' of the Psalmist (cxix), ought to be yet more pronounced on Christian lips. (e) When these preceding four elements of prayer

13

are assured, not before, comes the rightful place for *petition*. Said the writer of our first epistle of John, which so fully echoes the Fourth Gospel,

This is the boldness which we have towards Him, that if we ask anything according to His will He hears us.

'According to His will.' So that 'asking,' or 'begging,' is merely one seventh part of real prayer; and even that part is plainly conditioned. There is no Christian-warrant whatever for the loose notion that prayer simply means the right to ask God for anything, anyhow, for any purpose, just as the mood may be. Jesus said many times—'whatsoever ye shall ask in My name'—and that gentle but severe test applies to every petition, (f) But asking for others, *intercession,* is as real a part of prayer as any plea for oneself. The whole New Testament bears witness to this. The Apostle's testimony is specially plain—

Ye also helping together on our behalf, by your supplication; that for the gift bestowed upon us by means of many, thanks may be given by many persons on our behalf. (2 Cor. i. 11.)

The example of Jesus Himself is finally endorsed by the exhortation of James.[1] (g) Yet there is another element of true prayer never to be forgotten. Even that with which Jesus Himself concluded his own agonizing petition, and the Apostle hushed his thrice-repeated entreaty. As the Master said—'If it be possible, let this cup pass from Me—nevertheless, not My will, but Thine be done, so did the servant echo that *submission*—'He has said to me, My grace is sufficient for thee.' Real belief in the love of a Heavenly Father cannot but bring every sincere disciple to the same conclusion, however hard, beyond expression, the apparent failure of earnest pleading may

[1] John xvii.; James v. 16.

sometimes be.   These seven, then, *adoration, thanks-
giving, confession, resolution, petition, intercession, submission,* in their combination, alone make reality in
prayer. The word which best conveys that whole complexity, as distinct from the simplicity of monotonous
begging, is ' communion.'

(ii)   Another common but hindering fallacy, is that
prayer is a duty. From the Christian standpoint prayer
is no more a duty, than for our bodily life is eating, or
breathing, or sleeping. If a man does not want to live,
he need not adopt so violent a method as suicide. He has
but to cease from any one of these. But if he desires to
live, he has no choice. These are not duties; they are
absolute necessities. It is even so spiritually. If a man
is content with the animal life, which is really spiritual
death, he need not trouble about communion with God,
any more than his dog does. But if he would live the
truly Christian life, which in the New Testament is called
' eternal life '—or, as Paul put it, ' your life is hid with
Christ in God '—then he has no choice. Prayer is an
unmistakable *necessity*. He *must* cultivate communion
with God and ' pray without ceasing.' Without that,
the Christian life is as impossible as the body's life without food, or breath, or sleep.

(iii)   But that is far from all. As in bodily health
the necessity for food, and breathing, and sleep, is lost
in their *enjoyment,* so is it spiritually. No healthy man
takes his daily food, his nightly rest, his every breath,
from a sense of duty, or mere necessity. He enjoys them.
They are his comfort and delight. No more does any
true disciple of Christ pray—in the full sense of communing with God—because he ought, or because he must.
There is no more sense of compulsion than in any happy
child's companionship with his father.

> Prayer is the Christian's vital breath,
>   The Christian's native air,

and there is no more thought of necessity, than in breathing the fresh invigorating air of a bright spring morning.

(iv) But the true analogy takes us still further. The enjoyment and exhilaration which come from food, and rest, and fresh air, lead on always to something more. The enjoyment issues in better health. The rest and comfort restore *strength* for work. The inspiration brings nerve energy, and through this, burdens which seemed intolerable, become easy to bear. So, in the Christian life, duties which otherwise were irksome and opportunities of service which seemed impossible, become through real prayer as easy and happy as the daily toil of a strong man who sings at his work.

(v) The more thoughtfully these realities are appreciated, the more does a most precious truth emerge, namely, that Christian prayer is, after all, much more of an *attitude* than an act. Even as in a happy home where love prevails. There, between parent and child, sometimes an expressive word, or an occasional kiss, will emphasize love. But the deepest and most precious reality is the heart-attitude of every hour, which needs no words, but binds the mother to her boy, or the father to his girl, with inexpressible mutual trust. Such a heart-attitude of reverent love to God as an ever-present Father, is the very soul of Christian prayer. It will never be better expressed than in the word of Jesus Himself—

He who sent Me is with Me; He has not left Me alone; for I am always doing the things that please Him.—Father, I thank Thee that Thou hast heard Me. And I knew that Thou hearest Me always.

(vi) It must also be understood and appreciated, once for all, that such prayer as deserves the name, is always a matter of *quality,* not quantity. This could not be made clearer or more emphatic than in the words of Jesus recorded in Matt. vi. 7, 8. But it must be sadly

confessed that no precept of His has been ' more honoured
in the breach than in the observance.' What is pitifully
called ' persevering prayer,' has been largely based upon
an utterly mistaken interpretation of one of the most
beautiful of the stories told by Jesus. This is sometimes
referred to as ' The unjust judge'; sometimes as ' The
importunate widow.' But the common inference from it
was certainly not what Jesus intended to teach. He
did not suggest any *likeness* between God and the heartless judge who drove the poor widow to add quantity to
the quality of her petition. Much rather did He emphasize the *contrast*, between the judge's callous pro-
crastination, and the tender solicitude of a father's heart
which responds ' speedily,' that is, without any delay
at all. Painful repetition is never necessary to move
a father's heart. As a rule, in our human life, when we
feel most, we say least. At any crisis, one ' God bless
you,' thrilling with heart-reality, is worth more than
floods of fine speech with ornate embellishment. The
popular measurement of prayer's efficacy by the ' hours
spent upon our knees,' has done more than can be said,
to make it a drudgery for believers, and a repellent
mockery to those outside.

(vii) If the whole of the preceding may be summarized, it comes to this, that the heart-attitude which
constitutes the soul of prayer is independent alike of time
or place, of circumstance or temperament, of manner or
form. When it is once understood that Christian prayer is
not just an effort to see how much we can get out of God,
but lowly, loving, trusting, communion with Him, then
it may be truly and surely said that the time for prayer
is any time and always; the place for prayer is anywhere
and everywhere; the mood for prayer is whatever the
hour may bring. With this unspeakably helpful addition;
that as a little child wants mother most, and is surest
of her loving sympathy, at any special time of distress

or pain, so, if Jesus be true, when we feel most down-spirited, and least inclined for all that is highest and noblest, we may feel most sure of the tender sympathy of our Father! This always includes all that the sympathizing Master meant to convey to His depressed and bewildered disciples when He so tenderly and earnestly assured them that—'The Father Himself loves you—Let not your heart be troubled—believe in God, believe also in Me.'

This has been recently expressed with pathetic force by Dr. H. Fosdick. Referring to the benediction of communion with God, he says—

Such experiences come in prayer—not in saying prayers. There are times when we really pray, and know what the Master meant when He said—'I am not alone—I and the Father are one.' Long years ago, in a bitter experience of youth, I went to my earthly father to be helped. I do not recollect what he said, but only this, that he put his arm around me and promised to stand by me through thick and thin; so that whereas I came to him depressed, I went away rejoicing and sure of victory. How often, in solitary prayer, have we had that experience.

(2) Now as regards prayer from many hearts in unison. From the New Testament standpoint, there can be no question as to the meaning and value of united prayer, in public worship, or on special occasions. This has already been seen in the reference to 2 Cor. i. 11. Public prayer is both an act and an attitude. Coming together for such a purpose is a distinct action, and necessitates definite times and suitable places. But it is, after all, only the heart attitude which makes such an action to be real prayer. All the elements mentioned above are needed, and can never be ignored. When one really thinks about it seriously, public prayer in uttered words is a tremendous assumption. It is comparatively easy to believe, in the sacred secretness of private prayer which needs no words, that 'spirit with spirit may meet.'

But to believe that a flood of words, poured out at all sorts of times, by all kinds of worshippers, is really heard and heeded by God Himself—is a staggering exercise of faith. When all it involves is borne in mind—one only God throughout the overwhelmingly vast universe, in which our whole solar system is but a speck, whilst light travelling at 186,000 miles every second, takes thousands of years to reach us from other systems just within our view, and millions of years from yet other systems beyond them—it is not merely a staggering but an overwhelming thought, that He who is in, and through, and over ALL, should heed the cry of such infinitesimals as ourselves. Congregations may well sing

> God is in Heaven, and men below:
> Be short our tunes, our words be few!
> A solemn reverence checks our songs,
> And praise sits silent on our tongues.

Science can give us no warrant that we are divinely heard. How then can we dare to believe that we are not mocking ourselves with talking to the air, but are really in touch with the living God of all? The Christian answer must at least include what follows.

(i)   The teaching of Jesus Himself is unmistakable. He assumes both the possibility and the efficacy of united prayer—' Where two or three are gathered together in My Name, there am I in the midst of them.'

(ii)   The whole New Testament not only takes this for granted, but emphasizes it. Quotation would be superfluous, for it permeates all the exhortations and assurances of all the Apostles.

(iii)   It is also plain that it was the practice of all the early churches to meet together, after the analogy of the Jewish synagogues, for Christian prayer and praise. Such worship has never ceased in all the succeeding ages.

(iv)   In such assemblies, all the seven elements of

true prayer may be specially realized and intensified by the undeniable influences of human fellowship, more than they can be in solitude. The stimulus of public meetings is equally unquestionable and immeasurable. It may well lead to noblest heights and truest depths of devotion.

(v) There may be many methods and forms of such worship. The truly Christian spirit will make all allowance for differences of temperament, and taste, and capacity. The absolute essentials are reverence and sincerity, truth and love. Whether these are expressed in liturgical form as in a printed prayer-book, or naturally and freely as in ' extemporaneous ' prayer, is irrelevant. Great and lamentable as are the errors of Romanism, there can be no doubt that myriads of worshippers seek for the grace of God as truly at ' High Mass,' as in a Methodist prayer meeting, or a Quaker's silent hour. Whatever else is right, exclusive bigotry is always wrong, and far from the spirit of Christ. Yet it is impossible for any honest mind to miss the great lesson of Jesus in His talk to the Samaritan woman. ' Neither in this mountain nor in Jerusalem '—puts an end for ever to insistence upon any special kind of ritual as a spiritual necessity. ' God is Spirit, and they that worship Him must worship in spirit and in truth '—is at once the supreme test of reality, and the Magna Charta of Christian liberty, in all that relates to united prayer or public worship.

(vi) It is difficult to estimate aright the ' call to prayer,' which is so often made on special occasions, or in any great social or national crisis. Without doubt it is only for good that the spirit of prayer is enkindled and intensified throughout the land. But there is a real danger of representing God as the hard-hearted judge in the parable—only reached and moved by persistence. As shown above, Jesus emphatically contradicted that.

Ebenezer Elliott's well-known hymn is often sung with enthusiasm—

When wilt Thou save the people?
O God of mercy, when?

But few in the crowds realize how such words, as they
stand, involve both a moral impossibility and a reflection
upon the character of God. If He could so ' save the
people,' that is, by mere exercise of His will, surely, if
He be the Father whom Jesus asserts, He would have
done so long ago. According to Christ's Gospel, He is
always doing, in the ceaseless work of the Holy Spirit,
all that can be done to ' save the people '—apart from the
will of the people, and the influence of the Christian
Church. It would seem, therefore, that the real worth
of a call to prayer is rather to be found in the Apostle's
doctrine and practice—' We then as co-workers with God,
entreat you.' We do not know what may be the influence
upon either the mind of God, or man, from united
Christian appeal. But we do know that it is vain for any
number of avowed believers to assemble and multiply
words, unless these are accompanied by actions and
characters which express more plainly the desire that the
people may be ' saved.' It is a case in which the words
addressed to Moses, as recorded in Exodus xiv. 15, have
a far-reaching and perpetual application—' And the Lord
said unto Moses, wherefore criest thou unto Me? Speak
unto the children of Israel that they go forward.' The
same principle applies to every crisis in our life.

(IV) This brings us yet to one more query in regard
to prayer, which cannot be wholly overlooked. Since
petition is at least one of the main elements in prayer,
the question must arise as to how much it may avail to
bring actual answers to definite pleading. There is no
more difficult theme in all Christian thought, than the
seeming failure of many pure and unselfish petitions to
obtain the desired response. ' Unanswered prayer '
has always been a pathetic trouble for believers, and a

favourite sneer of sceptics. It would be sheer mental dishonesty, as well as callousness of heart, to ignore the many harrowing cases in which it seemed as if the ' heavens were as brass,' and Omar Khayyám's pessimism true.

> And that inverted Bowl we call the Sky,
>   Whereunder crawling, coop't, we live and die,
> Lift not thy hands to IT for help—for IT
>   Rolls impotently on as Thou or I.

And yet Christian faith is pledged to the attitude of James (v. 16).

> So then confess our wrong-doings to one another and pray for each other's recovery from illness. A good man's prayer, when he puts his whole soul into it, is very efficacious.

The oft-quoted words of King Arthur in Tennyson's Idylls are borne out by numberless experiences which cannot be tabulated. In very deed

> More things are wrought by prayer
> Than this world dreams of.

And there is sound philosophy, as well as patient faith, in the avowal that

> Blind unbelief is sure to err,
>   And scan His work in vain;
> God is His own interpreter,
>   And He will make it plain.

When, therefore, reverent trust in God, as Jesus reveals Him, is blended with honest and tender sympathy, the following considerations may at least help in hours of sincere perplexity. They are but suggestions, and must be estimated by each individual according to his own experience.

(i) After all, so far as real prayer, that is, communion with God, is concerned, petition, asking for some specific help or gift, is but one-seventh part of the whole. So that even if that should seem to fail, the greater part is left. Surely a true child's appreciation of a father's love and care, does not consist wholly and only in asking for and obtaining presents.

(ii) It is moreover no verbal evasion but the simple truth, that some petitions are most truly and tenderly answered by refusal. Would any father, meriting the name, give his little one an open razor to play with, because the child cried for it? Would any reliable doctor give his patient, just recovering from typhoid, solid food because he so hungered for it? If the Fatherhood of God be anything more than pious fiction, the most real answer to many of our petitions, is to let them go unanswered.

(iii) Some earnest and sincere petitions which are not answered as we so desire, may be answered in other ways, indirectly if not directly. Myriads of experiences would testify to this.

(iv) Lifes varied course through passing years, certainly also shows that to some prayers the answer comes, and must come, in after years, rather than in days or hours. The real benediction comes in personal character, as gradually, but as surely, as the growth of a little child into its later, fuller life.

(v) When all the other elements of real prayer are truly known and felt, there is nothing less than certainty, resting on the word of Christ Himself, that every such heartfelt desire is known, and heeded, by the Father of whom Jesus said so plainly that not a sparrow fell to the ground without His notice. Every loyal disciple may say as surely as did Jesus Himself—' I knew that Thou hearest Me always.'

(vi) It must be frankly confessed that in some special cases of human suffering and sorrow, when agonizing petitions have not brought the relief, or help, or healing, or deliverance, which were so intensely longed for, all that is suggested above will seem to be mere words, of little or no avail to heal a broken heart, or relieve a troubled soul. I remember only too many cases, in the course of the years, in which undeserved and innocent suffering, unrelieved in answer to anguished entreaty, seemed to make faith a mockery, and had to be left in the mystery of a darkness that could be felt. In such cases there is nothing for it but blind trust in the present, and the assured hope of the life to come. Meanwhile, this remains. No apparent failure of our anguished pleading, can ever be more tragic than that of Christ Himself. In His hour of bitterest darkness, and direst need, did He not cry—' Father, if it be possible, let this cup pass from me ' ? But it did not pass. As noted above, all that His echo of the Psalmist's mystery—' My God, my God, why hast Thou forsaken Me ? '—meant to Him we shall never know. But we do know that the black cloud passed away, and He entered into the ' light that never was on sea or land,' with ' Father, into Thy hands I commit My Spirit,' on His lips. Christian faith must ever acknowledge that—' It is enough for the servant, that he be as his Lord.'

(3) PUBLIC WORSHIP

From the very beginning of religion amongst men the custom of meeting together for some form of worship has obtained. It was specially manifest in the Jewish faith, and became a distinctive Christian practice. It is recorded that Jesus Himself regularly attended the synagogue, and the writer of the letter to the Hebrews (x. 25) assumes and endorses assembling for Christian worship. We are not, however, concerned here with the history of public worship, but with its continuance in our own days. There are thus four queries which call for consideration. (1) Why should united worship still be maintained as part of Christian faith? (2) What are the present-day facts as to its observance? (3) What is the explanation of its comparative decline? (4) What can be done to restore and develop it?

(1) As to the value, and even necessity, of public worship, for all the purposes of Christianity, the following principles seem to be unmistakable.

(i) An isolated Christian is a self-contradiction. For according to Christ's teaching, the Second Great Command is of equal force with the First, and requires social intercourse for its opportunity. Worship is an open recognition of both the great commands which constitute the Christian ideal. Without intercourse with others, Christianity is a self-centred delusion. Solipsism cannot be Christian.

(ii) The notion sometimes expressed that a man can worship God by converse with Nature, or by meditation at home, is plausible enough, but equally fallacious. (a) It entirely ignores the altruism which Jesus emphasized; (b) it also ignores His own practice, and the doctrine of the whole New Testament; (c) as a matter of fact, it is not done. With scarcely any exception, those who absent themselves from public worship, do so not in order that they may find higher inspiration elsewhere, but because they are not at all concerned about what worship stands for.

(iii) Christianity is nothing if not social, and the communion with others which is the essence of Christian character, becomes specially possible amid all the associations of worship. It is not a mere question of going to church ' to get good,' or to obey a divine behest, but is an opportunity to do good on the lines of Acts xx. 35, by means of mutual fellowship and sympathy.

(iv) Yet the personal element need not be ignored. In these days of rush and crush and turmoil through the week, it may be of greatest spiritual value to make sure of an hour when ordinary cares may be dismissed, and daily worries silenced, so as to make possible some real appreciation of things divine.

(v)   Such an hour, indeed, becomes as necessary as precious, not only for quiet thoughtfulness, but for the definite renewal of personal faith and the confirmation of convictions, without which the profession of Christianity is a mere name without significance, a shell without a kernel.

(vi)   For all purposes of higher thought and spiritual desire, there is unquestionably an inspiration in reverent and earnest public worship, which is as real as indescribable.   In every great assembly, as orators and politicians well know, the atmosphere is charged with possibilities of impression which are quite unknown in solitude.   All this may be utilized to the utmost in public worship.

(vii)   Another element of the case which must never be overlooked, is the opportunity afforded for teaching and learning, as well as feeling.   The need for these is plainly twofold.   There is even yet tragic ignorance amongst ordinary people as to what Christianity really means, in the light of to-day.   Whilst the Bible itself is so crowded out of private reading, that the 'lessons' read in public worship, are practically all that most worshippers know about its application to modern life. Outside the churches, the Bible is not read at all; whilst the knowledge imparted in schools is of little avail for spiritual purposes.

(viii)   Whether there are church bells or not, the regular assembling of a number of sincere and intelligent people for public worship, is in itself a protest against the prevalent Godlessness of to-day's environment, especially on Sunday, which cannot but be for Christians the Lord's Day.   It is a plea for something more than the feeding, or motoring, or general pleasure-seeking, which are fast coming to be in this country as on the Continent, the main occupations of that day.

(ix) Nor is that all. For the indirect influences of worship may be both great and far-reaching. A congregation that has been deeply moved and inspired, as well as taught in Christian principles, cannot just dismiss it all as nothing during the ensuing week. The stimulus to thought and feeling and character, goes on as surely as the ripple in a pond from a falling stone extends to its shores. It becomes a real contribution to that public opinion, without which our legislators tell us the highest ideals of civic and social welfare can never be attained.

(x) To all these must be added, last though not least, the full significance of the Apostolic phrase—'for this is the will of God in Christ Jesus, concerning you.' When Jesus said—'for such as worship in spirit and in truth, doth the Father seek to be His worshippers'—He set an ideal for all time before His disciples. As every normal child seeks for fellowship with his father, as well as with his brothers and sisters, so will all those to whom the words of Christ are sacred, prize the opportunity which public worship affords, to fulfil His ideal in drawing nearer to God and to each other on the Lord's day, than is often possible during the week. And experience abundantly proves the benediction of so doing.

(2) When it is asked with an open mind what is the present condition of things in regard to public worship, the true answer is to be found neither in pessimism nor in optimism, but a fair blending of both. It is easy enough to avow that there is a 'slump' in church-going; that the churches are empty; and the like. But such sinister estimates are at worst only half true. That there are very many, a majority, who 'go nowhere' on

Sunday, is manifest. Out of London's eight millions, not one million are in actual touch with any Christian Church, and much the same proportion obtains throughout the land. The Continent may be left to speak for itself. It is vain to try to conceal the fact that general indifference to religion is increasing. How far the large audiences which in some places go to ' Mass ' in Romish churches, as a complete expression of their worship, come into the account, is hard to say. There are also plenty of ' oncers ' in Protestantism. But disappointing as these facts are, they do not constitute the whole case. In very many instances the comparative emptiness of city churches is due to the development of suburbs, where numberless churches have been erected to meet the growing need, and are generally well filled. On the whole, however, it is impossible to deny that the tendency of to-day is towards decrease rather than increase, in the numbers of those who are regular worshippers. The situation is certainly serious enough to demand the most careful attention from all real Christians.

(3) As to the explanation of this tendency, the true and sufficient answer may be given in a word—the modern atmosphere. But this includes so many adverse influences that it is necessary, for the truth's sake, to face them frankly.

(i) The pressure of modern life, especially on nerve and brain, is confessedly great, and apparently increasing. The wear and tear of the week become very trying, and in numberless cases naturally create a disposition on Sundays to remain at home, if not in bed, at least in quiet. (ii) This disposition is confirmed immeasurably by the modern multiplication of newspapers and ephemeral literature of all kinds. These appeal strongly to the taste and capacity of the average man or woman who has had only a moderate education, and has no

definite religious convictions. A pipe and his paper are
the only Gospel that myriads of working men desire.
(iii) For those who are better educated, and have more
time for thought, it is much the same, on another plane.
The ceaseless flood of literature in every department of
thought, supplies endless opportunities and inducements
for mental enjoyment at home, superior to what, on
the average, can be found in listening to sermons. Unless
there is strong personal conviction, a recent book and a
comfortable arm-chair, will outweigh any suggestions
to go to a public service. (iv) The attractions and
distractions of modern life are continually increasing
—especially in the means of transport on Sundays. All
the opportunities for mutual visiting are now multiplied
through the lessening of cost, so that trips by rail, tram,
bus, motor-car, motor-cycle, abound to an extent never
dreamed of a generation ago.

(v) Whereas these distracting influences operate
mostly in summer when the days are bright and long,
there can be no question that through all the winter
months the latest development of wireless broadcasting
must and will tell increasingly, against attendance at
' places of worship.' When the weather is bad, or a
certain preacher is disliked, or a form of service is unattractive, it will be a temptation too strong for very
many, otherwise religiously inclined, to remain without
effort at home and enjoy excellent—though utterly
' secular '—music, and perhaps listen to some notable
preacher.

(vi) This will be specially the case if the public
service at the church usually attended, is cold and per-
functory, formal or heartless. There is an unmistakable
atmosphere in every religious assembly which either
attracts or repels. This must affect the attendance.
It is hard to describe, but it is as real as the physical
atmosphere, and as influential.

14

(vii) Outside the churches, the general spirit of religious indifference mentioned above creates another atmosphere which cannot but be felt. It arises from the practical materialism and craving for sensational excitement which have so largely developed during recent years. It needs no describing, but its influence in the opposite direction to public worship is immeasurable.

(viii) In addition to all these factors, what is known as preaching must, for all Protestant churches, be taken into full account. It is said that ' Romanists go to church to pray, Protestants to hear a sermon.' Unfortunately, too often, much cannot be thought of the spiritual quality of either proceeding. Certainly reality in prayer is not more necessary than true teaching, in public services. The potentiality of the pulpit is beyond measure. Whatever may be the fascination of good literature at home, nothing can compare with the inspiration of the living voice, when it is the instrument for the expression of truth emanating from a clear mind and a warm heart. But in these days, the mere flow of pious platitudes in channels of ancient phraseology, with the reiteration of hackneyed terms, is worse than useless for intelligent audiences. The young people of to-day in particular, will not come and listen for half an hour to things which are untrue, or seriously out of date. Ecclesiastical humdrum and intellectual childishness, which would not be tolerated elsewhere, will have to be banished from pulpits, if public worship is to retain its hold upon modern men and women.

(ix) In some cases, it is to be hoped not in many, the internal condition of a church may act as a real deterrent. In one case, certainly, which I remember only too well, the senior deacon of the church definitely protested in a church meeting against the people coming, and made it his great objection to the Pastor, that he was always endeavouring to win new members into the church. There is such a thing as religious snobbery; and there are churches where actions speak louder than words, to the effect that ' the poor are not wanted here.' Or even where such an attitude does not prevail, there may yet be petty jealousies, family bickerings, struggles for office, all of which tend to lower the spiritual atmosphere and prevent church services from being the attractive benediction which they ought to be.

(x) Yet another hindrance cannot be overlooked. It is useless to ignore the fact that the modern atmosphere is not only, negatively, largely religiously indifferent, but positively is being increasingly permeated with pronouncedly hostile influences. Downright denial of all Christian doctrines is to-day more wide-spread, more clever, more quietly persistent, and often more virulent, than ever before. The rampant propagandism of last century's ' Secularism' has only given place to the much more able, insidious, and implacable, energies of the ' Rationalist Press Association.' These are, indeed, never mentioned by ecclesiastical authorities, but are ceaselessly working, as quietly but as surely as the white ants, to undermine and destroy everything Christian. The suggestion that Materialism is dead, and that Christian spirituality is everywhere reviving, is but a pious mirage, as contrary to fact as soothing to the imagination.

(xi) To all the above must yet be added this serious consideration that in doctrine as well as in form of worship, Christian churches differ so much one from another. If a man is so disposed, he may easily justify his absence from worship—as to my personal knowledge he does—by the plea that he does not know where to go, because what is taught as God's truth in one church, is flatly contradicted in another. It is easy enough to say that he ought to decide for himself, as against abject and unworthy ' submission' to the bigoted dogmatism of Rome. But that means mental effort which he is not disposed to make. So he remains outside of all—unless some Christian worker should lead him to find help towards decision, in the public worship of some church where heart and head combine to make Christ's Gospel real.

(4) What then is the outlook for the future? What can be done to make Christian worship all that it might be for individual hearts and the community at large? Any helpful answer to such a query must involve three factors. (i) The general conduct of the service; (ii) the influence of the pulpit; (iii) the spirit of the whole church. Of these, the last two have been partly considered above. But with this added note. It is not enough that light and heat should be found in the pulpit, and harmonious peace, with warmth of heart, should prevail amongst church members. The unmistakable commission of Jesus to His disciples remains in full force —' Go and make disciples from all nations.' That is to say, all real discipleship is aggressive. The function of a Christian church is not merely to gather members and form them into a happy family, but to persist in ceaseless efforts to win others into the same comfort and help and hope. 'You are the salt of the earth, you are the light of the world,' Jesus said, and the figures of speech so truly express His whole intention, that a self-centred Christian church is a manifest self-contradiction. But it does not by any means follow that mission bands, or street preaching, or revival missions, are the only or best way to move the outer world. There may be many methods of appeal. If the unselfish altruism of any church be but real, the method will take care of itself.

But as regards (i) above—conduct of Christian worship, only a few suggestions can here be made. There may be many modes of worship, from the elaborate ritual of Rome, to the impressive silence in a meeting of the

'Friends,' or the living freedom of the Salvation Army. In this country the main division is between the liturgical method, as maintained in Anglicanism, and the spontaneous as practised in the Free Churches. In the choice between these, all allowance must be made for differences of training, taste, and temperament. One method may be as spiritual and helpful as the other. Yet these few notes seem to be called for, as having resulted from many years of observation and experience, from boyhood until now. There is no warrant for impeaching the sincerity of the devotees at the extreme liturgical service of the Romish 'Mass,' or its 'Anglo-Catholic' imitation. But it is impossible to avoid asking in how many cases it consists in the formal recital of words, rather than in realization of their meaning. The ordinary Anglican service is not merely liturgical, but indissolubly bound up with the Prayer Book, which by very many is regarded with as much reverence as the Bible. Yet very little honest thought shows that it is by no means satisfactory as a fixed form of Christian worship. Many may prefer the antique language in which the prayers are couched, but the theology involved will not always bear scrutiny. Certainly the mechanical cutting-up of the Psalms into thirty portions, irrespective of their significance, makes their public chanting in some cases as un-Christian as unreal. Besides which, constant repetition of the same words cannot but become monotonous, even if sincere. Whilst the invariable employment of the Magnificat, and Nunc Dimittis is as utterly inapplicable to, and unsuitable for, modern promiscuous congregations, as they were significant and impressive in their original occurrence.

Thus the need for the revision of the Anglican Prayer Book is overwhelmingly manifest, if it is to be a true and wise Christian liturgy for these days. But the swarm of difficulties at once arising, and the outcry against any change on the one hand, with the demand for sacerdotal change on the other, make such an attempt almost impossible—thus illustrating, once more, the potency of religious convention, and the dead hand of ecclesiasticism. The manifest attractiveness of the Prayer Book liturgy may be said to consist in the blending of four main elements : namely, reverence, symbolism, music, and custom. All these are certainly good in their place, and to a proper degree. But when they become substitutes for the exercise of mind in discerning truth, and the energy of heart in appreciating it, they cease to make worship either what Jesus intended, or what Christianity should embody.

There is, of course, no objection to a liturgical form of service in itself. But it must be truly Christian, and appropriate for the times in which we live. If a congregation is to be invited to join in responses, they must at least be such as the men and women and children of to-day can both understand and appreciate, not a mere repetition of words, however venerable through old association.

But for the majority of those who breathe the modern atmosphere of freedom and intelligence, the spontaneous form of worship, under proper conditions, would seem to be most suitable. There is manifestly more scope for reference to all the realities of our actual life, and the conflicts of the modern world. There is no reason whatever, save in individual behaviour, why there should not be as much reverence and beauty in such a method of worship, as in any stereotyped mediaeval forms. It is true that more depends upon the conductor of the service; but that is his own special responsibility. Whilst, as to the help of such beautiful music as forms so large a part of Romish and Anglican worship, it may be—and in numberless cases is—quite as capable of cultivation in a Free Church service, as in any cathedral whatever. Furthermore, hearty and earnest congregational singing

is even more inspiring than the most artistic rendering of
anthems by a trained choir. Whatever may be best in
concerts, or musical festivals, in public worship the needs
and capacities of the people have to come into careful
account.

When all the above is taken into fair consideration, it
only remains to add that the churches, at their best and
utmost, cannot possibly compel the modern world to
become Christian. But there is every reason to believe
that all buildings for worship in the land would be filled
with eager worshippers, if only all those who ' profess
and call themselves Christians ' were true, in all respects,
to their profession.

(4) PREACHING

The influence of the Christian pulpit mentioned
above is so serious a matter as to call for special consideration. Considered apart from the force of custom, a
sermon is really a strange event. A man occupies some
elevated position in a building whence he can reach the
greatest number with his voice, and there he is permitted
to say what he likes, without fear of interruption, upon
the greatest and most difficult of themes. He may keep his
audience almost as long as he pleases, or dismiss them as
briefly as he will. If a man has a message to deliver, it
is indeed an unparalleled opportunity, and has been
employed as such throughout all Christian history. In
our own time, preaching, in connexion with public
worship, is still considered the best method for the
maintenance of Christian faith and life. Every Sunday
thousands of sermons are delivered, under all kinds of
circumstances. To Romish and Anglican churches, congregations are drawn mostly by the customary cere-

monial. But with the Free Churches much more heed is
given to the preaching. Much also depends on the personality of the preacher. Familiar names such as Parsons,
Parker, Punshon, Hunter, Jowett, Clifford, Norwood,
stand for a host of others who have thus greatly
influenced their generation. But the problems considered
in the preceding section relative to the decline in church-
going, remain, and the question presses, why, if Christianity stands for a real Gospel, and is truly represented,
should not all the churches everywhere be always filled?
A leading daily paper asserts that the 'people do not
come, because they are fed up with preaching.' But that
is merely the usual superficial journalistic estimate.

As a matter of fact, preaching is, in many respects,
more difficult to-day than ever before. To an unprecedented extent, the modern sermon has to run the gauntlet
between keener criticism on the one hand, and grosser
indifference on the other. Some who occupy pews are
better instructed than the occupant of the pulpit; whilst
the multiplied attractions and distractions of even the
British Sunday, lead millions to ignore the preacher
altogether. The days when the *ipse dixit* of the man in
the pulpit sufficed to warrant any statement then made,
are gone for ever. More and more, even in the churches,
grows the disposition to challenge what he says, or, when
there is little that is questionable, to demand that his
sermon shall be reduced to a minimum.

And yet the sermon is a splendid opportunity, for
human beings are always more moved by the living voice,
than by any cold print. Why does not modern preaching
effect more? Answers are not far to seek, though difficult
to express in courteous charity. In Romish and Anglican
churches, as a rule, the sermons—generally about fifteen
minutes in duration—deserve the little attention they
get. In plain truth, they are too often mere pious piffle,
only fit for childish or ignorant hearers, simply tolerated

by thoughtful listeners. In the Free Churches more often, quantity is substituted for quality, and congregations are indeed ' fed up ' with platitudes. Happily, there are many exceptions to this rule. But the need for impressive appeal to men and women to-day from the Christian standpoint is so manifest, that it is scarcely possible to exaggerate the importance of such opportunities as sermons afford. When it is seriously asked why more is not thereby accomplished, honest reply must refer to three things; (i) misrepresentation in substance; (ii) faults in method; (iii) lack of forceful application.

(i) The main purpose of preaching has to be kept in view. It is not merely to keep a church together, like a happy family, by ' expository ' preaching, but to attract and move those who are without, so as to win them for Christian discipleship. Is the average preaching of to-day doing this? There are grave reasons for saying that it is not. And yet, as regards the substance of Gospel truth, the preaching of to-day happily differs much from that of a century, or even half a century, ago. All too often, in the days gone by, have the representations of God, and the dogmas concerning Jesus, together with the dire estimates of human nature, the demand for implicit belief in a verbally-inspired Bible, and the threats of everlasting punishment, all tended to alienate rather than attract the outer world, making the very name of the Gospel a by-word. Surely, however, though slowly, are preachers shaking themselves free from these ancient fetters, and striving to make known the real good tidings which come to humanity in Jesus Christ. In that change lies the hope of the Christian future.

(ii) But even where a winsome message of grace and truth is intended, it is in by no means few cases weakened, if not marred, by faulty failure in the method of its delivery. In only too many pulpits, the natural dignity of a thoughtful and earnest Christian teacher is set aside, for the superfluous dress, unnatural attitudes, and unhelpful mannerisms of a clerical caste. Whilst true elocution, that is, the art of speaking distinctly, intelligently, and forcefully—which should be the preacher's most effective instrument—is painfully conspicuous by its absence. So that even when the message is good and true, vast numbers do not hear, let alone understand, the unchecked torrent of inarticulate words which is sometimes called ' earnest ' preaching.

An even greater hindrance to effective preaching, no matter how good its substance, is the common practice of reading instead of speaking. No read sermon on earth, be the reader ever so good an elocutionist, can take the place of the living word which comes direct from the mind and heart of a true preacher, by means of voice and eyes and gesture, into the very soul of his hearers. Politicians know the truth of this, and it is the real essence of oratory. In some cases, may be, pulpit ' notes ' are permissible. But they are always as real a hindrance as crutches would be to a healthy normal walker. They inevitably detract from that directness of appeal which is the mainspring of effective public speech. To speak as sympathetically as plainly, it is thus that only too often faults continue in pulpits, through many a wearisome half-hour, which would not elsewhere be tolerated for five minutes. How seriously this detracts from the worth of preaching, no words are needed to show.

Surely all these failures, whether of substance or of method, can be and ought to be remedied. As regards the Christian message itself, there is to-day, thanks to ' Modernism,' rightly interpreted, a more real and inspiring Gospel to be preached than ever before. There is a far truer and better knowledge of both God and man, with all the breadth and emphasis and hopefulness which come from the scientific revelation of an illimitable universe. And there is more need to-day than ever that such a Gospel should be preached. Think of it all. The enormous increase of population; millions upon millions more of human personalities with all their powers for good or ill; the compulsory quickening of thought through the measureless and resistless growth of knowledge; the ever-increasing means of communication, nationally and internationally; these all create such a situation as the world has never before known. Meanwhile, the unspeakable horrors of the late awful war, followed as they have been by years of doubt and strife, national disasters and international distrust, with dire anxieties for the future, conspire to show how vain are all science, philosophy, politics, and sociology combined, to secure peace and goodwill amongst men, or provide any guarantee of a warless, happier future. But this is exactly what the Gospel of Christ *would* do—that is beyond controversy—if only it were rightly understood and faithfully obeyed.

(iii) To that end there is no greater human incentive than Christian preaching, when it is worthy of its high commission. But it will have to be not only true to the utmost and latest human knowledge, but purged from all unnecessary hindrances in delivery, and charged with the genuine fervour which only comes from passionate sincerity. It has been said that one main reason why theatres are full and churches empty, is that whilst actors take fictions and represent them as facts, preachers take facts and treat them as fictions. One of the keenest memories of my youth is hearing Mr. Bradlaugh declare in public, that if he believed what was being preached concerning eternal punishment, he would spend his whole life in ceaseless endeavour to save his fellow-men from so dire a fate. At least such an attitude is a protest that the mere heartless fulfilling of pulpit routine, can never do justice to the verities of Christianity. Like so many other things, preaching is really worth just what it costs. What

His Gospel cost Jesus Himself, is only told in such an utterance as Paul's overwhelming reminder to the Philippians (ii. 6, 7, 8). What it cost the Apostles and early Christians to preach and live, we know well. In others ways, but no less actually, must there be a double cost in these days, if modern preaching is to be what it ought to be for all Christian purposes.

For the cost to the preacher, and its result, it may save words to take a brilliant illustration. The wonderful effectiveness and far-reaching influence of the late Dr. Jowett's sermons needs no comment. To listen to him was to be moved to one's depths, and receive an unforgetable impression. But only his nearest friends knew what such preaching cost him. Speaking generally, in the pulpit more perhaps than in any other public position, it is personality that counts. But personality is not a mere matter of heredity. It is a complex reality which admits of and calls for cultivation to the utmost, through heart devotion no less than mental toil and physical sobriety. Whether a man's force of character is great enough to tell in the pulpit as elsewhere, depends not upon his heredity or environment, but upon the consecrating use he makes of both. It is the cost of so doing which alone will add the dynamic to his sermons.

But the cost of such preaching as is to count for something in the maelström of modern life, is not for the preacher only. It takes an audience as well as a preacher, to make a sermon worth hearing. Bad sermons may mean bad hearers, quite as often as a bad preacher. Mental indolence, heart indifference, petty thoughts, narrow prejudices, will suffice to ruin the eloquence of a Chrysostom, and make the tender wooing of a Jowett as unavailing as the thunders of a Parker. There is no more deadly heresy than the notion, alas too popular, that church-goers have only to ' get good,' that is to receive everything and give nothing, beyond a small money contribution. How often even an individual hearer may help or mar sincere and earnest preaching, every occupant of a pulpit knows. The effect of a sermon is not a queston of its length. Some discourses of ten minutes are nine minutes too long. Others are all too short when they occupy an hour. It is the hearer who makes a sermon long or short, quite as much as the preacher. There may be a happy and useful medium in this respect, but the modern heartless and mindless demand for shorter sermons, and ever shorter services, for mere brevity's sake, is but a device of Godless superficiality, against which every preacher who is loyal to his message and His Master, will stand firm. He will be no more browbeaten by the modern cynicism which sniffs at the ' foolishness of preaching,' than misled into empty verbosity by the hackneyed quotation of—' not by might nor by power, but by My spirit, saith the Lord.' For he will recognize always the three absolute essentials of his great task—truth in substance; wisdom in method; heart force in application. When, at real cost, he has so spent himself, in making clear and impressive the real Gospel of Jesus, he may be well content to leave the rest to Him for whom he pleads.

(5) FUNDAMENTALISM

A few years since, a whole series of pamphlets entitled ' Fundamentals ' was sent from America to almost every known Christian minister or clergyman in this country. They contained a many-sided and urgent repetition of what are generally termed 'orthodox' Christian doctrines. Of these booklets, it is said that some ten millions were sent out by two ' laymen ' in Los Angeles, at a cost of more than £25,000. Nothing in all religious history has more vividly illustrated the Apostle's estimate of some zealots in his day, in his letter to the Romans (x. 2)— ' I bear them witness that they have a zeal for God, but not according to knowledge.' The ability and sincerity displayed in these booklets is beyond question. But the whole enterprise is really a vast assumption, based upon a false interpretation of a phrase in the Epistle of Jude (ver. 3)—' contend earnestly for the faith which was once for all delivered unto the saints.' The inference is that Christianity consists of a complex stereotyped system of doctrines, ' once for all ' miraculously communicated from heaven, like Mohammed's Koran, only to be exactly reiterated thenceforth, for evermore. ' The faith,' to these advocates, means just these doctrines which they formulate, and no others. But certainly to many other Christians, equally intelligent and sincere, the faith means something very different. On what grounds do these ' Fundamentalists,' out of an unnumbered host of honest and competent thinkers on these great themes, assume that they are absolutely right, and all others entirely wrong? For indeed there are very many who differ very strongly from their dogmatic pronouncements. Not only Romanists and Unitarians, but Anglo-Catholics, Methodists, Congregationalists, Baptists, Presbyterians, and others, would all disagree in many respects with the ' testimonies ' which these vehement writers from America thus send forth.

Yet in the course of their polemics, there is also so much that is true and admirable. Hence it is no wonder that not merely in America but throughout Europe, the name has become familiar, and represents a religious movement which must be reckoned with. Fundamentalism is said to be the protest against a vast lapse from the true Christian faith, under the influence of the modern literary, historical, and scientific, closer scrutiny of the Bible. Its special anathemas are poured out upon the

' Higher Criticism '—which name, though in itself perfectly innocent and intelligible, is travestied into super-
cilious, ignorant and anti-Christian meaning. But besides
this, the general acceptance of the principle of evolution
is vehemently denied and raucously denounced, its whole
significance being stigmatized as anti-Christian.   The
strong feeling thus aroused came to a climax in 1925
as Dayton, Tennessee, where a school teacher was legally
condemned and fined, for teaching evolution in his school.
The conflict became tragic, through the sudden death of
W. J. Bryan, who had been advocate for the prosecution.
His final address, never delivered, but afterwards printed
and circulated, contained a five-fold denunciation of
evolution which speaks for itself, and will be estimated
presently.

But precisely the same attitude is taken by many
in this country. In particular, a section of Wesleyan
Methodism, calling itself the ' Wesley Bible Union,' has
undertaken a definite mission of protest, and issues a
monthly journal to that effect, characterized by ultra-
montane dogmatism and denunciation of all who differ.
Its principal mover has also published a volume entitled
The Bankruptcy of Evolution, which is only calculated
to impress the uninstructed. Still this attitude finds
many supporters in the ' evangelical ' section of both
Anglicanism and the Free Churches. Hence, even in this
brief retrospect it demands careful notice. The details of
theological controversy are here manifestly impossible,
but a fair and thorough examination of the whole Fundamentalist crusade warrants all the following statements.

(1)   Its loudly proclaimed mission is to set forth
a certain number of definite theological doctrines, as
being absolutely necessary to Christian faith in general,
and personal ' salvation ' in particular.

(2)   It is plain to every honest mind that the Bible
itself throughout, and all formulation of Christian doc-

trine, are liable to a variety of interpretations.   Out of these, one particular set is chosen, as being infallible and exclusive of all others.   All that does not coincide with Fundamentalism, is pronounced misleading, false, destructive of Christianity.

(3)   This special set of interpretations is not only sincerely maintained, but a vehement attack is made, in the form of heresy hunting, upon all who dare to differ from it.   These hunts are specially directed against some of the best known and most highly esteemed Christian ministers in the churches.   Such men as Dr. H. Fosdick, Dr. W. M. Forrest, Dr. Lynn Harold Hough, Dr. G. Jackson, may be taken as typical targets for the pious spleen of Fundamentalists—some of it expressed in language more suited for the race course or saloon, than for Christian advocacy.

(4)   But upon the face of it, Fundamentalists have no more right to claim exclusive infallibility for their conclusions because they are sincere, than all others have. For that matter, Thugs, Moslems, Buddhists, Jesuits, Mormons, are quite as sincere, and most of them quite as intelligent, as they are.   It is said that there are 350 different religious sects in England.   If so, it shows at least that mere sincerity, however intelligent and dogmatic, is no guarantee whatever of objective truth.

(5)   The basal assumption of Fundamentalism is that at a certain stage in the development of Christianty, a complete and final statement was reached as to doctrine, to which nothing can be added, and from which nothing can be withdrawn.   In support of this obscurantist attitude, it is quite a common practice—as mentioned above—for its advocates to quote the utterance of the Seer in Rev. xxii. 18, 19, as applying both to the whole Bible and to their own particular interpretation of it. Whereas any child can see that its only reference is to

the preceding utterances of that special portion of the
New Testament.

(6) Such an attitude involves definite and persistent
refusal to learn anything from the unquestionable and
irresistible increase in human knowledge, alike as to
history, science, and Biblical study. Dr. Forrest's avowal
is amply justified that—'the Fundamentalists will carry
it unanimously, that religion and ignorance are one and
inseparable, now and for ever.' Methodism in particular,
on both sides of the Atlantic, would be held fast bound
in the dead hand of John Wesley—in spite of his 'high
church' proclivities, along with his willingness to 'burn
all witches' and stake the whole inspiration of the Bible
upon witchcraft. Such childish obscurantism is as contrary to the teaching of Christ and the New Testament,
as it is to human welfare in general. Said the Apostle
Paul—'In malice be babes, but in mind be men.' But
if a babe does not learn more and better as it grows, it
will never be a man at all. The law of all life is growth,
whether physical, intellectual, or spiritual. The Christianity which does not grow in knowledge, as well as in
grace, is false to the New Testament, and useless for
humanity.

(7) In spite of the seeming harmony and rigidity of
Fundamentalism, there are many serious differences of
opinion among its adherents—who is to decide between
them? Not a few of them would now as emphatically
reject some portions of the 'Westminster Shorter
Catechism,' as would Romanists or Evangelicals. But a
century ago that statement was accepted as the final
expression of all Christian truth, and was much more
authoritative than any incoherent Fundamental declara-
tions can ever be.

(8) The main doctrine which is said to be absolutely
sure, essential, and unchangeable, upon which all else
depends, relates to the Bible. The usual phrase runs

15

' the authority and infallibility of the word of God.'
This really involves what is known as verbal inspiration, and regards all the sixty-six portions of the Bible as
equally inspired, and binding upon the Christian church
for all time, so that it can be quoted piece-meal for all
purposes of Christian doctrine.   This attitude has been
sufficiently estimated above.   By it Fundamentalism
stands or falls.

(9) From such an estimate and treatment of the
Bible, what follows?   In brief general summary, these
items.   The doctrine of God as Triune.   The acceptance
as literal history and exact science of the opening chapters
of Genesis.   The sudden creation and actual ' fall ' of
Adam and Eve in the geographical Garden of Eden with
the consequences for all mankind of ' original sin,' and
total depravity.   Through these, the whole human race
is doomed to be lost eternally.   Salvation consists in
escaping that doom through belief in the substitutionary
atonement of Jesus.   His real Deity was involved and
always present in His human incarnation.   His crucifixion
was followed by His physical resurrection.   After this,
came His Ascension, and then the enduement of the
Apostles with power at Pentecost for their world mission.
For all who hold this faith there is to be, after death, an
everlasting heaven.   For those who reject it, there is
only the prospect of a literal hell for ever and ever.
The eschatology of this summary has been estimated
above.   But in so grave a matter it seems really necessary
to substantiate statement by quotation.   Thus one of
the principal leaders of the W.B.U. movement previously
mentioned, deliberately printed his and its tenets in this
regard.

All Bible students are agreed that the Bible teaches with
unmistakable emphasis that the punishment of the wicked is to be
one of torment, for ever and ever, to be endured with a consciousness to which there shall be no rest.   This doctrine is inseparably

linked up with that of the inherent immortality of the human soul. If the doctrine of never-ending punishment be false, then I maintain that the Bible is a false book. To believe that the punishment of those who die in their sins will ever terminate, is destructive of the authority of Christ. The whole fabric of Christianity perishes, if the doctrine of unending punishment be not true.[1]

That at least is plain. The Fundamentalism which is committed to that, needs no further condemnation. But meanwhile, according to its vehement advocates, Christ is to come again in manifest terrestrial splendour, and on literal clouds of glory. In connexion with this there is to be—some say before His coming, some say after—an overwhelming spectacular Judgement Day, somewhere on earth, where all men, women, and children, who have ever lived, will literally appear in resuscitated physical bodies, to be judged according to their former earthly lives. Almost all Fundamentalists believe that such an event is soon coming to pass. Christ is then to reign on earth for a thousand years. It is enough to say that however sufficient this whole conception may have been for the middle ages, or even the eighteenth century, it is not believable now.

(10) Whilst it cannot be truly said that Fundamentalism ignores Christian ethics, or Christian character, it does undoubtedly regard orthodox belief as the prime requisite for salvation. The frightful declaration of the Athanasian creed has been mentioned above—but it is equalled by the anathemas Fundamentalism bestows on those who do not hold the divine nature of Jesus in the precise way which they define. No doctrine of the κένωσις can be tolerated; His absolute infallibility, in every meticulous detail, must be enforced. It must suffice here to refer to what has been said above on this theme, with the simple but far-reaching addition that, however

[1] *Wesley Bible Union Journal*, Sept. 1925.

desirable it may be to seek for truth to the utmost, the person of Jesus remains and will ever remain, theology's insoluble mystery. To speak of it as the 'Hypostatic Union' is only verbal jugglery. To denounce one's fellow-Christans, therefore, because they do not hold some one precise view, is as contrary to the whole spirit of the New Testament, as it is to the words and example of Christ Himself.

(11) In regard to all the doctrines of the Christian faith there is no warrant in the New Testament, and certainly none in reason, for adopting any one stage in Christian thought or history, as absolutely final, and only permitting reiteration. This is manifest enough in some respects. The cosmogeny of the Apostles and early Christians was unquestionably Ptolemaic; but the hardiest Fundamentalist dare not cling to that now. The knowledge we now possess concerning the antiquity of man and the age of the earth, cannot be either denied or ignored. There is no more reason for thinking that the Apostles and early fathers, or Councils of bishops, knew everything that need ever be known about God and man, than about astronomy or geology. Indeed, if the words of Christ recorded in the Fourth Gospel have any significance at all, they do distinctly intimate that under the Spirit's guidance, the truth concerning Himself and His meaning to humanity, would grow from more to more as time went on. Woe indeed to Christianity, if no advance is to be made upon the interpretations of the Gospel which were promulgated by Origen, or Augustine, or Cyprian; or, we may well add, by Luther, or Calvin, or Wesley.

(12) There is no question as to the sincerity and intensity of the religious experiences of many Fundamentalists. But unless they are based upon truth and fact, they are only as a castle in the air. A great deal may be assumed as beyond reasonable controversy. No Christian

Modernist would disagree with the Fundamentalist as to the validity of theism and human moral responsibility, or question the historicity of Jesus, and the general reliability of the New Testament. But besides these, there are two other requisites for a living and growing Christian faith to-day. (1) It must be true to fact, in the light of all that is proved to be reliable in modern knowledge, whether historical, scientific, or critical. (ii) It must also be true to what is actually before us in the frank and reverent scrutiny of the Bible. Its exegesis must be fair and thorough, corresponding with the latest and best results of modern scholarly investigation, unfettered by ecclesiastical traditions or ' orthodox ' convention. Without such full consideration, it is utterly useless to keep on insisting that the Bible is ' the Word of God,' and reiterating its infallible sufficiency.

(13) There is much to admire and appreciate in the strong protests of Fundamentalism against Romanism on the one hand, and Agnosticism on the other. But inasmuch as the representatives of both these cults are also intelligent and sincere, all such protests are invalid, unless supported by objective truth in all respects.

(14) Unfortunately, some of the main assertions of Fundamentalism are demonstrably false. In addition to the matters above mentioned, its whole attitude towards evolution is a blunder and a folly. To take one prominent and typical instance out of many others, what was the five-fold indictment of Mr. Bryan in the famous Dayton trial? A few moments' careful consideration shows that in point of actual fact, it was but five-fold delusion. Thus (i) it is said that ' evolution contradicts the Mosaic record of creation and shakes faith in the word of God.' Here, plainly, are four false assumptions. First, that the whole Bible without any qualification is the word of God; then, that Moses is the author of the opening chapters of Genesis; then, that

this record of creation is an exact scientific account of creation. Then, finally, that Christian faith is necessarily shaken by the acceptance of the principle of evolution. This, numberless Christian students to-day know to be untrue. Again, (ii) evolution is said to ' dispute every vital truth of the Bible '—which is also manifestly untrue. Then (iii) evolution is represented as ' diverting attention from pressing problems of great importance to trifling speculation.' It would be hard indeed to frame any statement more manifestly false. (iv) Evolution is said to paralyse the hope of reform, because it is ' a cult of heartless processes, its only programme for man being scientific breeding, with no place for the regeneration of the individual.' As to regeneration, enough has been said above in the section upon conversion. But taking the assertion as it stands, it shows either deplorable ignorance or wilful mis-statement, as every genuine student knows. (v) Finally, it is said that evolution would ' eliminate love, and carry man back to a mere struggle of tooth and claw.' But any man who claims to speak with authority, ought surely to acquaint himself with the truth as to his subject matter. How far from truth is this bald assertion, cannot be better shown than in the deliberately published conclusions of such experts as Profs. J. A. Thomson and P. Geddes, in their small but sufficient volume on *Evolution*, in the Home University Library.

The ideal of evolution is thus no gladiator's show, but an Eden; and though competition can never be wholly eliminated, it is much for our pure natural history to see no longer struggle but love, as creation's final law.[1]

[1] V. p. 247. See also Prof. Thomson's—*The Gospel of Evolution; Concerning Evolution; Evolution in its Relation to Religious Thought,* by Joseph Le Conte (Chapman & Hall); *Through Evolution to the Living God,* by J. R. Cohu (Parker, Oxford); *The Faith of an Evolutionist,* by T. A. Palmer (Allenson); with many more such witnesses.

The Fundamentalism which rests upon such shallow misrepresentations as these, is sufficiently self-condemned.

(15) The folly of Fundamentalism is further manifest in its childish attempt to prevent the spread of modern knowledge, whether scientific or otherwise. The Dayton onslaught only caused a smile of pitiful amusement throughout the world of intelligent people to-day, together with amazement that American Christianity should have so many unworthy representatives. Any attempt in these days to prevent the application of modern knowledge, scientific, historical, critical, to Christian principles, is as futile as the fabled folly of Canute's courtiers. Rather it is worse, for it tends to create unnecessary and unwarranted conflict between science and Christianity. In seeking to reduce rational faith to ecclesiastical superstition, it becomes an enemy to both Christianity and humanity.

(16) There is, moreover, a double tragedy about this whole Fundamental attitude. (i) It exposes Christianity helplessly to attack from modern opponents; whether in the rabid form of such gibes as those of the ' Literary Guide,' in its exhibition of militant ' Rationalism,' or the cultured aversion of some men of letters, such as those who recently carried on the stunt of the *Daily Express* concerning ' my religion.' (ii) It thus makes Christian faith unnecessarily difficult, if not impossible, for the rising generation of men and women, who are increasingly imbued with all the latest valid results from the investigations of science and criticism.

(17) It is, however, only too plain that the pitiful conflict to which Fundamentalism gives rise, will not soon come to an end. A Dr. J. R. Straton of New York has announced his intention of carrying on the work of Mr. Bryan, and maintaining a Fundamentalist crusade throughout the United States. He will doubtless have too many followers—like certain obscurantist leaders

in this country—to permit any hope that they will speedily be convinced of error, and face the modern situation with an open mind as well as with a pure heart. In this respect it resembles the other great enemy of rational and Scriptural Christianity which also claims the monopoly of truth. Yet the ecclesiastical, sacerdotal sacramentarianism, which finds its culmination in the audacious assumptions and persistent bigotry of Rome, cannot but conflict with some of the tenets of Fundamentalism. So that there are lamentable signs of a prolonged and bitter triangular conflict between Fundamentalism, Romanism, and Agnosticism. In that conflict, these three mutual opponents will sometimes be found strangely joining hands, in virulent opposition to that rational Christian faith for which Modernism, rightly understood, really pleads.

(18) One thing must be steadily borne in mind. When all discussions are over and all wrangling, religious or irreligious, comes to an end, the final Christian test of value, as to any creed, or standard, or doctrine whatever, is to be found in personal character—the ' salvation ' outlined above. Character not creed, character not mere personal experience, is the ' fruit of the Spirit ' which must grow on the Christian ' tree of life,' if its leaves are to be ' for the healing of the nations.' Whatever becomes of theological definitions, or orthodox shibboleths, all that is contrary to the Apostolic summary in Paul's first letter (ch. xiii.) to the Corinthians, is wrong, and definitely un-Christian. Bigotry is always wicked. The principle of his decisive word to the Romans (ch. xiv. 17, 18) is plainly applicable here also.

The kingdom of God is not eating and drinking, but righteousness, and peace, and joy in the Holy Spirit. For he that in these things serveth Christ is well-pleasing to God and approved of men.

(19) When the question then inevitably arises—

does it matter what a man believes?—the three-fold
answer is too manifest to call for lengthy discussion. (i)
It does matter to God, as the Heavenly Father who cares
beyond utterance for the best welfare of all His children.
He seeks, in Christ's own words, for those who worship
not only ' in spirit ' but ' in truth.' (ii) It matters unspeakably to each individual. For it is immeasurably true
that ' as a man thinks in his heart, so is he.' Ultimately
all character and conduct turn upon conviction. As a
rule, with few exceptions, what a man really believes he
acts upon; his words and deeds are but the expression of
his thoughts. (iii) Thus his belief also matters to his
whole environment. For all who surround him, in his
home or in his business, feel his influence. His beliefs or
disbeliefs cannot but make themselves felt, in all his
relations with his fellows. These are such platitudes that
the question above ought really never to be asked.

But when the query behind the question is as to
whether a man is condemned now, or will be doomed
hereafter, because of some mistakes in his creed, then
the negative answer is as plain as the whole New Testament can make it. The confession of Peter stands good
for all time, and covers all creeds.

Of a truth I perceive that God is no respecter of persons; but
in every nation he that feareth Him and worketh righteousness is
acceptable to Him.

It is unmeasured pity that the Church which professes
to depend so much upon Peter, has not learned that
Apostle's lesson. But it ought to weigh quite as much
with Fundamentalism as with Romanism. They ought
to know that in Paul's day the conflict concerning
orthodoxy turned upon circumcision, quite as keenly
and bitterly as to-day upon Biblical infallibility. Hence,
the significance of the Apostle's twice repeated declaration, that ' in Christ Jesus neither circumcision matters

anything, nor uncircumcision,' but the 'new creation' which means 'faith working within through love.'

(20) Finally, how far then is a man responsible for believing what is true, as against what is false? Nothing can relieve him of his responsibility for using his own powers of mind, as a moral being. Jesus put it strongly to His own hearers—'Yes, and why even of yourselves do you not decide what is right?' (Luke xii. 57). More than that; a man is responsible, as an honest thinker, for seeking for the truth, even when it is not easy to find. The Romish demand to hand over such responsibility to 'the Church,' is double delusion. For, first in order to do that, he must exercise the very judgement he is asked to give up. And further, the whole history, as well as present attitude, of that Church, show that its assumption of supreme authority over conscience is utterly contrary to the New Testament; whilst its decisions are no less contradictory to valid modern knowledge.

As moral beings, every man, woman, and child, is responsible, not only for such light and knowledge as he or she has, but for that which they all might have, if they chose to seek for it. When, however, a man has been brought to see and feel that certain facts and principles are true, in regard to the Gospel of Jesus, that truth must be his guide. Whether he be Protestant or Romanist, Fundamentalist or Modernist, Methodist or Unitarian, he is only justified in the degree in which he follows what he sees to be true. The words of the Psalmist—'Thou desirest truth in the inward parts'—find their everlasting echo in the Apostolic mandate—'Finally brethren, whatsoever things are true.' In this respect, each may rest assured of his acceptance with the Father whom Jesus reveals. All that remains is that when the convictions of others differ from his own, he should reverence their sincerity, and treat them as children of the same Father as himself, and equally beloved.

Once again, therefore, the Apostle's word truly sums up
the whole case—for Fundamentalist and Modernist alike.

Watch ye, stand fast in the faith, quit you like men, be strong.
Let all that you do, be done in love.

(6) MODERNISM

After what has been pointed out in the preceding
section, it becomes necessary to consider carefully the
Modernism which is now so naturally and often set over
against Fundamentalism. For the average Christian
believer to-day, there is a choice between three forms
of faith—Fundamentalism, Romanism, Modernism. It
is not necessary to explain the two former; but Modernism, is, for the majority, as indefinite as a mist and as
noxious as malaria. What is sometimes called 'liberal
Evangelicalism' is simply evangelical Modernism. The
first thing that must strike the mind of every intelligent
and honest observer, is that two of these sections are as
absolutely sure of their own tenets, as manifestly contradictory to each other. Meanwhile, the number is
growing—especially amongst the young who are now
increasingly better educated—who will not accept either
of these standpoints. The rising generation, indeed,
cannot but turn from all such rigid assumptions of
infallibility, by reason of the modern atmosphere of
history, science, and fact, which they are compelled
to breathe. Two questions thus press for answer.[1]
(1) What does Modernism really mean? (2) How does
it help Christian faith in the present situation?

[1] What follows here is largely taken from an article in the *London
Quarterly Review,* for April 1926, by the Editor's kind permission.

(1) In reply to these queries, Modernism may be viewed either as a plain fact, or as a religious attitude. As a fact, it is a general mental atmosphere, arising from the influence of modern knowledge and modern thought upon life as we now know it. It is manifest everywhere, and in all things. In everything except religion, it is rather welcomed than opposed. No one objects to a penny postage, or cheap telegrams, or fast trams, or wireless wonders, or flying marvels of transport. But when it comes to religion, the whole scene changes. Numbers of raucous voices at once declare that poison gas is upon us. An American D.D., speaking for many others, has just announced that—' if any teacher or minister advocates the evolution theory,' his church ' has no apology to offer for hanging the hides of the first cousins and defenders of the orang-outang, on the topmost telephone poles in the city.' But whether it is welcomed or scorned, Modernism, as a fact, cannot be denied, or evaded, or prevented.

As a religious attitude, it is as we have seen, viewed by very many only as a subject for multiplied anathemas. But as the late Mr. Pryke has said [1]

However acquired, the name Modernist has come to stay; and history offers not a few examples of the opprobious label being rescued from its lowly or unpleasing associations, and transformed into a title of honour and respect.

There can be little doubt that such transformation will eventually come to pass, because like Protestantism or Methodism—which were at first opprobrious names —Modernism, as a mental and spiritual attitude, stands for that which is true, and therefore, in the end, triumphant. Its simplest yet sufficient definition is *open-mindedness*. But in fuller expression, it is just

[1] In his interesting volume on *Modernism as a Working Faith*, published by Heffer.

the embodiment of that Apostolic ideal which has been
quoted more than once in preceding sections, but really
merits continued repetition for the sake of emphasis :

> In one last word, my brothers, whatever is true or honourable,
> just or pure, winsome or promising, if there is anything noble or
> praiseworthy, take these all into full account.

Thus Modernism represents the thought and effort of
those who see the prevalent corrosion of faith through
the modern atmosphere and endeavour to prevent or
mitigate it on behalf of a real Christianity. It is manifest
to all who are not wilfully blind, that *something* must be
done. Much of what has been taught and said, preached,
and sung, in days gone by, cannot now be maintained by
those who accept the Apostolic ideal. Neither Fundamentalism nor Romanism will stand the acid test of the
present, let alone of a severer future.

The issues involved are vast indeed. The main
questions are still, as they have long been, those which
relate to the Bible, to Christ, and to the Christian Church.
Each of these themes offers unmeasured room for earnest
investigation and great differences of conviction. This
will be sufficiently manifest from what has been said in
the preceding sections, with which doubtless many will
disagree. There is, however, voluminous enough discussion of these high themes elsewhere. But in regard
to them all, the characteristic feature of Modernism
stands out in unmistakable relief. It is emphatically
opposed to the chief boast of Rome, expressed in one
sentence of a recent Jesuit publication—' The Catholic
Church stands committed to this doctrine for ever.' Here
we have the usual—but none the less outrageous—
assumption of the great word ' Catholic,' as applying only
to the Romish section, and thus combining falsity with
bigotry. But in spite of history, and Galileo, the boast of
semper eadem unblushingly remains. Romanism is

ancient—nothing has been learned since its beginning.
Nothing will ever be. Growth in knowledge and its
application are anathema. In these respects, alas,
Fundamentalism follows in the wake of Romanism. It
also is absolutely sure; and is not open to change. It has
nothing to learn; and competes with Rome in the sweeping virulence of its denunciations of all who venture to
differ from its rigid creed. But it is tragic self-contradiction on the part of all such as profess to be guided by
the New Testament. Manifestly, on these principles,
Christianity would never have been born.

It is just here that Modernism, as firmly as modestly,
lifts up its head in protest. New converts we know
are given to excessive zeal, and of this, Mr. G. K. Chesterton has recently given a characteristic specimen in his
foreword to a Romish manifesto by Father Woodlock.
He avows that

> Modernism is the enemy of many things, but the thing of which
> it always seems to me the mortal enemy, is liberty.

Verily, such a deliverance takes the prize for zeal not
only without discretion, but without regard for truth.
Certainly 'Modernism is the enemy of many things'
—amongst them, lying. For, let the book in question
bear its own witness as to the absence of truth in this
sentence. Says Father Woodlock:

> No compromise on any defined dogma can even be considered,
> as a means of facilitating the return even were it of all the
> Christian sects reunited in one Protestant Church, which had
> secured, let us imagine, communion with the East. Whether to
> secure unity Rome would abate one jot of her defined doctrine, or
> derogate from the universal jurisdiction of her supreme Pastor,
> is wholly beyond the range of discussion.

That is Rome's and Mr. Chesterton's conception of
liberty! Of a truth, if it is not much rather, when

considered in all its bearings, narrow-minded bigotry and ecclesiastical tyranny, language has no meaning. And if this is Christianity, then the New Testament is the most misleading book on earth.

Modernism, on the other hand, is the very synonym of liberty. As such, it takes all the risks and enjoys all the benedictions of freedom. It differs from the preceding in being a living faith. For it appreciates growth, and where there is no growth there is no life. Naturally, and inevitably, there are differences and even extremes in its ranks; as in any large family there are unmeasured differences in form, temperament, and ability. But no parent worthy the name desires instead, that his children should be all of one mould, like dummies from shop windows. He prefers life with all its differences, in liberty and love. Modernism, however, is no more committed to the special views of extremists, than democracy is to the shouts of anarchists. No Modernist is bound to the opinions, say, of Professors Bacon or Kirsopp Lake, or all the views advocated in *The Modern Churchman*. He is only bound to two things, and that by his own definite conviction and deliberate choice. First, he accepts the New Testament records as substantially true, and reliable. Then, on its principles, he endorses the Apostolic summary of Christian obligation, namely, to seek and follow to the uttermost whatever things are true. The truth, the whole truth, and nothing but the truth, is the Modernist creed. This cannot be too plainly stated, or too often reiterated.

Unfortunately, it is here that both Romanism and Fundamentalism manifestly fail. For instance, Father Woodlock's book, above mentioned, states unequivocally, that

Adam—the first human being—was created in the supernatural state, because endowed from the first with the supernatural gift of sanctifying grace.

Now that statement is simply untrue. It not only sets on edge the teeth of every scientist, but is definitely contrary to fact. That should be enough. But the same applies to many other matters. Matt. xvi. 23 is continually referred to, but the Romish exegesis is demonstrably false. In John x. 16, Jesus did not say 'There shall be one fold.' Still less did He mean, as the context itself plainly shows, that His one 'flock' should consist of an all-embracing Romish Church. Nor did the Apostles ever contemplate such a possibility. There is no New Testament warrant whatever, nor anything approaching it, for the worship of 'our Lady.' So, with truth, we might go on and on. The boast that 294,000,000 'subjects' accept the supremacy and infallibility of the Pope, does not count for much when the mentality of most of them is fairly estimated. But in any case, such numbers say no more for the truthfulness of these Romish assumptions, than the fact that more than 200,000,000 Moslems believe as utterly in Mohammed, establishes the validity of his claims. Fanaticism has always had its crowds, and always will have; until truth comes to be everywhere triumphant. Which is not yet, nor will be for many a day.

Meanwhile, it is true that Modernism, as a mental and spiritual attitude, is both a refuge and a dynamic, such as this age unspeakably needs.

It is a real refuge for all earnest thinkers, in the following respects.

(i) It makes a clear distinction between the essentials and non-essentials of Christian faith. How real, and great, and necessary, a distinction this is, cannot be shown here in a few words. But readers of Mr. Pryke's book above mentioned, who will also study patiently *The Form and Content in the Christian Tradition,* by Dr. Sanday and Mr. Williams (Longmans) and *Doctrine and Principles* by C. E. Beeby (Williams

& Norgate), will find all the guidance they need. It is
well summarized in one sentence by Dr. Davison.

We must take care that we do not reckon among our fundamentals, 'facts' as to the world's origin and history, which simply
are not facts; and theories concerning man and God, which simply
are 'not' so.[1]

(ii) It clings to what it has held to be true, until
the contrary is proved. This sane and Christian principle was well expressed by that splendid scholar and
noble character, Dr. W. Sanday.

I do not disclaim the name Modernist. It describes justly what
I aim at being. I aim at thinking the thoughts and speaking the
language of my own day, and yet, at the same time keeping all that
is essential in the religion of the past. I fully believe that it is
possible to do this. If I did not think so, I should not be here.

(iii) It satisfies the Christian conscience in putting
truth always first—before all else, whether ecclesiastical
tradition or venerable association. It thus follows, at
any cost, not only the Apostolic injunction above quoted,
but the word of Christ Himself—'You shall know the
truth, and the truth shall make you free.' A very
different prescription, God be thanked, from that of
Rome per Messrs. Woodlock and Chesterton.

(iv) It is rational, in paying all due respect to
recent knowledge, whether historical, scientific, or
critical. As Dr. Davison put it—

The faith must not be mere feeling. If it is to overcome the
modern world, with all its various forces and interests, it must be
intellectually satisfying.

It is plain fact that 'the faith,' as represented by
Fundamentalism and Romanism, is so utterly unsatis-
factory in modern light, that it plays into the hands of
those who style themselves 'Rationalists,' and, in the

1 *London Quarterly Review*, January, 1926.

eyes of very many, establishes their claim to have exploded Christianity. Modernism strives to act upon the Apostle's principle—' I am speaking as to wise men, form your own estimate of what I say ' (1 Cor. x. 15).

(v) It makes room for that further growth of faith which comes through increasing knowledge of God. Not without ample reason did the Archbishop of Canterbury say recently, that ' the supreme need of our nation is a new understanding of God's character.' This has been sufficiently considered above, and finds its embodiment in Modernism.

(vi) It is impossible that there should come to pass the ' new understanding ' just mentioned, without giving rise to many deep and sincere differences of judgement between earnest thinkers. We see that neither Romanism nor Fundamentalism will allow them the breath of any new life. Where are they to find room to live? The refuge they need—and deserve—is open to them in Modernism. For herein the varieties of perception and conviction which cannot but arise when men are free to think for themselves, are not anathematized, but looked upon with a sympathy which is as far from easy *laissez faire,* as from ecclesiastical tyranny.

(vii) In this refuge, moreover, there is safety as well as liberty. For such Modernism confers immunity from external attacks which otherwise were serious, if not overwhelming. Its freedom from rigid dogmatisms brings with it complete deliverance from former fears as to the stability of Christianity under the onslaughts of agnosticism, or ' rationalism,' or secularism. The erstwhile thunders of ' Iconoclast ' and ' Saladin,' lose all their terrors; and the gibes of the *Freethinker,* and the *Literary Guide* become but occasions for pity. The sneers of bygone days at the Old Testament representations of the character of God, and the ' immoralities ' of some Jewish heroes, have lost their sting, and become positive reasons for Christian thankfulness and devotion.

(viii) Modernism thus meets the unquestionable need of the children and young people who are being better educated every decade. Mr. Pryke wrote most truly that

Until the child is helped to grasp the obvious fact that the Bible is not a book, but a library; that all the pictures of God contained in that library are not equally true; that some are frankly un-Christian, and therefore false; that the truth of every picture must be tested by the portrait of God presented to us in Jesus Christ—his mind will remain in a condition of muddle from which there is no escape, religion will be divorced from life, and his ideas of God at best will be chaotic, hazy, and departmental.

It is for want of such guidance that so many of our Sunday-school senior scholars are lost to the churches, and wander away into irreligion altogether.

(ix) It is not to be supposed that all the comfort and advantage of Christian Modernism can be obtained without cost. There are few emancipations more costly than shaking oneself free from the fetters of preceding religious notions, and long established forms of thought. Middle-aged or elderly folk in particular, deserve deepest sympathy when called upon to exchange ideas which have filled their minds through many years, for new and unfamiliar conceptions. And yet these same people do not shrink from so doing in other matters. They never sigh for a stage-coach in which to travel across the country; they never refuse to send or receive a telegram in case of need; they do not disdain the surgical help of X-rays; nor scorn the 'wireless' as a dangerous innovation. Why should they turn a deaf ear to the Master's own recommendation, to set a proper value, in Christian faith, upon 'things both new and old'?[1] No doubt it is the apparent cost that hinders.

But the gain is no less manifest. To be robbed of

[1] Matt. xiii. 52.

half a sovereign would in these days be somewhat grievous, for most of us. But if, on each occasion the robber left a sovereign by way of compensation, most of us also would have no objection to being often robbed. It is no fanciful symbol. The 'growing pains' which sometimes Modernism cannot but occasion, if borne with patience and wisdom issue, as with our children, in larger growth and stronger health. Meanwhile, in the whole often painful process of unlearning as well as learning, there is the assurance of the same sympathy on our great Teacher's part, as every good teacher feels with a pupil who finds his lesson hard, but does his best to master it. There is more room than ever for the Psalmist's prayer —'Open Thou mine eyes, that I may behold wondrous things out of Thy law.' That there are yet more wondrous things to be learned from Christ's Gospel, is guaranteed to every humble disciple by the assurance of Jesus Himself—'When He the Spirit of Truth is come, He will take of Mine and will show unto you.' 'He will teach you all things.' 'He will declare to you the things that are to come.'

But Modernism, rightly apprehended, as the open-mindedness which is willing to be taught, and anxious only to follow the truth, is no less a dynamic than a refuge. And in these amongst other respects. (i) It provokes to reality, where too often there has been only appearance; and stirs to life, where before, only dead formulæ or meaningless words have ruled. The extent to which some such transformation is needed throughout present-day Christendom, is an unmeasured tragedy.

(ii) It stimulates to the fullest use of all our highest faculties, in its open acknowledgement that for all believers and for all Churches, there is yet much to be both learned and unlearned, if the promise of Christ just quoted is to be realized. Very few ordinary Christian folk to-day ever set themselves to think how great and costly a conflict it must have been to the first followers of Jesus, who were all Jews, to alter, or put away altogether, so much of their previous religion in order to become His disciples. None of us have ever known anything like such a demand for mental and spiritual enlargement. It was to them a far more real Modernism than there can be for any Fundamentalist of these days. But out of the willingness to do as He said—'Come to Me, and learn of Me'—Christianity arose.

(iii) Once more let us listen to Mr. Pryke, as to one gone from us now, whose witness deserves to be borne in mind—for it is most emphatically true.

Apart from Modernism, Christianity has no future; since without that unification of religion with modern thought for which the Modernist is working, the gulf between the Churches and the man in the street must grow continually wider, until at length religion and obscurantism become interchangeable terms, and that unhappy identification of faith with credulity towards which many now appear to be drifting, shall have attained completion.

Such a warning is corroborated by Dr. Forrest, who writes from the midst of rampant Fundamentalism,

They assume an infallible Bible which cannot be proved. Ultimately, the force conservative religion has called to its aid will destroy it. Meantime, it will alienate from itself all those who will to know the truth. If they are reached by liberal preaching and teaching, such may be saved to Christianity. Otherewise the Fundamentalists will carry it unanimously that religion and ignorance are one and inseparable, now and for ever.

(iv) But more than that. Speaking positively and practically, Modernism enables all real Christians to work together for the common good, in spite of differing convictions and ideals. The great lesson of Luke ix. 39, 50, is scorned by Fundamentalism and Romanism, but is learned in humility and practised in love's charity, by Modernism. The pitiful instances of petty bigotry which are only too well known in the present life of the Churches, cannot occur under its auspices.

(v)   Thus it becomes the only hope for a really united Christendom.   It is as certain as our very life that the union which Messrs. Chesterton and Woodlock, with their co-religionists, pray for—absolute submission to Rome's dogmas and discipline—will NEVER be brought to pass.   Nor will the uniformity of thought and speech, in order to perpetuate bygone theologies, which is the *sine quâ non* of Fundamentalism.   From both of these quixotic schemes the true ' Catholic ' Church and the modern world alike, travel farther every year.   In Father Woodlock's book there are, however, two true sentences which may be endorsed:

> The only union that is practicable is a genuine sympathetic co-operation of all Christian bodies in the work of social reconstruction.   A sincere conviction of the *bona fides* of those who reject our personal beliefs, and cling to those we reject, ought to enable us to work like brothers for the healing of the wounds of the world.

' Ought to,' indeed, but does not.   As witness the refusal of Rome to have anything to do with the great Christian unsectarian ' Copec ' gathering at Birmingham, not long since.   All other ' denominations ' were represented, except the one with which the writer of the above words is identified!   Is further proof required to show that on such lines as he represents, the ' ought to ' comes to nothing?   Nor will it ever come to anything until and unless the open-mindedness of Modernism makes possible ' the mutual charity which should be the ever-present bond of union, even in a disunited Christendom.'

It is more than probable that the preceding outline will displease some readers as much as it will reassure others.   Whether, however, it provokes a smile or a frown, it may be well to close with a few certainties which are beyond challenge. Modern knowledge is continually growing, and will grow irresistibly in all directions, and will increasingly affect religion. As to what really is Christianity, and how it is affected, the Churches differ sincerely, deeply, permanently.   There is no prospect whatever of organic union. Nor is it necessary, for the purposes of Christ's Kingdom, that there should be. ' There are diversities of operations, but the same Spirit.' All that is possible, or indeed desirable, is the Apostolic ' unity of the spirit, in the bond of peace.' And that really is, in the thought and speech of to-day, the Modernism which puts the love and service of the Christ of the New Testament, in the keeping of His two Great Commands, above all else—literally ALL else—and so allows to every man the liberty, and lays on him the responsibility, of his own interpretation and appreciation of Christian truth. This attitude of mind and heart alone makes it possible for sincere believers to differ conscientiously and strongly, and yet respect each other sufficiently to make bigotry impossible, and mutual denunciation utterly un-Christian. The whole situation can scarcely be better summed up than in a recent statement by Dr. Horton, who has himself long illustrated what he says :

What our time needs supremely is a presentation of Christianity, equally removed from Romanism and from Fundamentalism; a presentation which the intelligence and reason and knowledge of modern men can whole-heartedly accept; a presentation which starting from the Christ who is ever the same, shows clearly what He has to say to new times and new truth. Men are irreligious to-day because the forms and the formularies of religion seem out of date. They become immediately religious, when the truth of Christ comes to them afresh and disencumbered. What is wanted is the bold and fearless statement of the truth, in relation with all we know and are learning of the universe to which we belong.[1]

[1] *Congregational Quarterly*, April, 1926, p. 171.

When that is done, in the spirit which we know He would approve of whom we speak, there will come to pass as real an answer as human nature now permits, to His own prayer—' That they all may be one, that the world may believe that Thou has sent Me.

IV

EPILOGUE

In reviewing the preceding pages, I cannot but acknowledge (i) the imperfection of each section; and (ii) the omission of many important themes which might well have been expected, and equally call for frank consideration.

(i) As to the former, I can only plead the inevitable limitations of space, and the desire to avoid the technicalities of verbal camouflage, for the sake of all those ordinary readers for whom this whole presentation of Christian truth is intended.

(ii) In regard to the latter, the great problems of Pain and Evil, together with the relations of Christianity to modern social problems, have been carefully considered in other published works[1] to which I must be content to refer—seeing that there is nothing in them which I would retract. In reference to other important matters such as Evolution; The Perversions of Christianity in Modern Christendom; the Approximations to Christ's Ideals represented in the various Churches; Democracy; Sociology; Sunday Observance; The Meaning and Worth of Holiness; Church Government ; Foreign Missions; Sports; careful consideration is given to these in a companion volume entitled: *Twentieth Century Christianity,* published by Messrs. T. & T. Clark.

[1] More particularly to *Parts II and III* of my *Christian Theism Justified;* also *Christianity after the War;* and *Part V* in *The People's Religious Difficulties.* All published by the Epworth Press.

For the present, the preceding summaries must suffice as my sincere and humble contribution to a true and living Christianity. They have resulted, indirectly, from years of thought on lines which the isolation of an orphan childhood and following experiences have tended to make independent. Directly, they are the outcome of eighteen months of enforced silence through laryngitis. I can but trust and hope that all the labour expended has not been in vain. I cannot apologize for using the same 'plainness of speech' which seemed to the Apostle Paul called for, in his second letter to the Corinthians (iii. 12). But I echo—*longo intervallo*—his further avowal, in the preceding letter (1 Cor. iv. 1 to 5), of sincerity of purpose and desire only to be true to what is true. The rest I leave in His hands who knows us as we are, and does not disdain the humblest service.

WORKS BY THE SAME AUTHOR

PUBLISHED BY THE EPWORTH PRESS.

Haeckel's Monism False.

Theomonism True.

The True GOD—Thesis for the London D.D.

Determinism—False and True.

Does it matter what a Man Believes?

Christian Reality in Modern Light. Fernley Lecture, 1916.

Why not Modern Unbelief?
Replies to Atheism, Materialism, Pantheism, Agnosticism, Rationalism, Theosophy, Buddhism.

Christian Essentials.

Father of All—the Christian Doctrine of God.

Does Faith need Reasons?

Why not Islam?—A careful summary of the history and tenets of Mohammedanism, with its modern relations to Christianity.

Christian Theism Justified.
Part 1—Reply to Rationalistic attacks.
2—Why does not God prevent all evil?
3—A fair estimate of the mystery of pain.
4—The assurance that God is love.

Why not Russellism?

Why not Eddyism—miscalled Christian Science?

Why not Mormonism?

Christian Truth concerning the Lord's Supper.

The Mystery of Painlessness.

PUBLISHED BY T. & T. CLARK.

The Miracles of Unbelief,

Reality in Bible Reading.

Twentieth Century Christianity.